P9-BZJ-805

Critical acclaim for *Becoming a Manager*

"Thought-provoking material for human resource and management development professionals."
—Judith Oppenheim, Vice President Human Resources,
The Forum Corporation

"A fascinating look at the journey from individual contributor to manager. Capturing the challenge and the fear, the mistakes and the victories, this book will give new managers a crucial perspective on their experience."
—Morgan McCall, The University of Southern California

"[Hill's] insights into the transformation process are obvious in her suggestions of helpful resources for first-year managers."
—*Industry Week*

"One of the finest descriptions of the agony and ecstasy of moving from salesperson to sales manager that I have encountered. This book should be 'must reading' for newly promoted managers."
—Edgar H. Schein, Professor of Management,
MIT Sloan School of Management

"Provides valuable insight into the challenges that new managers face. It is must reading for professionals responsible for management development as well as for the manager struggling to make the difficult transition to a new identity."
—*The Design Management Institute Newsletter*

"A remarkably sensitive and unhurried reading of managerial beginnings."
—Karl Weick, Rensis Likert Collegiate
Professor of Organizational Behavior and Psychology,
School of Business Administration,
University of Michigan

PENGUIN BOOKS

BECOMING A MANAGER

Linda A. Hill is an Associate Professor in the Organizational Behavior/Human Resource Management area at the Harvard Business School. Her consulting and executive education activities have been in the areas of managing change and innovation, managing interfunctional conflict, managing in the multinational corporation, and developing an effective leadership style. Organizations with which Professor Hill has worked include American Bankers Association, American Federation of the Arts, Bankers Trust Company, Bristol-Meyers, IBM, McGraw-Hill, Molex International, Textron, and General Electric.

Before joining the faculty at Harvard, Hill was a postdoctoral research fellow at the Harvard Business School and a special assistant to the president of Radcliffe College designing a research project on social change and the support systems for women. She was also appointed as an adviser to the federal Commissioner of Education and as a member of the *Blueprint 2000* Employment Committee for the Commonwealth of Massachusetts. She is currently a member of the board of directors of the New England Human Resource Management Group, the advisory board of the American repertory theatre, the board of trustees of Bryn Mawr, and a trustee of The Children's Museum in Boston and the Beth Israel Hospital in Boston.

Dr. Hill earned a Ph.D. in Behavioral Sciences at the University of Chicago. She received her M.A. in Educational Psychology with a concentration in measurement and evaluation from the University of Chicago. She has an A.B., *summa cum laude,* in psychology from Bryn Mawr College.

Becoming
a
Manager

MASTERY OF A NEW IDENTITY

Linda A. Hill
Harvard Business School

PENGUIN BOOKS

PENGUIN BOOKS
Published by the Penguin Group
Penguin Books USA Inc., 375 Hudson Street,
New York, New York 10014, U.S.A.
Penguin Books Ltd, 27 Wrights Lane, London W8 5TZ, England
Penguin Books Australia Ltd, Ringwood, Victoria, Australia
Penguin Books Canada Ltd, 10 Alcorn Avenue,
Toronto, Ontario, Canada M4V 3B2
Penguin Books (N.Z.) Ltd, 182–190 Wairau Road,
Auckland 10, New Zealand

Penguin Books Ltd, Registered Offices: Harmondsworth, Middlesex, England

First published in the United States of America
by Harvard Business School Press 1992
Published in Penguin Books 1993

20 19 18 17 16 15 14 13

Copyright © the President and Fellows of Harvard College, 1992
All rights reserved

THE LIBRARY OF CONGRESS HAS CATALOGUED THE HARDCOVER AS FOLLOWS:
Hill, Linda A. (Linda Annette), 1956–
Becoming a manager: mastery of a new identity/Linda A. Hill.
p. cm.
ISBN 0-87584-302-6 (hc.)
ISBN 0 14 01.7920 8 (pbk.)
Includes bibliographical references and index.
1. Career changes. 2. Management. I. Title.
HF5384.H55 1992
658.4'09—dc20 91–40612

Printed in the United States of America

Except in the United States of America, this book is sold subject to the condition
that it shall not, by way of trade or otherwise, be lent, re-sold, hired out,
or otherwise circulated without the publisher's prior consent in any form
of binding or cover other than that in which it is published and
without a similar condition including this condition being
imposed on the subsequent purchaser.

To my parents,
Clifford and Lillian Hill,
who encouraged me to be inquisitive
and to have an optimistic outlook on life.

Contents

Preface   ix

Introduction   1

I Learning What It Means to Be a Manager   11

   1 Setting the Stage   15

   2 Reconciling Expectations   51

   3 Moving toward a Managerial Identity   77

II Developing Interpersonal Judgment   93

   4 Exercising Authority   97

   5 Managing Subordinates' Performance   123

III Confronting the Personal Side of Management   155

   6 Gaining Self-Knowledge   159

   7 Coping with the Stresses and Emotions   187

IV Managing the Transformation   207

   8 Critical Resources for the First Year   209

   9 Easing the Transformation   245

Selected Bibliography   283

Appendix   305

Index   325

Preface

The goal in this book is to provide a forum for new managers to speak for themselves as they learn the art of management. Although we know much about what effective and successful managers are like, we know little about how they become that way. Here the odyssey of nineteen new managers during their first year on the job is recounted. Their experiences and observations are instructive, for they give us a rich and textured understanding of the challenges in becoming a manager.

This book is intended for individuals who are considering a managerial career, new managers, those responsible for developing new managers—line managers and human resource managers—and fellow academics and researchers interested in managerial behavior and development. Because this book is designed to appeal to a wide audience, it includes very little technical detail. Those interested in the theoretical underpinnings are encouraged to consult the notes and bibliography. The Appendix includes a description of the research methodology.

The fieldwork for this project was done from 1985 to 1988; analysis of the data and writing spanned an additional three years. A great many people made important contributions along the way. For reasons of confidentiality I cannot thank by name the individuals and companies who participated in this research. I am especially indebted to the managers and their colleagues who gave generously of their time and took me into their confidence. This book is literally theirs, for it tells their stories. My hope is that I have done justice to their collective insights and presented their words as they intended them to be heard. My appreciation also goes to the organizations that employed these managers. They provided access to personnel and confidential information. They supported the project and asked for no feedback or other return.

The individuals who are most familiar with this research and have seen it through from inception to completion are John Gabarro, John Kotter, and Jay Lorsch, colleagues at the Harvard Business School. I am deeply grateful to them. I have benefited from the thoughtful guidance and support of others at the school as well. Samuel Hayes and Benjamin Shapiro assisted me in selecting and gaining access to research sites. Numerous associates reviewed the endless drafts of the manuscript and continually challenged me to refine the analysis and description of my findings. In particular, I thank Anne Donnellon, Robert Eccles, Richard Hackman, Morgan McCall, and Richard Walton. I also express my gratitude to Dean John McArthur and the directors of the Division of Research for offering me the time and resources to complete this work.

For the past few years, I have had the opportunity to present my research at professional meetings and corporate training programs and in a consulting capacity. I acknowledge the countless academics, executives, and managers whose observations and questions helped me interpret my findings and ascertain their implications. The confirmation received from the managers I met was most welcome. They reassured me that my findings were consistent with their experiences, helped them better understand those experiences, and suggested things they could do to capitalize on on-the-job learning.

Many have made invaluable contributions to the production of this book. Barbara Feinberg not only graciously shared her expertise as an editor, but also saw me through the emotional travails of writing a first book. My research assistants—Jaan Elias, Nancy Kamprath, and Melinda Conrad—helped me in preparing the manuscript, from locating misplaced references to critiques of the clarity and logic of the argument. My special thanks go to Hilary Gallagher, Carolyn Saltiel, and Rose Giacobbe and her staff in Word Processing. They patiently typed numerous drafts of the manuscript, often under pressure.

I also wish to acknowledge my friends for their good humor and understanding over the years, especially my dear friend, Lorraine Delhorne and my "dinner group"—Judy Bodie, Joline Godfrey, Diana McClure, Janice McCormick, Barbara Toffler, and Rose Zoltek Jick. And, I want to thank my husband, Roger Breitbart, for his affection, unstinting confidence in me, and substantive insights on my presentation and style.

Becoming
a
Manager

Introduction

*Do you know how hard it is to be the boss, when you are so out of
control! It's hard to verbalize. It's the feeling that all of a sudden . . .
it's the feeling you get when you have a child. On day X minus 1, you
still don't have a child. On day X, all of a sudden you're a mother or
a father and you're supposed to know everything there is to know about
taking care of this kid.**

This observation was made by a new branch manager in a
securities firm. He had been in his new position for only one
month. Before promotion he had been a broker for thirteen
years. He was a star producer, one of the most aggressive and
innovative brokers in his region. Neither he nor his peers were
surprised when the regional director asked him to consider a
management career. New branch managers were generally promoted from the ranks for competence and achievements as individual contributors.

He thoroughly enjoyed being a broker, and had never seriously considered management. The money had been "real
good" for the past few years. He worried intermittently, though,

---

*Unless otherwise identified, all quotations are either direct statements by the
managers in this study or reconstructed from interview notes. Many are
slightly altered to protect anonymity. All names are disguised.

about burnout from the unrelenting pressure—"Will this bull market last forever?"—or boredom as the years went by. Reflecting on the four branch managers for whom he had worked, he concluded he had some insight into what it took to be an effective manager. In fact, several times he had commented that if he had been in charge he would have known how to fix things so that he and his fellow brokers could perform to their full potential. He decided to find out more about the branch manager opportunity, and eventually chose to pursue it. When the branch assignment came through, the branch manager took him out for a congratulatory lunch and welcomed him to the "big leagues." Over the next week, as he distributed his clients to other brokers, he felt moments of intense panic, but there was no turning back. He was giving up his "security blanket." After a short time on the job, he lamented that he might have "bitten off more than he could chew."

That experience is by no means unique. Indeed, the promotion to manager is a pivotal juncture in a business career, for both the individual and organization. It is frequently both a reward for good performance, and also a means by which to infuse talent into the managerial hierarchy. But the odyssey from individual contributor to manager is often difficult, full of horror stories about promising careers that wither along the way. In spite of their established qualifications as individual contributors, many new managers never adjust successfully to managerial responsibilities. First-line management is the level in the organization from which come the most frequent reports of incompetence, burnout, and excessive attrition.[1] The human and financial costs are staggering for both the organization and those who fail to make the transition.[2] Even those who make it find that the first management job remains a potent memory as long as 25 years later.

Despite its ubiquity and importance, we know surprisingly little about the transition to management. Very few have studied the manager's earliest experiences—the first months or year on the job.[3] This is the topic of this book: What do new managers find most challenging? How do they learn to be managers? On

2

what individual and organizational resources do they rely? Although the shelves are stacked with descriptions of what effective and successful managers are like, there are few books on how they get that way.

THE NEW MANAGERS

This book follows nineteen managers through their first year. All participants were new sales and marketing managers, fourteen men and five women. Ten were branch managers in a securities firm and nine were sales managers in a computer company (see Appendix for a detailed description of the participants and the research methodology).

Before the promotion to manager everyone in the study was an individual contributor, otherwise known as a specialist, producer, or professional. Their primary responsibility was to perform specific technical tasks; their contribution to the organization was *individual,* depending primarily on personal expertise, experience, and action.[4] In contrast, a manager is formally in charge of the organization or one of its subunits. His or her primary responsibilities include supervising others rather than directly performing technical tasks. The distinction between individual contributor and first-line manager is often blurred, for first-line managers often perform technical work. It is the formal authority over others and the attendant rights and duties that differentiate the manager from the individual contributor.

The new managers were first-line field sales managers in their organizations. They were directly responsible for day-to-day management and supervision of field sales representatives in their territories and were accountable for achieving specific sales and marketing goals. The job descriptions for both included developing the sales organization; creating a healthy work environment; establishing standards of performance; evaluating, rewarding, and developing subordinates; acting as liaison between their unit and others in the company; interpreting and enforcing corporate policy; and representing the company to the community. Neither group had responsibility for specific accounts, but they were expected when necessary to call on clients with the assigned sales representative.

Both groups worked for *Fortune* 500 corporations. By almost any financial indicator, their companies were leaders in their industries. They were, however, undergoing significant change in response to an increasingly competitive and volatile business environment. Consequently, managerial roles in both companies were becoming more complex and demanding. Managers were held accountable for a broader array of financial, strategic, and human resource outcomes. They were asked to pursue not only short-term financial objectives, but also long-term strategic initiatives. They were expected to focus not only on revenues, but also on profits. The securities firm, after deregulation of the financial services industry, was moving from a product to a service focus. The computer company had recently instituted programs on cost control, service, and quality. Both companies consequently emphasized providing leadership, developing subordinates, and maintaining long-term partnerships with clients.

The securities firm managers (SFMs) and computer company managers (CCMs) and their positions differed significantly. The SFMs were managing retail salespeople who were independent players selling an intangible product (financial instruments) to individual and small business accounts. The CCMs were responsible for institutional salespeople who sold large data-processing systems to commercial accounts. They were members of a sales team that included systems analysts and administrative and operations personnel over whom the CCMs had no formal authority. The SFMs were general managers, with profit-and-loss responsibility for an entire branch. They were expected to plan strategy and execute programs for their work units. The CCMs, though, were responsible only for the sales function; most of their goals were still revenue- and not profit-oriented. They were expected to build sales and marketing programs for their unit consistent with the branch strategy. The span of authority and autonomy, and hence the change in position, was much greater for the SFMs than the CCMs. Not surprisingly, the SFMs had more experience as individual contributors than did the CCMs.

Despite these differences, the new managers provided strikingly consistent accounts of their first experiences.* We examine these recurrent themes in the managers' first-year biographies in the following pages.

FINDINGS

Although countless articles and books offer counsel on how to develop managerial talent, few have been based on empirical research. And few look at the phenomenon from the new manager's perspective or consider on-the-job developmental experience.[5] Most are how-to manuals outlining the knowledge a manager needs about the content of managerial work. Most treat management development from the single dimension of task learning: acquisition of necessary competencies (the knowledge and skills necessary to fulfill managerial functions) and establishment of key relationships. Becoming a manager is largely presented as an intellectual exercise, albeit a demanding one.

A pointedly different dimension in the development of a new manager emerged from the research described in these chapters. Here, new managers speak for themselves as they learn a new craft. Their experiences and impressions unveil a richer understanding of the challenges. Listening to them, it becomes clear that the transition to manager is not limited to acquiring competencies and building relationships. Rather, it constitutes a profound transformation, as individuals learn to think, feel, and value as managers (see Exhibit I-1).

---

*Their experiences were, of course, diverse. Each manager's experience was shaped partly by personal characteristics such as prior experience, skill, and managerial style, as well as by situational factors such as company, office size and strategy, and profile of subordinates. Still, we can see clear central tendencies or patterns. By central tendencies, I mean that the majority (fifteen or more) or most (ten or more) of the new managers responded or behaved consistently. In Chapter 9, we examine some of the more salient differences in their experiences.

Exhibit I-1

Transformation of Identity

From	*To*
A specialist and doer. Directly performs specific technical tasks. Strongly identified with those tasks.	A generalist and agenda-setter. Orchestrates diverse tasks, including finance, product design, and manufacturing or organization. Strongly identified with a business or the management profession.
An individual actor. Gets things done mostly by one's own efforts. Strongly identified as relatively independent.	A network builder. Gets things done through others, including subordinates over whom one has formal authority. Strongly identified as highly interdependent.

The new managers described the transformation vividly, weaving tales of coping with the stresses of transformation, reluctantly letting go of deeply held attitudes and habits, and timidly experimenting with new ways of thinking and being. They discussed not simply what happened, but how it felt.

The managers began to make the psychological adjustment as they tried to make sense of and struggled with their new agenda-setting and network-building responsibilities. As an outgrowth of taking action, they mastered four tasks of transformation:

- Learning what it means to be a manager
- Developing interpersonal judgment
- Gaining self-knowledge
- Coping with stress and emotion

Through on-the-job experience they began to understand and accept their new responsibilities (learning what it means to be a manager) and to acquire the task (developing interpersonal judgment) and personal (gaining self-knowledge and coping with stress and emotion) competencies necessary to meet them. The managers' expectations of their new job were incomplete and simplistic. They had to reconcile these expectations with the daily reality of managerial life and with the seemingly unending and confusing demands of their new subordinates, bosses, and peers. Over time the managers began to develop personal theories of management: a set of assumptions and hypotheses about the managerial role. They became aware of these theories as they reflected on their actions and decisions. In turn, these theories came to guide their future behavior. Unequivocally, the managers asserted that the most demanding task learning of the first year had to do with the "people challenges." Through the problems they encountered and their interactions with others they began to develop interpersonal rules of best managerial practice. But it was the personal learning more than the task learning that the managers found most unsettling. The first year of management was a period of considerable introspection and personal growth. They matured as they confronted previously undiscovered truths about themselves and were relieved to see that adults, like themselves, do change and develop. Not surprisingly, a major order of priority was learning to cope with the stress and intense emotion associated with their new position and the evolution of a new professional identity.

Although it was possible to distinguish conceptually among the four tasks, the managers dealt with and learned about them more or less simultaneously. By "learning," I mean the sort of learning after which an individual conceives of something in a qualitatively different way, and which has lasting influence. Moreover, this learning goes beyond the intellectual sense: it involves being acquainted with something experientially.[6] The lessons were learned as the managers confronted the daily litany of interactions and problems in their new assignments. And they were learned incrementally, gradually. Sometimes the managers were aware that they were learning, but most often they were not. The learning consisted principally of "gradual and tacit change"; with the accumulation of evidence and experience came the erosion of one set of beliefs, attitudes, and values and buildup of another.[7] The building-up process was one of iterative refinement and revision. Warren Bennis, an authority on managerial learning and development, writes, "A person does not gather learnings as possessions but rather becomes a new person with those learnings as a part of his or her new self."[8]

Like individuals who must suddenly face the transition to parenthood, the managers had to learn on the job, and it was a critical and overwhelming job at that. They were responsible for the lives of others, yet they had to make decisions and act before they understood what they were supposed to do. And like new parents, the managers were transformed by the experience. As they confronted and mastered the challenges, they came to view themselves and the world differently.

Most of the new managers in this study were successful. Of the nineteen, their superiors felt that all but three "made it" through the first year. In other words, they were well on their way to making the fundamental transformation required. But even for this group, the first year was neatly summed up by a manager who had served in the Navy: "It was one hell of a tour of duty."

NOTES

1. See Badawy (1982), Bayton and Chapman (1973), Beiker (1986), Dougherty (1984), Falvey (1989), Flamholtz and Randal (1987), Lorsch and Mathias (1987), London (1985), Medcoff (1985), Webber (1991), and Webster (1983).
2. It was difficult to obtain accurate figures on the costs to organizations of new manager incompetence and turnover. McCall et al. (1988) report that one company estimated a failed general manager cost $500,000, not counting the negative effect on business revenues (p. 110). "General manager" in the McCall et al. study referred, however, to senior-level managers.
3. Nicholson and West (1988) in their study on work transitions, observed that the literature on career transitions is in its infancy, with a very thin empirical base on which to build theory (p. 14). Extensive research has been done, however, in two related areas: organizational socialization and careers. For a summary of the literature on organizational socialization, see Louis (1990). For reviews of the careers literature, see Arthur et al. (1989) or Driver (1988).

4. Other individual-contributor roles include investment banker, physician, computer programmer, engineer, and accountant. Such individuals often have low-level assistants or secretaries for whom they have some supervisory responsibility, but their primary assignment is to perform some specific task or technical work.

5. Notable exceptions include Akin (1987), Burgoyne and Hodgson (1983), McCall et al. (1988), Mumford (1987), Nicholson and West (1988), and Schein (1978; 1987). Medcoff (1985) observes:

> Most analyses of how to train the technologist to become a manager look at the technologist from outside and prescribe ways to train him. More analysis of the technologist's point of view is badly needed. Such an analysis would yield rich insight about how, when and where to have him develop himself toward and within management (p. 21).

6. Theorists have discussed various types of learning. Burgoyne and Hodgson (1983) identified three types:

> Level 1 learning occurred when a manager simply took in some factual information or data which had an immediate relevance but did not have any long-term effect on their view of the world in general. . . . Level 2 learning, on the other hand, was when a manager apparently learnt something which was transferable from the present situation to another, i.e., he had changed his conception about a particular aspect of his view of the world in general; the aspect in question being, however, situation (as experienced by the manager) specific. . . . Level 3 learning was when a manager seemed to learn or become conscious about his conceptions of the world in general, how they were formed, or how he might change them. Level 3 learning is not, therefore, situation specific (pp. 393–395).

By learning, I mean that covered by Levels 2 and 3.

7. The conceptualization of role transitions as involving both unlearning the old role and incorporating the new is described by others, including Lewin (1935) and Schein (1961). Burgoyne and Hodgson (1983) studied "natural learning and managerial action" and discovered five processes of learning: 1) specific learning incidents; 2) evoking and extending "personal case law"; 3) gradual and tactic change in orientation or attitude on the basis of cumulative experience; 4) deliberate problem-solving and learning; and 5) reflective learning (pp. 394–395). My findings were consistent with their report that most managerial learning could be categorized as "gradual and tactic change . . . on the basis of cumulative experience."

8. Bennis (1989), p. 38.

I

Learning What It
Means to Be
a Manager

To tell the story of the new managers' experiences properly, we must start where they started, by asking what it means to be a manager and what a manager does. In this part of the book we consider how the new managers came to understand that the managerial role was distinct from the individual contributor role and how they began to embrace it.

The new managers learned through experience what it meant to be a manager—first, from their prior experience as individual contributors (observing their managers at work) and then, from their interactions with others while performing the functions and activities of management. Throughout their first year on the job, the managers reframed their understanding of what being a manager meant as they confronted the inevitable problems that came with their positions and the expectations of those with whom they worked.

They encountered many surprises, positive and negative,

along the way. As the managers learned about the realities of managerial work, they were plagued by a particular kind of surprise that arises when tacit job expectations are not met or features of the job are not anticipated. The problems and expectations that did not fit their existing frameworks provided an incentive for them to further refine and modify their understanding. They grappled with three critical sets of problems: (1) how to reconcile their initial expectations of management with the realities of a manager's daily life; (2) how to handle the numerous conflicts with their subordinates; and (3) how to make sense of and meet their superiors' ambitious demands. With each surprise and each reframing, the managers better understood the complexities of the managerial role and moved toward a managerial identity.

Because the new managers' understanding of what it means to be a manager was a distillation of expectations, their prior expectations, and the different claims of those with whom they came in contact, we must understand what those expectations were. In Chapter 1 we consider a blueprint of the managerial role and then the expectations of the new managers, their subordinates, their superiors, and their peers. (Unless otherwise specified, by peers I mean associates in other functional areas.) We concentrate on the managers' prior expectations and those of subordinates, because these are critical in the new managers' first-year experiences.[1] The blueprint of the managerial role serves as a reference point by which to identify similarities and differences in these expectations.

With this background, Chapters 2 and 3 document the evolutionary unfolding of the managers' experiences as they learn what being a manager entails. It is an emotional tale, for not only does their behavior change (what they do and with whom), but also their attitudes are transformed (their mindset, priorities, and sources of self-esteem). In Chapter 2 we focus on the new managers' experiences in the first half of the year, reconciling their expectations with the reality of managerial work and with subordinates' expectations. In Chapter 3, we watch as the managers' conceptions of their role become more complex and sophisticated in the second half of the year. Not until then do they begin to really integrate superior expectations into their understanding of managerial work and to adopt a more managerial identity.

Acknowledging superior expectations led them to appreciate more fully what it meant to be the person with the ultimate authority and accountability for the welfare of their unit. They began to recognize their place in the organization and to accept their agenda-setting and network-building responsibilities. As they began to integrate the myriad and often conflicting expectations of those with whom they worked, they began to forsake a once dearly held identity and in its place embrace another.

NOTES

1. As stated earlier, the sales managers were functional managers and their subordinates were all salespeople. The branch managers were general managers and had subordinates in different functional areas; sales, administration, and operations. Still, in speaking of their subordinates the branch managers were oriented almost exclusively toward their salespeople. In the discussion that follows, "subordinates" refers to salespersons unless otherwise indicated.

1

Setting the Stage

THE MANAGERIAL ROLE

Initially the new managers had no real idea of what they had gotten themselves into. They could not appreciate the complexity and breadth of their new role. One of them reported:

> I didn't have the slightest idea what my job was. I walked in giggling and laughing because I had been promoted and had no idea what principles or style to be guided by. After the first day I felt like I had run into a brick wall.

No wonder the new managers found it difficult to make sense of and define their new role. Distinguished practitioners and academics have produced volumes about managerial work and proposed a variety of conceptualizations. One thing about which they all agree is that the managerial role is complex and demanding. It is a boundary-spanning position into which are built inherent tensions. Managers must juggle diverse, often ambiguous, responsibilities and are enmeshed in a web of relationships with people who often make conflicting demands: subordinates, bosses, and others inside and outside of the organization.[1] As a result, the daily routine in management is often pressured, hectic, and fragmented.

They have to figure out what to do and how to act in all this apparent chaos of great uncertainty, diversity, and interdependence. Consequently, the managers have to develop and continually update agendas for the work unit. These agendas provide the framework and parameters within which they act. Kotter, an authority on managerial work, describes these agendas as made up of loosely connected goals and plans that address long- and short-term responsibilities (for these managers, long term means one to five years) and many issues: financial (such as sales, expenses, income, and return on investment); business (such as product refinement or new product development, inventory levels, and market share); and organizational (such matters as organizational design, policies on human resource management, and management of subordinates' performance).[2] To implement their emerging agendas, managers must establish cooperative relationships with and among people in their networks.

As individual contributors, the people in this study had, in a sense, one agenda: direct performance of technical work; that is, selling products and services to specific clients. To meet this responsibility, of course, they had had to attend to their relationships with customers, bosses, and sometimes peers (the CCMs in particular had a limited number of peers with whom they had to cooperate to get tasks done). But their contributions to corporate goals were based primarily on individual thought and action.

Promotion to management, though, meant a major leap in scope, more people, dollars, functions, products, and markets to be managed. The managers' contribution to corporate objectives was based on their influence on an entire unit. They had to get their work done through others. Consequently, they had to build and maintain larger and more diverse networks of relationships (including an entirely new group: subordinates). As the people with formal authority, they were accountable for making sense of and integrating the varied agendas of their constituencies. It was their task to form and negotiate agendas and orchestrate the work of those in their networks to complete those agendas and thereby gain the ends that their organizations desired.

A CONSTELLATION OF EXPECTATIONS

We begin this account by describing the new managers' initial expectations about their new roles—what they thought their most important responsibilities would be. Then we examine the points of view of key members of their internal networks: subordinates, superiors, and peers. The findings reported in this chapter are based on my first interviews with the various parties during the managers' first weeks on the job. What follows is the result of my analysis and interpretations of responses to two open-ended questions: How would you describe the manager's job? What is the manager supposed to do? Although the individual perspectives of managers, subordinates, superiors, and peers varied, clear consistencies appeared. In this chapter, these recurring patterns will be discussed. Important differences in the views will be presented later.

The new managers and those in their networks saw the managerial role differently. Each group's perceptions were biased to suit their interests. The new managers' initial expectations were shaped primarily by their motivation to move into management and by their experience as star producers. Hence, in defining their new role they focused heavily on their newly acquired formal authority and the agenda-setting responsibilities associated with sales. In contrast, they played down the second part of the role equation, that they were now primarily responsible for people, not the task. Their impression of their agenda-setting and network-building responsibilities therefore was impoverished.

The subordinates, on the other hand, made light of the managers' formal authority and stressed the managers' role as working through or with others. The subordinates defined the managers' agenda-setting and network-building responsibilities in a self-serving way: the managers' task was first and foremost to make sure the subordinates' personal agendas were fulfilled. The subordinates were most concerned that the managers not encroach on their territory and autonomy, and provide the context and resources the subordinates needed to derive success and satisfaction from their work.

The superiors, as you would expect, had the most comprehensive and most grounded view of being a manager. But they too revealed a bias. They emphasized the manager's role as one of formal authority, especially the accountability it implied for everything occurring in a work unit. Because the superiors had their own agendas and counted on the managers to contribute to them, their principal concern was that the managers deliver on whatever goals the superiors set for them.

We spend little time on peers' expectations, for the managers devoted little attention to them. Like the others in the managers' networks, their peers defined the managerial role according to their own priorities. Because they held the formal authority, the managers were responsible for making sure that not only they, but also their subordinates, recognized and addressed their peers' interests and requests.

In other words, each group had its own frame of reference to help make sense of the Byzantine maze of managerial work. We need to understand these frames, for they determined what each group chose to attend to, and as will become apparent, how they behaved.[3] Exhibit 1-1 summarizes the varied definitions of the managerial role that we found, using as a reference point the conceptual model of managerial work presented earlier.

Exhibit 1-1

What It Means to Be a Manager: A Conceptual Model

Managerial role	Constituency			
	New managers	Subordinates	Superiors	Peers
Agenda setting				
Financial	x		x	
Business	x	x	x	
Organizational		x	x	
Network building				
Subordinates	x	x	x	
Superiors			x	
Peers			x	x
External others			x	

THE NEW MANAGERS' EXPECTATIONS: MANAGER AS BOSS

When asked to describe what it meant to be a manager, nearly all the managers began by discussing management's rights and privileges, not its duties. They generally began by stating explicitly that being a manager meant being *the boss*:

> A manager is the person in charge.
> The manager is the person in power, the authority, the expert.
> Being the manager means running my own office, using my ideas and thoughts.
> You're on the other side of the desk. You hold their [the subordinates'] careers, their jobs, in the palm of your hand, so to speak.
> It's [the office] my baby. It's my job to make sure it works.

Their replies were quite consistent: it meant being responsible and accountable, having power, and being in control. Most managers attributed their motivation to become managers above all to the opportunity to exercise power and control; having those, they assumed they would gain much-desired autonomy to do what they thought best. They would no longer be "burdened by the unreasonable demands of others":

> Now, I'll be the one calling the shots. I like to have my own way, but the issue is not power over people. I just want the authority to control my own life.
> I want to give *my* ideas a chance.
> I worked for many managers through the years and I wasn't happy with most of them. I began talking a lot to people and told them my philosophy about managing, and finally I said, I have to try it. I want a chance to treat people the way I always wanted to be treated.

With formal authority came decision-making responsibility and accountability. Most saw decision making as a major function in their new role as *the* authority figure:

> I'm paid to make decisions. The buck stops here.
> The ability to make a good decision, support it, and stick by it. The managers who have difficulty are the ones who struggle with making decisions, have trouble making them, and then have buyer's remorse after they make them—they say, Was that really the right decision? You just can't do that.
> In this business you can't play around. You have to be in charge because the well-being of the client and the firm is in your hands. Period.

From these quotations we see that the new managers focused mainly on decisions about sales and business, not people. They routinely spoke of only two kinds of people-management decisions: hiring and firing subordinates. Even potential interpersonal conflicts were often reduced to questions of technical judgment. One manager anticipated that she would be called upon frequently as arbiter in disputes between subordinates and customers. In her account she described her job as "making sure the right business decision is made" and maintaining the customer relationship. She said nothing about how her actions might affect her relationship with her people or their development. Like the rest of her group, this manager saw the implications of the first aspect of the managerial role, formal authority, more clearly than of the second, getting work done through others.

Setting Agendas

Manager as sales leader. As the boss, the new managers felt their primary responsibility was to provide "sales leadership"; the manager "drives the business." Because they were in the sales function, that translated to "brings in the sales":

> I'll be the sales leader. I've got to absolutely keep coming up with the big sales ideas. You don't become the sales manager until you can handle the customer. I've matured my skills so that I hope I can negotiate better from the sheer number of customers I've dealt with.
> The job is 80 percent sales. I love sales. I've got to know the products and help my people build an approach to sales. I have to give them specific ideas and suggestions on how to sell and I've got to run effective meetings that impart the necessary information and motivate them [the salespeople] to sell the product.
> My priority is to drive the business, bring in the revenue, no matter what it takes.

In short, most managers contended that sales leadership was their "ultimate responsibility." They felt confident that their future subordinates, superiors, and customers held the same assumption:

> My boss pays me for making my quota and for customer satisfaction.
> The bottom line is that he [the boss] expects me to make the numbers.

My role is to make them [subordinates] rich . . . give them accounts, product training, and sales skills. Some want it handed to them, some want to work for it. Most think it best that I leave them alone and let them perform.

The customer is always right; I've got to make it [what the customer wants] happen yesterday.

The customer comes to me to make the tough decisions and exceptions that my people can't.

Three pivotal responsibilities of the sales leader come out in the new managers' descriptions of their role.[4] Their first obligation is to "provide opportunity"; that is, to distribute accounts, clients, or quotas. Besides providing opportunity, they are expected to provide sales ideas efficiently and promptly, information about what would sell, and tricks of the trade on how to sell:

My people know that time is money. They want me to give them the goods [information] with as little intrusion as possible.

My reps want me to be responsive. They come to me because they are having difficulty with deciding what the next step should be, to strategize and see if I can use my expertise or clout to help them follow through.

The final responsibility of the sales leader they stressed was medium- and long-term planning:

It's my job to pay attention to the strategic horizon for our territory. I have to have the two-year plan at least, some sense of where the customer needs to be. Every good marketeer has a vision, just like every good businessman will have one that he can't totally articulate, but he has in mind a picture of where this customer ought to be going.

I set the goals for the territory after analyzing and developing a strategy for our segment. . . . A lot of them [subordinates] have trouble thinking about what our customer should be doing. They'll think about what a customer is doing and I have to judge if they are doing the right thing.

The managers believed their subordinates would evaluate managerial performance primarily by the opportunities and sales

ey provided, but their superiors would place more
wei.. on planning.

In discussing sales leadership, the new managers showed
some appreciation for the distinction between being a doer and
being a manager. Just as they emphasized formal authority, they
saw agenda setting as a managerial prerogative. It was their right
as boss to set critical parameters within which their subordinates
would work, specifically to distribute accounts and set quotas.
They also relished their new planning responsibilities—caring
about the long term; they liked "doing strategy." Again, as boss
it was their job to set the direction for their unit. Moreover, the
new managers understood that in fulfilling their new roles, they
might have to run interference among the people with whom
they had to work. They acknowledged that their subordinates
and superiors might have different priorities. But as we see, they
focused on only a subset of their agenda-setting responsibilities,
those relating to the financial and business arenas, not the organization or people.

Building Networks

Manager as supervisor.   The new managers generally
defined their new positions by their responsibilities, not their
relationships. Starting out as managers, they did not appreciate
the distinction between being primarily responsible for people
rather than the task. For although they had identified some of
their newly acquired responsibilities, they had little sense of
those they were supposed to give up, specifically, direct responsibility for the technical task.

Still, almost all the managers mentioned the people management responsibilities of their new positions. By "people,"
however, they meant subordinates by and large, not superiors,
peers, or other principals outside the organization. Notice also
that in speaking of their subordinates, they mentioned almost
exclusively their salespeople. Even those who were general
managers and had subordinates in different functions—sales,
administration, and operations—displayed this bias. As we have
seen, for the new managers, managing subordinates mainly

meant exercising sales leadership. And sales leadership in turn meant their agenda-setting obligations specifically for financial and business matters.

Clearly then, the new managers were not attuned to their network-building responsibilities. They understood that they were responsible for supervising their salespeople, but they focused on the more formal and administrative aspects of managing people, which many labeled "personnel," such as staffing and completing performance appraisals. They fretted that their personnel responsibilities would be inordinately demanding of their time and energy. Most managers, asked to define managerial responsibilities, did indeed comment on the need to motivate the work force.[5] A few even mentioned the manager's role in "creating the right atmosphere" or "leading the team" in the organization. They could not, however, describe in much detail what they saw as their responsibilities in these areas. They simply mentioned them. They became visibly excited and often expounded in detail, though, about what they hoped to accomplish in the sales leadership and decision-making arenas.

Manager as administrator. We have seen that the new managers concentrated mainly on their new rights and privileges. Reluctantly, they accepted one of the duties that they identified as coming with authority, and that was administration. They defined administration as routine communication activities such as paperwork and exchange of information. The administrator's role was associated with their more negative images of the manager's job. They were quite vocal about their concerns. Their administrative responsibilities seemed to be constraints that interfered with their autonomy and stole precious time from more important responsibilities:

> Managers are bureaucrats, paper shufflers, parasites who get in the way.
>
> My worst manager was just an administrator. He spent all his time in his office with the door shut, pushing paper.
>
> I never want to think of myself as a manager. If I ever do, I'll lose my edge. You're in a field marketing job, not a staff job. So you're really riveted toward getting the marketing stuff done; everything else is overhead to you.

When they were feeling more magnanimous, the new managers defined administration as a secondary, yet essential, managerial function. They referred to it as a necessary evil: "A manager's job is to drive the business while staying within company policies and procedures."

The new managers saw their administrative responsibilities as serving two purposes. They were the organization's way of ensuring that business was conducted in accordance with company and legal requirements. The securities firm managers were more sensitive to the administrative role than those in the computer company: "We deal with money and are very tightly regulated." They acknowledged that the branch manager was considered the key to a brokerage house's effort at compliance, because he or she was in the best position to monitor brokers.[6] The administrative procedures protected them as well as the company from inequities and misconduct:

> When a company is fairly big, you have to create a paper trail.
>
> There is a structure and set of ground rules on how to operate—rules that you know as a rep. But soon I'll be on the other side of the desk. I'll have to be more objective and less creative. I'll have to follow some structure. You're trying to create an environment of uniformity not only among the people in your branch but across the division and company.
>
> The manual puts everything on the manager's shoulders. I get fired if one of the brokers is a crook and I don't catch it. . . . To protect my hide I've got to follow the procedures.

As some of the new managers mentioned, the administrative procedures were the organization's way of continually collecting and updating information about what was happening in the field and the marketplace. The managers expected that their administrative responsibilities would mean a lot to their superiors and be considered intrusive by their subordinates and customers. The latter two constituencies would expect the manager to "buffer them from bureaucratic red tape."

Manager as politician. All the new managers were uneasy about managing relationships with superiors and peers, especially about meeting objectives the boss gave them. They felt the best way to please the boss was to produce results, specifically by meeting the sales quotas for their territories. Producing results translated into providing sales leadership. Very few of them mentioned the need to devote time and attention to building a cooperative relationship with the boss or to negotiate with him or her about an appropriate agenda for their unit. They saw the boss's agenda as an imposed one, with which they simply had to live.

The new managers had very little to say about managing peer relations, and that reflected a rather cynical point of view. For many, managing these relationships fell under their administrative role, filling out the often tedious paperwork that peers in other functional areas might request. Networking was tolerated as a necessary evil, "keeping the administrative monkey off [your] back": "If you know the right people, you can get things done. You won't be held up by silly rules and procedures." This was a chore at which they hoped to spend little time.

With some disdain, almost all expressed the need to manage office politics. Many spoke of the problems peers could create for you, if they wanted to. Some recited tales of peers obstructing and even sabotaging each other's efforts. Those who had witnessed such events spoke of the need to behave diplomatically and make no unnecessary enemies. This tactic often meant not sharing with a peer what they honestly thought about their ideas or requests and, for some, doing a favor for a peer even when they "had nothing to gain personally." But as with superior relationships, few talked about proactively managing peer relationships. Only a handful seemed to appreciate the advantages in actively building trust, credibility, and cooperative relationships with peers. And even they seemed to feel such activities were a luxury.

Summary of New Managers' Initial Expectations

For all the new managers, the decision to pursue a managerial career had been a very thoughtful one. Before starting the new position, each had systematically thought about and discussed with various people what their job responsibilities would be. Still, their expectations of a manager's job were incomplete and simplistic. Admittedly, they recognized many of the managerial functions and some of the tensions inherent in the managerial position (such as those between sales leadership and administrative responsibilities). They did not, however, appreciate the full range of demands that would be made on them, and the ambiguities and inconsistencies. For them, the managerial role was mainly one of formal authority and managing the task, not the people. One new manager admitted, with some chagrin, that after a year on the job his initial image of the job was of being "the lead salesperson with the final authority and accountability."[7] Why did they not fully recognize the people management activities, especially supervising and coordinating others' efforts—the duty that researchers and experienced practitioners define as *the* basic distinction between being an individual contributor and a manager?[8]

The managers' initial expectations were partly influenced by information gleaned during their selection and promotion. Many took hints from conversation with their soon-to-be bosses and human resource personnel, and from reviews of practices in evaluating managerial performance and of compensation. (To protect confidentiality of the research sites, we do not present the exact text of the job descriptions.) Almost all descriptions they read or heard explicitly referred to the management responsibilities they would inherit. The information the managers gathered from these sources, though, usually emphasized end results rather than the actions they would need to take. The latter interested them most. As others have reported, formal job descriptions often consist of general exhortations about *what* management is, with little guidance on *how* a manager should perform his or her work.[9]

Instead, the managers' expectations were profoundly shaped by their motivation to become managers and by past work experience. In their initial conception of what it meant to be a manager, they emphasized the manager's rights and privileges instead of the duties. It was the rights and privileges—the authority—that had attracted them to management. As we will see in Chapter 2, the new managers were also reluctant to give up the *doer* role, with which they were comfortable and from which they had derived much personal esteem. The managers conceived of the managerial role as doing more of what they had been doing all along, only now they would have more power, control, and accountability.

Moreover, like most of us, the managers relied heavily upon past experience to make sense of their new position.[10] As individual contributors, they had worked closely with managers who held the very positions in which they would soon find themselves. The average new manager had been a producer for eight years and had reported to five managers. One confidently stated that he had seen it all. But, as we know from extensive research, experience can saddle individuals with a myopic view of their current circumstances. The managers' experience was an imperfect lens with which to make sense of their new position. They had experienced the managerial role only from the perspective of an individual contributor; their identity was still that of producer, not manager.

That the new managers had suffered few disappointments or setbacks in their careers appeared to prejudice their understanding of what being a manager meant. The cliché "success can be blinding" fits here. The managers had been star producers; in fact, they had been promoted to management mostly as a reward for outstanding performance. It was through the eyes of a *star* producer who had worked with bosses "awful and superb" that they came initially to define the role of manager. Because of their considerable technical expertise and high motivation, they depended less than the average salesperson on their sales managers for support and guidance. One manager said he "had succeeded in spite of most of [his] managers." Isolated by this star status, the new managers had limited first-hand opportunities to observe their managers handling the interpersonal difficulties that can arise in working with less proficient subordinates. And because they had been successful they had encountered relatively few difficulties or conflicts with superiors or peers. Researchers have found too that people learn more from their failures than their successes.[11] We're inclined to take the time to reflect on ourselves and our situation only when adversity strikes. Until they had to choose whether or not to pursue a managerial career, the new managers had little incentive to take a hard look at what their own managers did.

The new managers were in for major surprises. One lamented at the end of his first month that he had "taken the job under false pretenses." They would have to reconcile their expectations with the realities of managerial work, with the constituencies they would work with: subordinates, superiors, and peers. Next, we consider the subordinates' expectations.

SUBORDINATES' EXPECTATIONS: MANAGER AS PEOPLE MANAGER

For the new managers, the critical distinction between individual contributor and manager lay in authority and accountability. The subordinates saw the critical differences as in the second aspect of the managerial role, getting work done through others.[12] According to the subordinates, they were responsible for the task and tactics, and the manager was responsible for people and strategy. Indeed, the theme prevalent in the subordinates' remarks was that managers were "in the business of people management."

The subordinates believed the managers' job was to "support" their subordinates, who in turn, were responsible for the task. Whereas the managers saw the manager as boss, for the subordinates the manager was a facilitator. The manager's job was to create the conditions for subordinates' success. Most subordinates expected to be treated as "independent business[people] with [their] own small piece of the action":

> The manager is given a piece of the business to run by his boss. He has to break it down into a smaller piece and say, "Okay, here is your piece of the business. Here is your opportunity to attain a goal. After you have a chance to swallow it, show me your plan on how you are going to do it. Within it tell me the resources you need and what help you need from me to make your quota." And once in a while he

may have to kick me in the ass to make sure I'm going in the right direction.

The subordinates seemed to feel that the managers were to take the broad view. They were responsible for creating a positive work environment and for solving problems that the subordinates found intractable. I asked the subordinates how the new managers were to create such an environment. Four themes emerged from their responses: managers were to provide sales leadership and keep the organization running efficiently; managers had two agenda-setting responsibilities: to provide team leadership and manage relationships with others (in the organization, clients, and the community) and to build networks.

Setting Agendas

Manager as sales leader. Like the new managers, the subordinates defined sales leadership as a critical management function. They contended that technical expertise specific to their products was essential for sales management; a manager gained credibility by experience and reputation as a producer. One of the manager's first duties was to provide opportunity by distributing clients or territories and establishing quotas. This goal could be accomplished equitably and realistically only by someone who knew the market and products at first hand. They also expected the manager to provide sales ideas and guidance:

> What do I need? Ideas about how to get new clients and how to get into the cycles. How to handle the downtrends, really specific suggestions. When I wasn't producing much, I needed ideas of where to go, how to target a different group, help developing a script that fits who I am. [My manager] helped me find a way of meeting people because he figured out that I was better face-to-face than in a phone call. And it is important that a manager pick up on the good that you are doing too.

> A good manager is always providing fresh new ideas, such as how to take advantage of conference call technology.

The good manager gives direction and information about what works and takes the problems away.

The third sales leadership responsibility was planning. Most of the subordinates mentioned the manager's role in developing the unit's marketing strategy and approach:

You've got to have a sense of their strategy. . . . Hers is to get more information to the customer, more profiling, more public speaking at seminars: get out in front of the public more than we have done in the past. Also, try to sell a broader base of products. Get the insurance out there and take away the bankers' clients.

He's got to take care of the big picture so that we don't have to worry if we are on track. I just have to worry about the best tactics for getting the product out the door.

The subordinates believed a vital managerial role was to continually monitor what was going on in the organization and competitive environment and update their agendas appropriately.[13] The subordinates were keenly aware of their dependence on the manager for such information, to which they themselves did not have access (this goal is even clearer in their discussion of the manager as liaison).

It was the manager's job to think of the long term so that the subordinates could concentrate on meeting short-term goals. The subordinates stressed that the good manager was not simply reactive, but proactive. They counted on the manager to alert them to and prepare them for major changes in the future. It was the manager's responsibility to anticipate future opportunities and potential problems and plan accordingly, so that the organization could adapt without unnecessary interruption:

This is a fast-paced business. One day you're the leader, the next day you're last in the pack. The manager has got to keep up with the latest trends and prepare us for them.

[One of my best managers] used the superhighway analogy. We were moving up the superhighway to the top of the mountain and along the way there are signs such as slow, curve, narrow bridge, stop, and guard rails. He makes sure we abide by them so that we don't fall over the cliff. If the wheels go off the road, he gets us back on track. He charts us through the dangers.

Manager as organizer. The subordinates alternately described the managerial role as providing sales leadership and as maintaining an efficiently run organization. They felt that both functions were part of the manager's job, creating a context within which the subordinates could flourish.

Most expected the manager to be the organizer, to design and maintain an efficient and stable organization: setting up the structure, systems, staffing, and training that would achieve a steady and orderly work flow.[14] The managers ensured that office operations ran smoothly so that their subordinates could stick to the job of selling. Most claimed that staffing and training were especially important managerial responsibilities in building an efficient organization. In the professional service industries, many pointed out, employee talent was a key factor in success. It was imperative then that the manager make good hiring decisions and provide new people with the necessary training:

> You need good people around to compete with and share ideas with.
> If your manager doesn't know how to select talent, it brings down the whole office—not right away, but inevitably. People stop exchanging ideas, customer complaints skyrocket, and profits and morale go down.
> [Bad hiring decisions] expose the rest of the office to unsuccessful people, and the office needs to view themselves as a collection of successful professionals.
> We are in a people business. The manager has to hold the hands of the new people and train them so that they are headed toward doing a high-quality business.

Even in their discussions of the new managers' agenda-setting responsibilities, the subordinates emphasized the organizational or people aspects. For them, management was getting things done through others and the associated network-building responsibilities.

The subordinates thus saw the managers' role as "setting

the stage, the framework, and the strategy [they] were going after." Most of the subordinates saw two final managerial responsibilities as fitting into this role: building and maintaining effective networks both within and outside the unit.

Building Networks

Manager as team leader. The subordinates expected the new managers to create a "healthy office climate" in which their professional and personal needs would be recognized and addressed.

> This can be a frustrating business. You have a lot of personal rejection and you take the risk since you are on commission. You need a leader to give you strength when the frustrations get out of hand.
> You want an upbeat, optimistic environment.
> When it stops feeling like a good place to work, good people walk.
> A good manager is one about whom, when you are shaving in the morning, you have good thoughts. His influence sticks with you when you are not at your job. . . . A bad leader, on the other hand, undermines your efforts in subtle ways. He gives you no guides that motivate and support you.

Subordinates suggested that a manager could create a positive environment with "team leadership." One subordinate said, "the really good manager doesn't think of himself or herself as a manager, but as a leader." Many felt that inattention to these responsibilities of leadership, or to efforts to build good relationships with and among the subordinates, was a primary explanation for low morale and high turnover, hence, poor productivity.

Subordinates had difficulty pointing to specific managerial behaviors or activities as "leadership behaviors." Instead, they seemed to feel that a manager's leadership or lack of it permeated everything the manager did. This attitude was revealed in the manager's general tone and style. As others have found in research on leadership, these subordinates were constantly screening managers' actions, seeking leadership clues. One set of clues to which the subordinates were most sensitive had to do with the managers' perceived feeling for them as individuals:[15]

> You feel motivated to go to work. You want to cooperate. You feel a part of the team.
>
> He [the manager] knows how to get you to cooperate, even if you really do not want to.
>
> Leaders maintain respectful relationships with rapport and communication. They relate to the people.
>
> He [the manager] is the role model. If he is up, you're up.
>
> The manager, more than anybody else in the branch, stands for professionalism.

Leaders were "committed to their people as individuals." The subordinates expected their managers to be committed to both their short- and long-term development, not only as producers but also as individuals. Whereas the managers defined success as financial advancement, the subordinates defined it more broadly. Financial success may have been their primary drive, but the subordinates also valued three other types of success: recognition, both formal and informal; career development; and psychological well-being:

> It is his job to help me execute both my marketing plans and my personal growth objectives.
>
> You always knew he [a branch manager held in the highest esteem both by account executives and senior management] cared. He didn't just look at your numbers, but at your results.
>
> They [leaders] don't get too hung up on the numbers. They don't just talk business or chastise you for not doing enough. They have your best interests at heart. . . . They'll support you and not just look out for their own net gain.

The subordinates proposed that to be a leader meant to be a "counselor of sorts." They observed that at times it was impossible to distinguish between personal and work-related interests:

> She should offer guidance, a friendly ear. You should be able to go to her office and have it out sometimes, and she should listen to all your complaints and be sympathetic.

> He has got to ask how things are going at home or about
> my outside interests. He should go out and have a beer with
> you, not just keep his cool with the unit. . . . He has to show
> he doesn't just care about himself and is just self-centered.

In short, from the subordinates' point of view, the manager
was there to serve the subordinates' needs and worries first and
foremost. Providing team leadership, the manager could meet
both their personal and professional interests, relieve their anxieties and fears, and address their hopes and dreams. Most subordinates expected individual attention from their managers. Interestingly, the subordinates' notion of "team" was simplistic.
Team generally implies some notion of coordinated or synergistic activity. For the subordinates, though, it seemed to suggest simply cohesiveness. Because they valued personal autonomy very highly, their reading of "team" is probably no
accident. For the subordinates, the managerial job was largely
about building networks with them or, as we see in the next
section, on their behalf.

Manager as liaison.   The final theme about the managerial role revealed by the interviews with subordinates was that
of manager as representative of the unit. The manager, formally
in charge of the unit, was uniquely positioned to represent his
or her organization to those outside the unit, both within and
outside the company. In other words, the subordinates did acknowledge the new managers' authority when it was convenient
for them. When they thought of the manager as the boss or the
authority figure, the subordinates thought of the manager as
their liaison with the outside world. As part of their people
management responsibilities, the managers were expected to
build and maintain relationships actively with the people outside
the unit upon which it depended. The subordinates appeared to
see two related liaison roles: buffer and advocate.

Both the managers and the subordinates believed the manager was responsible for protecting them from illegitimate or
unnecessary requests from other parts of the organization. Specifically, they complained that the corporate and regional offices
often made unreasonable demands on those in the field.

Many of these requests involved administrative tasks. The

subordinates found those tasks even more distasteful than did the new managers. Most proudly admitted that commissioned salespeople like themselves were notorious for their tendency to "procrastinate when it came to paperwork." One sales representative said, "Frankly, I resent it." Most thought administration was a managerial responsibility and that they should be shielded from such "staff intrusions and regimentation": "My time is money for me and the firm. I should be involved [with administration] as little as possible."

Many of the subordinates adamantly claimed that they should be guarded from office politics, a managerial purview. Managers were expected to be advocates for their subordinates; they were responsible for speaking on behalf of their organization and securing resources, rewards, and recognition for those under their supervision:

> The exceptional manager always looks out for his people, gains access to the prime resources and company perks.
>
> You know . . . 50 percent of the time that I [a subordinate] go after something, I know where to get it, but because I'm not the manager making the call, they're not responsive to me. I can call and get told No. The manager can call and be told Yes.
>
> [The manager] is our public relations agent. He is our link to the outside world.

Many of the subordinates said that the managers' ability to procure resources and rewards was based only in part on their position of authority. It was also greatly influenced by the managers' credibility and network of relationships. Subordinates supplied many anecdotes describing how difficult their jobs became if their managers lacked credibility and contacts. One subordinate blamed one year's "unrealistic quota" on the manager's poor relationship with senior management:

> If [my manager] doesn't manage his boss, then we're put under unreasonable pressure. . . . The quota for the branch will be set too high and he won't be able to renegotiate it that easily. He doesn't chat up to the boss enough or talk us up

enough. I bet his boss doesn't even really know what is going on down here. It is the manager's responsibility to develop relationships with the outside community as well. It is important for him (the manager) to get out there and sell us to the community. Exposure. He creates the perception in the community that we stand for quality.

A manager's professionalism—how he carries himself in the community—should be an important focus for him. He should be a role model and provide the proper image to the community and participate in the community. My first manager provided the image, but didn't participate. And the next one participated but had the wrong image; he was very sloppy.

[The manager] is completely anonymous to the community. He has no visibility. It's tragic. The firm does not have major penetration. He should be as well known as the local banker, but he is not as committed to the community as he should be. He is also not sensitive as to how to integrate himself. He bought a Honda in a Ford town.

If a manager devoted enough attention to relationships with those outside the unit, then potential conflicts among subordinates and others outside the unit (with individuals in the company or with clients) could be avoided. The subordinates acknowledged that some conflicts would inevitably arise, no matter how well the manager maintained the web of relationships. When the subordinates could not resolve such conflicts, they expected the manager to intervene as their emissary:

You have to know that he is behind you and will represent you fairly.

They [managers] should be responsive. If I come to them and say I'm having difficulty with the next step, they should agree to help me and follow through. They can add their credibility when I have to go back and talk to the client.

For the subordinates, the manager was their link with the outside world. The new managers had access to information and resources they could not acquire independently. The subordinates expected the managers to recognize and devote much attention to their role as boundary-spanner.[16]

Summary of Subordinates' Expectations

The subordinates may seem to have had a more fully developed and accurate picture of the managerial role than did the new managers, especially the notion that managers got things done through others. This impression is particularly perplexing, for the managers had recently been subordinates themselves. But the subordinates accentuated the differences between the roles of individual contributor and manager that best fitted their interests. They did not want the new managers to infringe on their job as doer with primary responsibility for the task. Many observed that new managers were often reluctant to let go of their old role:

> Most of them [new managers] really enjoy selling and being a part of the process, being involved with the customer. As a result they are really attentive to the customers. Most of them are hams. . . . My manager for example enjoys standing before customers. And they enjoy taking control, and if you are not careful and stop them, they can lose control of themselves . . . "I'm directing this one." I find they do enjoy it so much that they can get their hands right in it. . . . They are so much in the game. They really want to play; just sitting on the sidelines is not enough. Be a coach—no way.
>
> Their classic mistakes. . . . They do my job [selling] or worse yet become bean counters. . . . Then you can only hope that you outlive them [that is, that they soon get transferred to another office].

The new managers of course were aware of these tensions; some even mentioned them explicitly. But their focus was elsewhere, on their newly acquired authority. Moreover, as we see in Chapter 2, they seemed to find the doer-manager distinction too threatening to fully contemplate; it meant giving up a comfortable and highly reinforced identity. A central theme in their experience was the dogged struggle with subordinates about their respective responsibilities.

For the subordinates, the quintessential managerial role was to create a supportive environment within which they could prosper professionally and personally. Whereas the new managers were blinded by their focus on management's rights and privileges (authority and control), the subordinates were blinded by their focus on the duties of management, especially those affecting subordinates. As a result, the subordinates downplayed the manager's position as authority figure over them. They failed to acknowledge fully the manager's ultimate responsibility for the unit's welfare and the associated right to supervise (influence and control) subordinates' behavior. The subordinates also saw the manager as liaison rather narrowly. They made light of the manager's obligation to balance subordinates' needs with those outside the unit.

SUPERIORS' EXPECTATIONS: MANAGER AS BOSS

The new managers' superiors held the most comprehensive and accurate view of what it means to be a manager. Of course, they were managers themselves. In fact, many reminisced about their first days as managers, recalling how "wrong and naive" they had been about the new world they were about to enter. The superiors often were visibly amused by the new managers' common misconceptions. But as we will see, the superiors' point of view about the managerial role also reflected their biases.

Like the new managers, most superiors emphasized that the manager was the one with formal authority and decision-making responsibility. The manager was above all the one who had final accountability in his or her unit:

> They [the managers] are the ones responsible. As far as I'm concerned, it [the unit] rises and falls on how they handle it. No one else can take the blame or the credit.
> They have to think like a businessman; act like they own the business in the way they run it.
> They are responsible for the whole ball of wax; everything.

Although the new managers had focused on the privileges that came with formal authority, the superiors emphasized the duties—the accountability. The superiors counted on the new managers to pull their weight in contributing to the superiors' agendas. Hence, the superiors stressed that managers were paid for meeting the objectives set for them—both the unit's short-term sales plans and the company's strategic goals:

> It's not good enough just to make the numbers in terms of quota and profits. Commands come down [from the most senior management] each year. Each year a theme stresses one issue or another such as asset gathering or productivity. Six or seven key things come down. Some are easily measurable, and some are not. But all are key.

This distinction was one the new managers saw as less vital. Although they talked about planning for the long term, as we have seen, most considered meeting short-term sales objectives the clear priority.

Setting Agendas

Manager as businessperson. In their interviews the superiors specified goals for which they intended to hold the new managers responsible. The list covered financial, business, and organizational matters. They admitted that they were probably giving the new managers "too many high-priority items" for them to realistically pay attention to. Moreover, they claimed that some of the goals were in conflict.

To their minds, a vital part of the manager's role was to make trade-offs and manage the resulting risks, for the manager was a "businessperson" who took the broad point of view. One superior said, "I expect [him] to run [the branch] as if he owned the business." The superiors emphasized that there were no right answers, just better and worse answers to the many issues that the new managers would find on their plate.

Most superiors emphasized that, in order to meet the numerous and varied objectives he or she was given, a manager had to formulate and follow a well-thought-out plan. This agenda was the manager's guide, the framework within which he or she balanced the inevitable trade-offs among competing priorities. In fact, nearly half of the superiors explicitly mentioned agenda setting in defining the managerial role. Without an agenda, the superiors contended, the new managers would make poor decisions on where to put their time and attention. The superiors, unlike the managers, were extremely conscious of the pressures that time and conflicting demands would put on the new managers. Moreover, they were aware that the managers initially would feel swamped and overwhelmed because they would not know how to make the necessary judgment calls. Judgment would come only with time and experience, principally from the "school of hard knocks."

Building Networks

Manager as team leader. Ultimately, the superiors defined the manager's role as managing people, not the task. Like the subordinates, the superiors observed that the new managers would be slow to understand this distinction. If the managers were to implement their agendas, they had to build and manage relationships with their subordinates first and foremost and with those outside their unit.

Many superiors considered the managers' team leadership responsibilities to be their most precious and elusive ones. The manager's effectiveness was mainly determined by meeting his or her leadership responsibilities. The superiors appeared to believe that managers brought into accord the objectives of the subordinates and the larger organization by leadership. Many superiors spoke of the new manager's need to create team spirit, to rally the troops around the unit's goals. Most stressed the manager's responsibility as role model:

> The manager sets the tone. The unit can only be as good as he is.
>
> A good manager raises expectations in the office and creates a good mood instead of a mediocre one through subtle pressures.

41

The superiors proposed that leadership responsibilities were especially significant for first-line managers. This manager was the representative of the organization who had most contact with, and therefore influence on, the producing center in this business, salespeople. The companies' marketing strategies strongly depend upon effective first-line sales managers.

Admittedly, "leadership" seemed a catch-all phrase for the superiors, covering many activities associated with communicating and motivating subordinates to achieve corporate goals. When the superiors referred to these responsibilities, they focused on the manager's need not simply to control subordinates, but rather to gain their commitment.

> The critical difference between exceptional and average managers—the exceptional managers motivate, develop, and lead people even though they've got to drive the business.

Many superiors acknowledged that some of the most experienced sales managers shirked these responsibilities of leadership.

Manager as integrator. Like the subordinates, most superiors felt the managers' interface responsibilities were crucial. The superiors, however, saw these responsibilities as more of a two-way street than did the subordinates. The managers were responsible for seeing that information and resources flowed in both directions, as needed. The superiors argued that the new managers were responsible for understanding and empathizing with the needs and interests of other critical people outside their units. They must communicate these needs to their subordinates and address them in formulating their units' objectives. The superiors expected the managers to equitably negotiate and integrate their units' interests with those of others.

Manager as administrator. Most superiors felt that, consistent with their emphasis on the new managers' role as integrator and on their accountability, the managers were to work within the organization's procedures and ground rules. As managers, they represented the company's interests. They must therefore fulfill their administrative responsibilities and thereby protect the company's "reputation and capital":

> The manager's job is to make lots of money for the company, without getting into trouble.
>
> Administration is risk management. It keeps you within the company's boundaries.

For the superiors, of course, protecting the company's interests could be very personal: "protecting [the boss's] hide." Most superiors described incidents in which a manager had gotten them into "hot water." Understandably, the superiors did not cherish such memories.

From the superiors' perspective, the manager's administrative job was designed to integrate the manager into the organization. Not only was administration the manager's way of communicating with others in the organization, it was also the way in which the rest of the organization informed the manager about its priorities and feelings. The managers failed to appreciate that interpretation of administrative procedures. They felt their administrative capacity was mostly a nuisance. As we see in Chapter 8, the managers frequently did not understand the reasons for administrative policies and practices and missed the signals that those implied. Once again, they were not especially oriented to meeting strategic corporate needs.

Summary of Superiors' Expectations

Like the new managers, the superiors began by defining the managerial role as one of authority and decision making. As the formal authority and the "nerve center" for his or her unit, the manager was uniquely placed to see to it that important decisions reflected the best current knowledge and the organization's goals. Hence, the manager was the only individual in the unit permitted to make strategic decisions; that is, to commit the unit to significant courses of action. For superiors, the managers' function was vital because it was integrative. Leadership was crucial for bringing together the subordinates' and the organization's goals. The superiors seemed to imply that a manager's formal authority represented only potential power. Leadership was the way of realizing this potential power. The superiors saw the manager's job in all its complexity: "In some ways, it's an impossible job. A manager is a jack of all trades, a chameleon, who has to please everybody."

The manager's job was to reconcile others' numerous and often conflicting expectations, to balance and manage trade-offs. Accomplishing the job required equal amounts of "expertise [technical knowledge], analytical ability, and interpersonal and group dynamic skills." The latter were critical; only by effective network building could the new managers implement their agendas.

PEER EXPECTATIONS:
MANAGER AS NEGOTIATOR

Peer expectations can be covered briefly. By peers, I mean associates in other functional areas and in the corporate or regional offices. The new managers paid little attention to their peer relationships. Not surprisingly, the peers looked on the new manager as a formal representative for their unit and as a boundary-spanner. They seemed to define the managerial role more by its relationships than its responsibilities. As outsiders, not in the new managers' direct chain of command, they experienced the managers' agenda-setting and networking responsibilities as so intimately intertwined that they are discussed together.

As the individuals with formal authority for the unit, the peers depended on the new managers to communicate their needs to their subordinates. They expected the managers to take into account their interests when planning for their unit. The peers were frustrated by this dependency; most complained that they were largely at the mercy of the new managers' good will. In both companies, those in field sales and marketing had access to more sources of power, both formal and informal. Field sales managers had more direct control over critical resources and contingencies and clearly had more prestige and status than those in other areas. And according to many of the peers, the systems for performance appraisal and compensation were not designed to "really hold [new managers] accountable" when they ignored peers' interests. When I asked the superiors if this perception were accurate, most agreed it was.

The peers believed that the good managers understood their place in the larger organization. These managers put much time into meeting with and building relations with those in support functions. A few of the peers described how they had worked with managers who seemed to "include [the peers] on the sales team" or treated them as partners. They saw such managers as the exception rather than the rule. Many peers predicted that the managers would not fully appreciate the critical contributions peers made to the organization or how to utilize them effectively.

The peers wanted the managers to see to it that desired information and resources were forthcoming from either the managers themselves or their subordinates. If the manager did not set clear expectations for his or her subordinates to provide such information and resources, "it wouldn't happen." The peers recognized that the salespeople often saw their requests as unimportant or even illegitimate.

Many of the peers also described how conflicts frequently arose between themselves and the subordinates. To meet customers' requests, the subordinates would often try to get the peers to make an exception to company policy or procedure or garner extraordinary corporate resources. Because they had formal authority, the managers were to arbitrate any disputes that then arose. The peers expected the managers to take the broader, more objective view, "what is best for the company," and weigh the facts accordingly.

CONCLUDING REMARKS

Now we have seen what being a manager meant to the new managers and those with whom they would work. Let us close by revisiting and elaborating on Exhibit 1-1, in which I summarized the parties' initial expectations with a conceptual model of the managerial role. This time we look at what being a manager means, using the language, with all its nuances, of the different constituencies (see Exhibit 1-2).

Exhibit 1-2

What It Means to Be a Manager:
In Their Own Words

Managerial role	*Constituency*			
	New managers	*Subordinates*	*Superiors*	*Peers*
Agenda setting				
Manager as boss	x		x	
Manager as sales leader	x	x		
Manager as organizer		x		
Manager as businessperson			x	
Building networks				
Manager as supervisor	x			
Manager as administrator	x		x	
Manager as politician	x			
Manager as people manager		x		
Manager as team leader		x	x	
Manager as liaison		x	x	
Manager as integrator			x	
Manager as negotiator				x

What a hodgepodge to make sense of, even after these points of view are organized into categories and illustrated by extensive quotations! The new managers obviously had their work cut out for them: learning how to be a manager was a formidable task. They had to make sense of complex, often conflicting, and demanding expectations.

The learning was also emotionally unsettling, for the managers had to *act* as managers before they understood what that role was. Only by acting would they know what their new assignment entailed. Indeed, they were faced with a frustrating paradox. They were trying to learn to perform a role whose meaning and importance they could not grasp ahead of time. They were eager to master their new responsibilities, but they did not yet know what they had to learn. Plato captured this dilemma in a dialogue between Socrates and Meno about virtue. Meno asked:

> But how will you look for something when you don't in the least know what it is? How on earth are you going to set up something you don't know as the object of your search? To put it another way, even if you come right up against it, how will you know that what you have found is the thing you didn't know?[17]

In Chapters 2 and 3, we look on as the new managers discover what they were looking for; that is, what management was really all about.

NOTES

1. My conceptualization of managerial work was most heavily influenced by the work of Kotter (1982), Mintzberg (1973), Sayles (1989), and Stewart (1982; 1987). One of the most widely accepted models of managerial roles is that of Mintzberg (1973). In a pioneering study of managers at work, he described ten critical managerial roles that fell into three groups: those involving primarily interpersonal relationships, the *Interpersonal Roles;* those primarily about transfer of information, the *Informational Roles;* and those involving decision making, the *Decisional Roles.*

> In essence, the manager is an input-output system in which authority and status give rise to interpersonal relationships, that lead to inputs

(information), and these in turn lead to outputs (information and decisions) (p. 58).

Moreover, Mintzberg carefully documented that the managerial role is a complex and demanding one into which inherent tensions are built:

> Organizations require managers not only because of imperfections in the system and unexpected changes in the environment, but because a formal authority is required to carry out certain basic, regular duties. The ten roles suggest six basic purposes of the manager—to ensure the efficient production of the organization's goods and services, to design and maintain the stability of organizational operations, to adapt the organization in a controlled way to the changing environment, to ensure that the organization serves the ends of those persons who control it, to serve as the key information link between the organization and its environment, and to operate the organization's status system (p. 99).

2. Kotter (1982), p. 60.

3. See Bandura (1986), Louis (1980), Schön (1983; 1990), or Wood and Bandura (1989) for discussions on how an individual's frame of reference influences his or her behavior. These researchers find that individuals in new situations construct their own version of reality and respond to their subjective reality as if it were objectively true.

4. One would think the new managers would have defined a fourth responsibility to be the distribution of rewards. In both companies the salespeople were commissioned; hence, their financial rewards were determined primarily by companywide compensation policies. Still, the new managers did have some discretionary funds and resources for distribution. In later months the managers began to appreciate the power not only of these discretionary funds and resources but also of nonmonetary rewards such as recognition programs.

5. There were some notable exceptions; these managers will be discussed in Chapter 8.

6. Compliance is the name given to surveillance against broker fraud and to maintenance of integrity in the brokerage industry. Branch managers were charged with guarding against many types of broker malfeasance, including churning (doing more trading in an account than warranted), misrepresentation (failing to properly convey the risks of an investment), and unsuitability (recommending investments not in keeping with an investor's financial position).

7. It is instructive to compare the new managers' expectations about management with descriptions in the literature on managerial work. Luthans et al. (1988) identified three "traditional management activities": planning, decision making, and controlling and two "routine communications activities": exchanging information and handling paperwork. It is interesting that Luthans et al. defined planning, decision making, and controlling as the traditional management activities. Clearly, the new managers would agree with that description. Luthans et al. would say that they conceived of the managerial role primarily as traditional management activities, and routine information. But the new managers failed to fully appreciate the significance of the other two types of managerial activities that Luthans et al. described: networking and human resource management.

8. Kraut et al. (1989) looked at the similarities and differences among managerial jobs at different levels in the organization. They found that for first-level managers, managing individual performance was rated the most important activity. They also report that representing one's staff was ranked equally high by all levels of management.

9. See Carroll and Gillen (1987) for further discussion of this point. They argued for conceptualizing managerial work based on how managers do their work, not simply what they do.

10. Researchers have found that people rely upon their experience to help them understand and cope with new or stressful situations. See Langer (1989).

11. See Bennis (1989) or Argyris (1991).

12. Although the inexperienced and more experienced subordinates identified the same managerial roles, they weighed them differently. For the current discussion, these differences are not important. They are quite relevant, however, to the discussion in Chapter 5 on interpersonal judgment and are considered there.

13. Their description of the manager as monitor was quite similar to that of Mintzberg (1973):

> The manager as monitor . . . is continually seeking, and being bombarded with, information that enables him to understand what is taking place in his organization and its environment. He seeks information to detect changes, to identify problems and opportunities, to build up knowledge about his milieu, to be informed when information must be disseminated and decisions made (p. 67).

14. The subordinates' discussion of this managerial responsibility was closest to Mintzberg's (1973) description of the manager as resource allocator (p. 86).

15. For instance, Kouzes and Posner (1987) report that subordinates rely upon four measures of credibility: honesty, competence, looking ahead, and being inspirational.

16. Sayles (1989) observed:

> Nothing legitimates and substantiates the position of leaders more than their ability to handle external relations. Above all else, leaders control a boundary, and interface. From the point of view of the subordinates, the leaders typically are the link with the outside world, whether the world of financial support (the bankers and investment community) or the world of upper management (where salary increases and increased budgets are born). Respected, admired leaders are those who can deal profitably with outsiders and bring back benefits and protection (p. 44).

17. Plato (1956), p. 128.

2

Reconciling Expectations

Throughout their first year on the job, the new managers reframed their understanding of what being a manager meant. Each reframing represented a further refinement and enrichment of their appreciation for their new role. Over time, through this process of continual reframing, the new managers began to move toward a managerial identity.

In Chapter 1, we saw that their initial framework was of the manager as the formal authority and stressed their agenda-setting responsibilities in financial and business matters. They generally overlooked the other aspect of their new role: getting things done through people or their network-building responsibilities. Surprises in three critical areas provoked them to re-think the managerial role.[1] The first was learning what the manager's daily life was really like. The second was their subordinates' expectations, which forced them to confront what getting work done through others meant. The final area was

51

superiors' expectations, which helped them understand both the opportunities and constraints of being the formal authority.

We now address the new managers' first six months on the job, as they struggled with the first two problems. Their initial task was to reconcile their expectations with the realities of daily life as a manager. Their expectations of power and control were inconsistent with the workload, pace, and dependence on others that they encountered. At the same time, the new managers were preoccupied with making sense of their subordinates' expectations. They were perplexed by their subordinates' apparently contradictory expectations.

After the first six months, most managers had learned to expect some overload, ambiguity, and conflict in the managerial role and that being a manager brought as much dependence as authority. And as they worked to please their subordinates, they became uncomfortably aware of the differences between being a manager and a doer, and of being responsible for people rather than the task. As they coped with the inevitable conflicts with subordinates and customers, they began in earnest to *unlearn* what it meant to be an individual contributor. Only as they gave up that identity could they begin to accept their identity as manager.

Because this story is told from the new managers' perspective, it is not especially neat or straightforward. The managers learned only as much as they needed to learn, when they needed to learn it—that is, when they encountered a problem or surprise. Consequently, the order in which they learned a lesson varied. They took charge of their new positions at different stages in the business cycle. Each manager's territory had its own market and subordinate dilemmas to manage. Some had to set and distribute sales quotas or make major personnel decisions such as hiring and firing early, and others did not face these tasks until the year's end. Only a handful had to handle lawsuits brought by customers or an exodus by key subordinates.

However, certain problems and surprises were bound to, and did, occur by various junctures in the year. In the very first days and weeks on the job, all confronted the daily realities in being a manager. Within the first three months, almost everyone had dealt with a significant conflict between subordinate and customer or subordinate and peer. And all but one of them received their first performance appraisal from their superiors in the second half of the year. Hence, the new managers' experiences are presented in their *general* order; that is, the order in which they confronted typical dilemmas. Because their learning was iterative, much like peeling an onion, we revisit some issues time and again. But each time, the new managers' framework for the managerial role will be more highly developed and more definitely grounded in reality.

DISCOVERING THE DAILY REALITIES OF MANAGERIAL WORK

The managers' first step was to learn that the managerial role was indeed distinct from that of the individual contributor. This step might seem obvious, but the managers were genuinely surprised by the discontinuity between producer and managerial roles and between their expectations and the realities they experienced in managerial work. The remarks reproduced here are those of new managers, who only weeks before had told me how eagerly they looked forward to their new positions—the authority, the power, and the control:

> My first day . . . I unloaded my stuff and packed my desk, got it organized, set up files—and really didn't do anything. I was kind of bored for the first few hours. I really had nothing to do; I hadn't gotten much direction from my boss. . . . The first two days were like that. My door was open. I didn't want my reps to come by and see me just sitting there twiddling my thumbs. I thought, how can I look busy? I started cleaning up the desk and putting in more files. I knew I should be busy, but I just didn't know how to do it on my own. . . . Then I started inviting the reps in when they walked by and asked them a little about their accounts and told them I just wanted to get on board. I did that for the first few days, talking customer strategies and reading all the memos so that I could keep

busy. . . . I kept thinking: I'm bored, I think, and it's odd to be on this side of the desk. . . . Then I made my first big decision. I told a rep to radically alter his marketing strategy for handling an account that would turn out to be one of our most competitive. After a while more people started stopping by. It began to dawn on me that I had walked into a pressure cooker; there were a lot of big problems. They were expecting some Houdini acts very quickly, never mind that you have to find out who your reps are and about their personalities, who your support people are; you're just introducing yourself and getting to know all the customers. It was very frustrating, the first two months on the job. There was a lot of pressure on me: What's going on here, what's going on there? It really takes a lot out of you.

This statement captures the experience shared more or less by all the new managers. Being a manager did not *feel* like what they had expected, and they did not *feel* that they knew what they were doing. From these feelings of anxiety and uneasiness, they surmised that "managing is not at all like producing." Within the first month they were able to articulate the critical differences between the manager's daily routine and that of the individual contributor. Thanks to this assault on their ideas about the manager as the formal authority, the managers began to ponder what they had gotten themselves into. For now, most could not delineate, with any confidence, what their new role entailed.

Workload and Pace of Managerial Work

When asked to describe what a manager does, the new managers spoke feelingly about the stresses in their new positions. Management seemed a world of overwhelming confusion, of overload, ambiguity, and conflict (in Chapter 7, we examine the emotional consequences of these themes).

Above all, they were struck by the unrelenting workload and pace of being a manager. When asked what advice he would give to someone considering a management job, one of the managers commented: "This job is much harder than you think. It is 40 to 50 percent more work than being a producer! Who would ever have guessed?"

One described as dazzling the leap in scope and scale and the open-endedness of his new job responsibilities. None felt comfortable defining the responsibilities; however, they were convinced that the list was unreasonably long. Management was "a job that never ended," "a job you couldn't get your hands around." On a typical day, they worked on many problems simultaneously from the insignificant to the important, were constantly interrupted, and had to manage dozens of brief interactions with many people:[2]

> You have eight or nine people looking for your time . . . coming into and out of your office all day long. Who is going to come in with the real hot one today and how do I escalate myself to listen to that one today, because I can't listen to all eight or nine?

Because the managers assumed before promotion that coordination and planning would be among their chief functions, the first few months on the job were disillusioning. Most described themselves as firefighters. They were too preoccupied with current problems to devote time or energy to thinking about potential problems, much less figuring out how to prevent or prepare for them.

From the first weeks, nearly all the managers were confronted with the reality that the manager's job was probably too big to handle alone. The illusion of mastery would prove difficult to forfeit, however, and would plague them throughout the first year. A basic assumption was that they would be the experts on everything. They did not realize that even the most exceptional managers could not be such experts.[3] Moreover, they failed to fully appreciate that overload, ambiguity, and conflict were inherent in the managerial role:

> Once I get my arms around this job, or should I say, if [he laughed nervously], everything will fall into place. Then I'll be the coordinator, controller, not necessarily in that order,

all the time. Someone who is close enough to the action to feed the right information and provide some answers.

I expected to come out of the starting gate with the knowledge . . . now I find I'm out here inventing the wheel.

At first, many thought these aspects of managerial life would go away as they learned how to do the new job. But by their third month on the job, two themes appeared in the managers' descriptions of the job's challenges. The first was the need for stamina and sheer energy. The second was the need to organize and manage their time wisely. They began to suspect that time would be one of their most precious resources.

To be a good manager you need loads of energy, mental and physical. . . . You're always on the go. Things can change all of a sudden. You may get a call in the morning and suddenly a computer went down. You have a competitive situation, and that is all you need is to have a computer breakdown. You have to change your focus. But you have to be aware of that and say what the real issue is and what the most important thing today is, and I have more things than I can do, anyway. That is the one thing I have noticed about this job, you always have more things than you can realistically do. It is always a matter of setting priorities and saying what is real for today.

Management as Dependence

An even more unnerving realization about managerial life soon arose:

You will no longer be evaluated on your own production, but instead on that of the people who report to you. . . . When I was an account executive I was in control of my own little world. My pay was commensurate with my efforts.

By the end of the third month, most managers were beginning to realize that being a manager was as much a position of dependence as of authority. The relation between personal efforts and control over results was more indirect and tenuous.[4]

Asked to describe what she disliked about her new job, a manager stated:

> The fact that you really are not in control of anything. The only time you are in control is when you shut your door, and then I feel I am not doing the job I'm supposed to be doing, which is being with the people.

For most, the feeling of dependence was overwhelming and even menacing during the first months, as they came to realize that their subordinates "were not as motivated or capable" as they:

> I had been talking and talking to this rep about how to handle a client and he wasn't getting it. I began to break into a sweat. It hit me what people meant when they warned me that when I gave up my book [his accounts], I gave up my security blanket.
>
> Probably the biggest difference [from being a producer], is now I depend on people—it's almost like a car cylinder—me and the six people reporting to me. I've got six cylinders and I've got to have all cylinders operating, and if one goes, it hits you. . . . You're so used to being the only inhibitor. You define your own parameters and your limitations, but the other six define the parameters and motivations, and you try to alter their behavior and get them to increase their ambition, but basically that is real hard to do.

Feelings of dependence and loss of control were a persistent theme in the new managers' discussions throughout the first year.[5]

WHY THE SURPRISE?

For the first few months, the managers saw no way of reconciling their expectations with reality. As they contrasted expectations with reality they admitted exasperatedly that they had accepted the job based on erroneous perceptions. They wondered how they could have been so far off base: "It was as if I had entered an alien world."

Why were they taken aback by their first experiences as manager? As individual contributors, they had worked closely with managers who held the very positions in which they now found themselves. Also, all had participated in formal selection and orientation programs. They were genuinely surprised, though, by the discontinuity between the producer and manager roles and between their expectations and the realities of management.[6]

As we have seen, the new managers' experiences had created perceptual filters that led them to attend to selected aspects of managerial work: "I knew the job from the outside looking in. It's a totally different story now that I am on the inside!" From the outside looking in, they had seen the power and control that came with formal authority and not its limitations and dependence.

Only by living through their first days on the job were they able to uncover some of their assumptions about managerial work. Because they had thought little about managerial exigencies of daily life, when confronted with them they made some interesting discoveries. They had assumed that as managers their lives would be more "organized and orderly" than they had been as producers, for they would be the ones "with the most power and therefore in control." They had assumed that authority meant independence, autonomy because "you get to make the decisions." The new managers were experiencing the kind of surprise that arises when tacit job expectations are not met or when features of the job are not anticipated. One manager said he was "doubly surprised." Job aspects not previously considered important stood out because their presence or absence was experienced as undesirable.

RECONCILING SUBORDINATES' EXPECTATIONS

The new managers had to reconcile their expectations (conscious and emergent) with reality, and they also had to reconcile the "often inconsistent and downright conflicting expectations"

58

of the constituencies with whom they worked: subordinates, customers, bosses, and peers. For the first half of the year, most concentrated on understanding and meeting their subordinates' expectations. They relied heavily upon past experience to make sense of the new. This natural tendency was reinforced by their spending most of their time with subordinates. Consequently, this was the group to whom they *felt* most beholden. To illustrate this phenomenon, one manager observed:

> Jack [his boss] would kill me if he heard what I am about to say. What is my role, truthfully? It is to protect my reps and to keep my customers happy even if they aren't buying. That's the way I minimize my personal losses.

Prior to their promotions, the new managers felt they knew what their subordinates expected of them: "I may have the title, but I am still one of them. I know how they think."

As we saw in Chapter 1, the managers could not have been more mistaken. *The* major sources of feelings of overload and ambiguity throughout the first year were their subordinates' expectations. Those predictions proved to be the managers' most difficult piece of the managerial puzzle to assimilate—to do so meant unlearning or giving up their identity as producers, a difficult proposition at best. Their discoveries about managerial work and their feelings of impotence made it a very unnerving prospect. But during the year the managers did gain insight into the subordinates' point of view. Gradually they recognized the complexity of their subordinates' expectations, both from interaction with subordinates and reflection on their own experiences as producers. As they did so, they came to understand what it means to get work done through others.

Discovering Subordinates' Needs

For the first half of the year, the new managers had a one-dimensional view of subordinates' expectations: helping them achieve rewards, principally financial. Although the managers felt they understood subordinates' expectations about what they were supposed to do, they did not understand the subordinates' views about *how* they were to achieve this goal. The subordinates seemed to want them to "keep out of the way and let them do business," but the subordinates also seemed "very needy"; they could never get enough of the managers' attention:

> If I went out on the floor and asked if I spent enough time with them, 100 percent of them would say I did not spend enough time with them.
>
> I could tell a big area of dissatisfaction for them [the account executives] was the amount of personal time I gave them. They simply wanted more of my time.

At first, the new managers did not know what to make of this apparent conflict—subordinates wanted the manager to "leave them alone, yet be fully involved." By the third month, almost all managers had "helped [subordinates] solve substantive [technical] problems that had come up" and found themselves caught in the middle of a conflict between their subordinates and other members of the organization or about a company policy or procedure. From these encounters, the managers began to understand what their subordinates meant by "involvement." The subordinates expected them to act as problem solvers:

> The challenge. . . . You're faced with a lot of different situations, problem situations. You've got to sit down with them [subordinates]; you've got to analyze, propose solutions, and then implement those solutions.
>
> You know you have employees reporting to you. For the most part when they come in, they're going to have problems. Typically, they want you to get involved. They can be really challenging and time-consuming.

The managers observed that their subordinates sought their assistance about a variety of problems. The subordinates expected answers and decisiveness:

> They don't want me to undermine their efforts. When they give a problem to the manager, they don't want it thrown back at them or the facts thrown back at them. That would be

a waste of their time, and time is money. They want it fixed now.

They should have ability to make a good decision, support it, and stick by it. The managers who have difficulty are the ones who struggle with making decisions, have trouble making them, and then face buyer's remorse after they make them—they say, "Was that really the right decision?" You just can't do that.

The managers soon realized that a major aspect of solving subordinates' problems was serving as their liaison with those outside the unit:

I'm the advocate for them to the rest of the company. I understand now what I need to do, and the words and the buttons and all the different structures that need to get pushed, so that I can be helpful to those guys, so that they don't have to see it, so they can keep their blinders on and keep marching after the business.

When asked at the end of the first months what a manager was, most no longer responded "being the boss" or "being the person in control." Instead, they mentioned a "troubleshooter," "a juggler," and a "quick-change artist." All emphasized solving problems, making decisions, and providing resources as their primary responsibilities:

The reps see me as their problem solver, when they face an obstacle, need help, or need another resource to make quota. They expect me to help with the analysis of the account, be the referee, tell them their options, and provide the resources. If necessary, I have to protect them from the customer, shield them from above, from requirements that come down.

My people expect me to assist them with market strategy and act as their interface if necessary.

I pave the way for my people with product specialists, financial experts, the regional boys, whatever.

For the new managers, the critical competencies required to be a manager now included not only time management and the ability to set priorities (which they had learned by coping with managerial work) but also problem-solving ability (still primarily about technical and business matters), decisiveness, and knowledge of company resources.

From the third month to the fifth, most managers wholeheartedly embraced the roles of problem solver, buffer, and provider of resources and, in a way, abdicated their responsibilities as the formal authority. And as in the last quotations above, most were beginning to appreciate that they were at the nexus in a web of relationships. But their conception of the manager's role reflected a downward focus. They unconsciously began to lose sight of their role as company representative and to appreciate only one side of their responsibilities as integrator, those affecting their subordinates:

> It is my job to shield them from the company.
>
> I'm not going to push products down their throats even though that is what the [regional] office wants.
>
> I've got to keep all the staff bureaucracy totally away from them . . . keep the staff orientation off their hands. Only give them what they need to know, that's all that should be in their in-baskets.
>
> My job is to protect them from headquarters so that they have time to sell and to sell them to the organization so that they get the recognition they deserve.

From the subordinates' perspective, the managers were now on their way to understanding their new role. The subordinates had formerly defined the sales leadership and liaison roles as key managerial responsibilities; now they expected the manager to be responsive to their needs. And like the new managers, the subordinates had advocated a rather one-sided view of those interface obligations.

The definition of manager as problem solver was consistent with the new managers' prior notions of the manager as authority and sales leader. As problem solvers, they could simultaneously act out the roles of expert and decision maker and "legitimately slip back into the producer role" (a manager's statement about his earlier behavior after one year on the job): "What I like best is when they come in and say, 'Here is a problem, what can I do about it? What do you think?' They value my opinion.

They want to hear my view; the greatest compliment is when they use my ideas."

The new managers' focus on their problem-solving responsibilities was consistent with their short-term orientation toward meeting "tangible" obligations.[7] Most seemed to be quickly absorbing the managerial tendency to gravitate toward the more active aspects of their work—the ones that were current, specific, and well defined.[8] They preferred the active because they were much more likely to achieve "those all too rare feelings of progress" and mastery while working on the more active elements in their jobs.

> It's very satisfying to have a problem presented to you that they've worked on and cannot solve. And with your experience you get involved in the thing and they resolve it quickly. They're happy and you're happy. I'd say that is what I enjoy most.

The subordinate of this manager commented on the manager's behavior:

> He jumped right in and took over. . . . He did the absolute worst thing he could do—he became the lead salesman on *my* account. . . . It's common among rookie managers; they make a fundamental mistake, I guess because it is the most comfortable thing for them to do.

Forging an Identity

The new manager was unaware of his subordinate's displeasure. The managers had come to understand what their subordinates wanted them to be involved in, but they had yet to understand when involvement became interference in their subordinates' eyes. Overidentifying with their subordinates kept them from seeing that their interests and thus their role might differ from those of their subordinates. They had yet to see the difference between doer and manager.

In the first six months or so, a major source of conflict for the managers was the discrepancy between subordinates' and customers' expectations. The managers soon understood their customers' expectations. From the customers' perspective, their managerial functions were to be company representative and negotiator. Most of their customer interactions required them to be arbiters in disputes between subordinates and customers:

> As a manager you unfortunately don't get much customer contact, although it varies with personal style. The problem lies in casual, not operational contacts: where a problem arises, you need to get involved, get something done beyond the day-to-day issues. Also, you are more broadly involved with the customer about where they should be making significant financial investments.

From their experience as very successful salespeople, the new managers "knew that the customer was always right," and expected the manager to "make it [what the customer wanted] happen yesterday." The managers may have been too eager to oblige. To do so meant making a sale, and, equally important, it meant an opportunity to "regress" to their old role as producer and "do what they knew they were good at, pleasing a customer," at the same time feeling like the boss because they exercised the final decision:

> I like going out with the rep, who may need me to lend him my credibility as manager. I like the challenge, the joy in closing. I go out with the reps and we make the call and talk about the customer; it's fun.
> You don't get much customer contact on this job, and I miss that a lot. You can't go in face-to-face and establish rapport with a human being. . . . I look forward to the times when I get to go along with the rep because he has a problem.

The customer, more than any others with whom they came in contact, seemed to treat the new managers as "the boss"—the one with the power to make the tough decisions such as making exceptions to company policy or acquiring extraordinary organizational resources. According to one new manager: "Managers need to handle highly sensitive direct contacts with clients. They have to make on-the-spot judgments. They have got to be strong enough to resolve those conflicts."

Whenever they spoke of their responsibilities to the customer, the managers became animated. They emphasized handling customer contacts professionally, for the "ultimate responsibility was customer satisfaction and future business opportunity."

The new managers soon learned, however, the "negative fallout from pleasing the customer." One described an "ungrateful rep, who had not even thanked [him] for dropping everything and getting in there and closing the deal, after [the subordinate] had almost blown it." Subordinates did not always react well to having the manager "step in to save the day," even if it meant "simply modifying and not overriding their decisions or actions." Furthermore, the subordinates "seemed to resent" time spent with the customers. One manager fretted:

> I go home some days and complain to my wife that I'm just returning phone calls to irate customers all day. And she says, "Well, that's part of your job; you're expected to do this." But that puts me in a tough conflict. I've got to close my door to talk to customers because it is usually a touchy subject. You know out there they [his subordinates] think you're doing nothing. I am in here doing a job, but I know that out there the perception is different.

At first, the managers did not know what to make of their subordinates' reactions to their "assistance." Most of the time a subordinate, usually a seasoned and successful salesperson, helped the managers see the error of their ways. Almost every new manager could recall one or more conversations with subordinates about their tendency to "interfere." The earlier and more frequently they got this feedback, the sooner the managers began to appreciate the difference between doer and manager. One manager described these incidents:

> He [one of the biggest producers in the office] came and said he thought I took the customer's side too often. He showed me his message pad, with no messages. But I had sided with the customer who claimed for weeks he had never

been able to get through. . . . He asked if I'd ever once considered that the customer wasn't telling the truth. . . . I have to admit it was a fair question. . . . I started getting heat from the troops. They trod lightly, joking about my doing the job all by myself and calling me the most overpaid rep in the company. . . . But I knew what they were getting at. . . . I was rationalizing that I had mainly young reps and so they needed me. . . . I was milking that one for all it was worth.

The managers were quite shaken by these encounters. Another manager remarked:

When did it happen? Just yesterday I was a rep like him. Already I've forgotten what it is like out in the field and I'm one of them [management]. . . . I remember that when I was a rep, there were times when I called my manager; there was a right time to use them.

Another manager observed: "I hated when *my* manager became the lead rep on my seven accounts. He wasn't selective about the customer situations he got involved in."

The feedback from their subordinates and their substantial workloads forced the managers to confront the issue of what being a manager meant:

I knew I had to become a silent partner; that is the appropriate managerial role in a customer environment. . . . I knew it was going to be hard to do if things didn't seem to be going right.

In the first four or five months on the job, whenever a rep came in with a problem, I was intent on gaining credibility with the reps, having them like me, and gaining their trust. When they came in with a problem, I'd grab it and run with it. Now that I have more experience, when they come in with a problem, I sit back and ask them questions and let them find the answers.

The account executives expect me to enhance their ability to do business and then get out of their way. The manager's job is to make sure things run smoothly and to be a resource if they need influence in other parts of the organization. I should initiate and know whom to call to deal with specific problems.

From first-hand experience the managers knew all too well

how frustrating and counterproductive it was for a manager to take over a subordinate's account. To meet their own needs, they had been making a mistake they deplored in others. Now that they had been made aware of their behavior, many promised to make the effort to resist the temptation. Doing so, however, required almost constant vigilance during their first year, and they would often revert to the doer role.

At about the same time, after four to six months on the job, many managers began to question their role as the technical expert for the unit. They had trouble keeping up with new product developments because of their workload. They did not have time to immerse themselves in technical detail. They saw that, in time, they would no longer be on the cutting edge and therefore, might not be in the best position to know which product would meet a customer's needs. This was a brave and painful admission—it implied that soon the managers would no longer have the expert knowledge to be a successful producer. One manager began to wonder what "it means really to be a sales leader":

> I was raised on stocks and bonds. Now we're trying to wean the old brokers from those and get the younger brokers to sell the packaged products. I had to have ideas about how to sell the packages even though my business was still of the old school.
>
> Our array of products had grown greatly even in the short time I'd been a manager [six months] and would continue to grow. From a technical standpoint, my credibility of being able to put together the right marketing strategy, go out and call on the customers, my value to the reps would go down. . . . All you can attempt to do is to keep up with it at thirty thousand feet instead of knowing it at ground level.

Many reported that they began to emphasize the strategic, not the tactical aspects of sales leadership. They also began to appreciate that they should directly intervene only in especially difficult situations:

> I provide the big picture of where they're [the subordinates] headed so that they can get through the peaks and valleys.

I was spread too thin. I had no choice but to cut back to a hands-off style—getting involved in exceptions only. It was a relief really to back off and work at arm's length.

I put my sales hat on only when a rep was *really* in trouble.

Most new managers were beginning to understand their agenda-setting responsibilities for organizational or people matters.

Reclaiming Formal Authority

Besides the conflicts between subordinates and customers, the managers had to mediate subordinates' conflicts with others in the organization. Understandably, in the early months the new managers often sympathized with the subordinates more than with customers in these conflicts. Many conflicts were brought on by the subordinates' inability to secure some organizational resource (and the consequent conflict with someone elsewhere in the company) and their reluctance to follow company procedures or policies. The managers began to receive telephone calls from people in other parts of the company blaming them for their subordinates' behavior. They came to resent having to cover for and "take the heat" for their subordinates. They began to hold their subordinates accountable for "creating unnecessary work" and other problems.

Most soon realized too that, because of their dependence on their subordinates, their subordinates' behavior exposed them to risk:

What do I like least . . . ? That one of my brokers could get me fired. In other words, as good a manager as I am—or as I will be, I should say—I could have a broker do something illegal or wrong, and that would get me fired. You see, when I was in production, I could always run a good ethical business because I was the only one running the business. But as a manager I work with—work for—sixty brokers. And any one of them can get me fired. Because that broker, without my knowledge, might have done something illegal, causing a huge problem. Someone has to be held accountable—guess who?

The risks they took as producers were no longer possible:

> It's a tough business [as a producer]. You're paid to go after the business. I wasn't conservative in every situation; I just made sure I didn't get caught.
>
> You've got to change your morals (morals is the wrong word), but you've got to change your guidelines or outlook on how you make decisions. When you're a rep there is a white area which is okay to use. There is a black area that you aren't allowed to use. Then there is a gray area in which you can operate. . . . The gray area is a lot smaller when you're a manager.

The new managers were beginning to understand their responsibilities as the one who had formal authority in their unit, and to appreciate their place in the larger organization. Again, they were learning that with authority came constraints:

> I have less freedom as a manager. I have to be a conformist, whereas before I prided myself on getting results by being a nonconformist. . . . Yeah, can you believe this out of a guy who has been fighting the system all these years? I play it close to the book.
>
> I can't be an unflinching supporter [of the subordinates]. I've got to be objective.

Of course, subordinates often did not graciously accept "no" as an answer to their requests. Many acknowledged that "you have to have a big ego in this business." But they also recognized that their subordinates did not "have the big picture." As managers, it was their obligation to see that the organization's broader interests were met. Handling these disputes with their subordinates, the managers were getting their first real taste of thinking broadly and strategically; they were beginning to appreciate how their decisions were linked to those of the larger organization.

Giving their subordinates negative feedback made the managers better acquainted with their role as the authority and representative of company interests:

> [Giving a performance evaluation] it finally hit home that I had been elevated to boss. They treated me like a manager; they tried to impress me.

I asked one of them to come in, just to sit and chat and tell me what he did, so that I could get a handle on how he was doing and how I could help. I tell you, the man had his blue suit on. He had his power tie on, and he had everything all bound up in his document case to make a formal presentation. I never put that much stock in images, and to have him do that—that was just an eye-opener. I just accepted it—what can you do?

The day before, I was on the battlefield with them, on the floor day after day. . . . Then review time came around. They changed their view of me. All of a sudden I became someone who threatened their survival. . . . It was quite an exercise; it forced me out of the mode of friendship and made me look at how I perceived results. It caused a great deal of soul-searching, and I really wondered if I could do it. You hold their job—their career—in your hands, so to speak. They have an inbred fear.

In assessing subordinates' performance, again the managers were forced not only to accept the idea that their interests could be different from those of their subordinates, but also that the subordinates had a "narrow perspective." A manager provided this example:

I talked to two clients last night. I had just done a mailing to 5,000 of our best customers, telling them about our new product, and that if they wanted to contact their broker about it I thought it would be worth their time. Or they could call me directly. Some of them are calling me. Last night about 8:30, when I had finished my work, I called the ones who had called me and talked about the product. The brokers wouldn't call about this product because they didn't understand it and why it was so important to the company's future. This was a way to get them to learn the product for fear that they might be asked about it and they wouldn't know anything about it.

Evaluating subordinates' performance was truly a rite of passage for the new managers. And if they had to severely reprimand or fire a subordinate, the lesson was one not easily forgotten: "I had joined a new fraternity," and "Not only was I no longer one of the gang, I was the enemy."

Manager as Primarily Responsible for People

From their experience in handling subordinates' conflicts and feedback, the new managers' image of their role and identity was evolving radically. Their identity put them in "no-man's land"; they were neither producer nor manager. One reported that he often felt bewildered. Slowly and reluctantly they were relinquishing the doer role and coming to know what it meant to be responsible for people.

About halfway through the first year, most managers began to talk as if they were in a "support" or "facilitator" position. At the end of his fifth month, one of them ruminated:

> Funny you should ask that question. What the hell am I supposed to be doing? Every day I think it is something different. I'm paid for making my quota, but my job is to support and develop my people. . . . What do you make of that?

Earlier in the year this manager had described his job as being a problem solver. At that time he had generously interspersed the word "support" in his discussion. This time, however, "support" meant something different, something broader. Supporting their subordinates meant more than simply solving their immediate problems; it also meant providing the subordinates with the knowledge and skills they needed to do their jobs. Because the managers could no longer do the selling themselves, they had to choose and train subordinates who could do so:

> After you have coped with somebody else's hiring mistakes, you see the importance of taking the time to get the right people. . . . You are only as good as your people.
>
> My success is my people's success and vice versa. . . . You have to invest in training them and not just think of the short term and impose your solutions on them. . . . The effects of a bad manager who hasn't developed his people are immediately apparent. They can execute but they can't initiate.
>
> My job is to persuade the customer to buy a product. I go through the reps to do that. I've got to convince the customer that he or she wants our business. . . . I have to do some handholding and training to make sure the rep focuses on customer satisfaction.

71

>Does a manager produce? I'd say, yes. As many demands as the manager has on his time, I think his primary responsibility is people development. Not production, but people development. And I think that while you're developing people, you are producing through them at the same time.

For the first time, many explicitly defined themselves as people managers—they were responsible for training and developing subordinates. The new managers were also beginning to recognize their long-term as well as short-term responsibilities; training and development were investments. They began to devote more time and attention to hiring, training, and development. (That is not to say that they were devoting enough time or the right proportion of time to these matters. Even by the end of the year, their subordinates and superiors still felt the managers could improve in these categories.)

From their subordinates' requests and complaints, the managers began to realize that their subordinates expected them to care about "their whole person":

>I was getting feedback—not-so-subtle feedback—from my people that they felt they were getting a lot of guidance in marketing, but they wanted more attention to personal development—the career perspective—and more feedback on how they were doing day by day—you're doing the right thing or you're not doing the right thing—to get ahead.

>They want me to facilitate their efforts; to help them execute their marketing plans and personal growth objectives. I have to be a sounding board for both, to help them assess options and resources, and understand how to get what they want in the short term and the long term.

>They [the subordinates] are interested in making money, sure, but they are also interested in getting ahead, in recognition by the company, in enjoying their job.

>I think the first thing they expect is support. They expect that if they're out doing their job as they think it should be done and as it has been outlined for them, that they're going to get my support. If they make a mistake, they expect me to go through that mistake with them, to do what needs to be done to correct it, but not to chastise or punish them for mis-

takes that were made unknowingly, mistakes that I call legitimate.

In other words, the managers were becoming aware of and sensitive to their subordinates' psychological needs:

> You've got to get behind the numbers [quotas] and see what is really coming. You've got to break the numbers barrier.
>
> Now I have a very clear perception of what they want from the boss: they want all kinds of exposure to them, visible exposure, sales ideas; talking about sales is just part of it. They want jokes, [to] be asked about themselves, a lot of involvement, and that is the toughest part of this job.
>
> They want the door to be always open, whether it's here [in the office] or at home, whether it is in the business day or on the weekend, so that when they have a problem that is business related or personal, they can call me. I try to get them comfortable that they can talk to me about anything and that it doesn't go any further. Anything.

Numerous researchers have observed that new managers consider dealing with people problems rather than technical problems to be a poor use of their time and effort, and until they relinquish or unlearn this attitude, they cannot succeed as managers.[9] The managers were taking another critical step. They no longer defined their subordinates' "neediness" as illegitimate. Instead, they accepted that responding to subordinates' psychological needs was part of their job, albeit a part they were still uncomfortable handling: "Some days I feel more like a psychiatrist than a manager. A boss can't be a friend. They've got it all wrong."

Most managers were more comfortable with their formal people management skills (such as training and development) than their informal ones (such as counseling and leadership). The former skills were more consistent with their notions of being sales leader; they were sharing their technical expertise with others. The latter skills were difficult to grasp and articulate. Besides, they "didn't know how to do them." Most soon argued that people problems of all kinds were the toughest part of their job:

> The people psychology part is the most challenging. I don't know if I like it. I hadn't realized, because I had my book [of clients], how hard it is to motivate people or develop them or deal with their personal problems.

The managers began to mention among their responsibilities motivating their subordinates, and a selected few brought up leadership. That they were now even giving lip service to these ideas is significant. All were surprised that it was so difficult to get people to do what needed to be done:

> You've got to have the ability to listen, respect people, let them be individuals, get them to trust you, and at the same time give advice and be sensitive to business and personal issues.

CONCLUDING REMARKS

As we have seen, the managers began to confront the difference between their old and new roles, not by choice but of necessity. First, they had to deal with the realities in the manager's daily life. Discovering that their predictions about their routine were grossly inaccurate, they began to revise their conceptualization of managerial work to reflect its reality. In making and living with the consequences of decisions, especially conflicts involving their subordinates (subordinate against customer, subordinate against the organization, performance reviews of subordinates), the managers began to move toward a managerial identity. As they were forced to act, to manage conflicts between themselves and their subordinates, they came to appreciate what it meant to be primarily responsible for people, not the task, and to discover *their own* interests as managers. Forced to make decisions against their subordinates' wishes, they began to separate themselves from the subordinates—they began to see the difference between being a manager and a doer, and to reclaim their formal authority.

NOTES

1. My analysis of the new managers' way of reframing their understanding of the managerial role was heavily influenced by the work of Bandura (1986; 1989) on social-learning theory, Louis (1980; 1990) on sense-making, and Schön (1983; 1990) on the reflective practitioner.

2. The new managers' first impressions were reminiscent of Mintzberg's (1973) discussion of managerial work:

> Because of the open-ended nature of his job, the manager feels compelled to perform a great quantity of work, at an unrelenting pace. Little free time is available and breaks are rare. Senior managers, in particular, cannot escape from their jobs after hours, because of the work they take home and because their minds tend to be on their jobs during much of their "free" time. In contrast to activities performed by most non-managers, those of the manager are characterized by brevity, variety, and fragmentation. The vast majority are of brief duration, on the order of seconds for foremen and minutes for chief executives. The variety of activities to be performed is great, and the lack of pattern among subsequent activities, with the trivial interspersed with the consequential, requires that the manager shift moods quickly and frequently. In general, managerial work is fragmented and interruptions are commonplace (p. 51).

3. In their work, McCall et al. (1988) found that this was a common and strong misconception for the less-experienced manager:

> This approach assumes that it's a manager's responsibility to be the expert, to master the content of the assignment, and to direct others accordingly—a technical manager for all seasons, a walking encyclopedia of business brilliance. Some might call this arrogance, and it may be, partly, but more often such a belief results from the fear of giving up control, of being exposed as a nincompoop, or the worst fear of all—being wrong with everyone watching (p. 34).

4. See Flamholtz and Randall (1987) for a description of just how stressful managers find this aspect of managerial work (p. 15).

5. Schein (1978) found that for first-line managers the outstanding feature of their new position was the "reality shock . . . that people [could be] roadblocks to what they wanted to do" (p. 95).

6. See Louis's (1980) work on career transitions for a discussion of different forms of surprise experiences and the challenges in adapting to them (pp. 237–238). Individuals are surprised when they find a difference between their

expectations and subsequent experiences in a new situation. Louis says expectations can be conscious, tacit, or emergent.

7. In this vein, Falvey (1989), in an article on the producing manager, made this observation:

> No matter how much personal discipline someone possesses, it is human nature to do more of what they do best. Thus the accounts always win, and the people to be managed always lose out (p. 44).

8. Mintzberg (1978), among others, finds that the pressures of managerial work encourage such an active orientation.

9. See Schein (1987).

3

Moving toward a
Managerial Identity

From the sixth month to the ninth, most of the new managers began to focus more fully on their bosses' interests. They had managed conflicts with their subordinates (therefore, they no longer overidentified with the subordinates) and had been on the job long enough to have some results for which they felt accountable. They had gone through a business cycle (at least quarterly results were in) and had discussed their performance with their bosses. (Some had formal reviews, but most had only informal ones.) Many said the honeymoon was over. The lessons of what it meant to be the formal authority were coming home to roost. They began to accept their agenda-setting and network-building responsibilities and to behave, think, and value more like managers. At the end of Chapter 2, we saw them flirting with their new identity; we now see them begin to embrace it.

LIVING WITH ULTIMATE ACCOUNTABILITY

The message the managers heard from their bosses was that they had full responsibility and would be held accountable for everything that took place in their unit. In conversations with the superiors they felt the "full pressure of having to make the bottom line," and they had expected to hear just that:

> He was giving me complete flexibility to hang myself. He told me he wouldn't question any of my expenses; he never would. He would let me do whatever I wanted to, but then at the end of the year he would hold me accountable. If I wanted to spend some money and make an investment in the office, I could. I just bought a $9,000 personal computer. That's a lot of money. He didn't say a word, but I'd better be able to show what kind of revenues it generated.
>
> If I commit something in a big way and it turns out wrong, it will hurt my career. . . . Every move I make is a risk to my career, just as we subject the customer to risks.

Many described these conversations about their authority and accountability as "exhilarating and scary" at the same time. From the interviews, it seemed that during this period they craved the autonomy and opportunity to make decisions, but still did not feel on top of their jobs, recognizing that they had a great deal to learn. They became anxious and returned again to their preconceptions about the managerial role: they were supposed to be experts at everything. Consequently, the managers often found conversations with their bosses confusing and worrisome. They reported being surprised by both the variety and subjectivity of criteria that their superiors used to evaluate them. They were especially struck by their bosses' priorities. According to their performance plans and the company compensation policies, the new managers were "paid for making quota and customer satisfaction." Their bosses, however, devoted a "disproportionate" amount of time to issues other than the quota: "It was as if he defined my job as: 50 percent people development, 30 percent sales and product leadership, and 30 percent administration and compliance."

From the interviews it appeared that the managers saw

their superiors as evaluating them principally by four criteria: what the managers were doing to implement company strategy, their future plans for their unit, how they were treating their people, and how they were getting along with others in the organization. The first two criteria have to do with setting agendas and the others with building networks.

WHAT IT MEANS TO BE THE AGENDA SETTER

As described in the introduction, both companies that served as research sites in this study were undergoing significant organizational change. They were moving toward profit and service and away from revenue and product as their focuses. Hence, cost cutting was becoming a top priority and whole new families of products were being introduced to meet demands for customer service and quality. Most of the bosses questioned the new managers explicitly about how they intended to implement the new company strategies:[1]

> Costs! Costs! Costs! Every little debit and credit! That is all he cared about. . . . But if you don't bring in the sales, costs don't matter.
>
> He didn't see why I was not selling more of the products [the corporate office] was pushing. But my brokers were complaining that I was shoving them down their throats.
>
> I knew the company wanted my reps to try to sell a whole round of products to the customer. But the reps like to sell only what they know and what will move out the door quickest. . . . They know what pays for their bread and butter.
>
> He noticed my people were still doing a large percentage of small trades and holding too many small accounts. Couldn't I tell from the change in account exec compensation that the company wasn't interested in encouraging that kind of business any more? What was I supposed to do, tell the account execs to dump half their clients?

The managers often tried to justify their actions to their superiors:

> On the surface it looked like I was ignoring company directives. I was over budget for my expense ratio. . . . The

manager before me had a different philosophy. He was a number cruncher. I felt the people needed to be recognized because they had gotten less recognition than they should
have. . . . He listened to my story, but he kept shaking his
head. . . . No excuses.

The superior's retort was that the manager was "being soft
and not living up to his responsibilities." From the forcefulness
he saw in the superior's remarks and the threat to downgrade
the manager's performance rating, he soon concluded that it was
his job to articulate and see to it that the firm's strategy was
implemented. Many of the other new managers received similar
feedback from their superiors. Because they had been so eager
to please their subordinates, most had gone beyond their bud-
gets and had often neglected directives to focus on products or
services their subordinates did not want to sell. Now, it was
being brought home, one manager said, that they were expected
to be team players.

WHAT IT MEANS TO BE THE NETWORK BUILDER

Not only were many of the superiors apparently displeased
that the managers had not fulfilled their agenda-setting responsibilities, but most also complained about their network-building
performance. In fact, from the new managers' perspective, their
superiors spent the lion's share of their conversations discussing
people management and leadership:

> Every time he called he kept talking about what I was
> doing about hiring, training, and motivating my people . . . I
> wanted to talk about new sales ideas I was working on.
> He admitted I was paid for maximizing revenue, main-
> taining a high level of customer satisfaction, and developing
> my people, in that order. But he said from day to day I should
> reverse the priorities. What you invest today in people, you'll
> reap tomorrow. The quotas are sort of arbitrary measurements
> for compensation.
> He made it very explicit. My overall evaluation would
> be no higher than that for my people management. That was

the highest priority. The second element was marketing our products to the customer in a way that would sustain growth, and the third element was doing things that would get us into new areas, like applications or software.

He kept pointing out that this is a people business.

Because the managers by this time had come to accept, in part, their people responsibilities, they were not taken aback by these comments as they might have been earlier in the year. In fact, recalling their first conversations with their new bosses (when they were hired), many remembered that the bosses had mentioned people management. Nonetheless, "I didn't think he [the boss] took it so seriously then."

Still, many were put off at first by the weight their superiors placed on managing people; conversations with their superiors fed their insecurity about being dependent upon others. "Am I really just a highly paid personnel manager?" one manager had asked his boss. His boss had replied, "No, you're paid to be a leader."

Superiors were more than willing to elaborate on what they meant by leadership. The managers recalled these definitions when I asked about their conversations with their superiors:

> Hiring. Training. Personnel problems in the office. Motivating. Deciding about conflicts between customers and account executives. Satisfying the egos of thirty salespeople and fifteen support people. Having a people orientation, willing to be involved in the challenges of dealing with people.

> The people side of the business, career manager, foreman, take care of all the little details but also create an atmosphere that people will excel in. That atmosphere depends on a lot of things. The general attitude I project.

> Hiring. Developing. Vision and esprit de corps.

> Making sure people are happy, working hard, doing things that are right for themselves and for the company, and really providing the tender loving care that keeps them going strong.

Many managers reported that they intuitively understood what their superiors meant by leadership and why they regarded it so highly. Many commented that as they listened to their superiors they thought back on some of the best managers they had worked for; those managers had demonstrated real leadership qualities. But they felt these people had been the exception, not the rule: "Leadership is a luxury, not really a necessity." Consequently, they felt their superiors were making somewhat unreasonable demands. One pointed out that he had just recently discovered he would "have to motivate people, that they would not want to do the right thing." He had yet to figure out how to "go about actually motivating such people."

During the latter half of the year, the managers reported that their relationships, not just with their subordinates, but also with others outside their units, were becoming more of an issue with their bosses. This trouble often came up in talking about their way of handling administrative responsibilities:

> My numbers were good, but my boss kept harping on why he was getting so many complaints from corporate about me . . . I hadn't filled out all their mundane forms on time. What he didn't understand is that if I had used up all my time on those bullcrap reports, the numbers wouldn't have been so good.

> He spent the whole time asking me about a scrap I got into with the legal department over a customer contract. My rep couldn't get the guy to cooperate and so I had to call and chew him out.

> He bawled me out. . . . He asked me if I knew how people looked at me. How was I spending my time on peer relationships? People perceived me to be interested only in my own patch, my turf, my people. He said I had some trading off to do. In short, he said, they perceive you as exploitive, self-centered. And it will come back to haunt you.

In these instances their superiors talked to the managers about the value of building and maintaining good relationships with others in the organization. Most stressed being proactive in doing so:

> His point was that I was the coordinator who had to keep everyone informed about what was going on in my area, what things we needed to do, what resources we were lacking. He told me to be more aggressive in representing my patch.

> To prove to me why I needed to really know the adminis-

trative procedures, he showed me some tricks. . . . We are always looking for money around here. If you are going to be measured on performance—how well you do profit and loss—a lot of money can be found in this firm if you know what you are doing. Inherent in the system of reporting revenues and expenses are deficiencies. If you are not following them closely you can cost yourself a small fortune and never know it. . . . I had to smile because he showed me how to claim something that really didn't belong to me from a charge point of view and get a rebate for it. . . . I guess it is worth watching the administrative point of view.

Although the managers could appreciate their superiors' point of view, most still saw office politics as, at best, a poor use of their time, and their administrative responsibilities as uninteresting:

There are only so many hours in the day. I don't care to use them striking up great relationships with the home-office people. My boss is great at that stuff. But he wants to be the top person in the region. Me, I'm just civil. Now I spend two hours a week on it, though, because my boss wants me to.

Politics are not my arena. It's the company's responsibility to see to it that people are rewarded, promoted, and praised for the right reasons.

I do the staff work because my boss dictates that I do it. It is mundane day-to-day kinds of things. It's a part of my job and part of pleasing the boss.

The managers found the bosses' position about managing relationships with others in the company and implementing company strategy inconsistent in many ways with those of their subordinates. They appreciated their superiors' position. As described earlier, the managers themselves had done battle with their subordinates over some of the same issues. But for the first time the managers were feeling the full weight of being caught in the middle, which Roethlisberger called being the "master and victim of double-talk."[2] The first-line management position poses unique problems: the first-line manager is at once at the bottom of the heap and yet no longer "one of the guys." The managers were just beginning to appreciate the challenges of reconciling rank-and-file demands with those of senior management. They were moving toward richer understanding of their interface responsibilities:

> Let me tell you about the dilemma for first-line managers. A lot of people warned me that it was the toughest job in the company. When you're in the field because you're dealing with all the reps and all the customers, it's very much like you're a rep. But at the same time you now have a second line of management that is putting forces on you. The staff is breathing down your neck. You've got all the responsibilities of management and staff work that comes with managing the people, but you still have all the tactical things with customers—marketing strategies, and the like.

Being held accountable for a unit was a burdensome responsibility.

ADOPTING A MANAGERIAL IDENTITY: THINKING LIKE AN AGENDA SETTER

Not until almost the end of the year did many of the managers fully appreciate what their bosses had been trying to communicate to them. They had been overwhelmed at first by the sheer number of criteria on which their superiors were evaluating them. Superiors' expectations were described as a mess, inconsistent, and ambiguous. Others complained that their superiors were being unrealistic: "She wants only superstar offices." In time, as they received additional feedback on their performance and began to feel some mastery over the job, most were able to make sense of their superiors' demands, distilling them into a coherent message. The superiors expected them to be businesspeople, not salespeople:

> It's like I'm running a subsidiary, roughly a $50-million business. My boss works at the holding company and he expects me to run it. He expects me to do everything and you have a net result of a positive return.
> I'm running my own business.

Once the managers began to see that they were running a business, they realized that their role was to be generalists. To cope with all the challenges, they would have to broaden their perspective and be aware of the "total context" of the business. They would also have to adopt a long-term orientation. They reasoned that as salespeople their primary goal was making the numbers, a short-term objective. As managers, though they still needed the numbers, they had to take the longer view of business potential and people development. They began to display even more interest in their long-term agenda-setting responsibilities:

> I was back at the home office for a few days answering questions. I realized that I didn't know all I needed to know. I need a wider perspective on what I was doing and what my competition is doing, now and—if I could figure it out—in the next few years. Otherwise they can eat me alive if I'm not ready.
>
> I had to expand my horizons and think about what I wanted for my group two, three years from now. . . . [For example], what is the size of the market going to be? What do I want my share to be? What kind of expenses can I maintain and still be competitive?
>
> Next year . . . I'll need to take the longer view in adopting a strategy for each person I have. I'll need to better understand our business environment and customers so that I can balance the potential of the environment and the people. I'll set some long-term targets next time around.

As the managers began to incorporate the superiors' point of view and reconcile it with the numerous expectations of the others around them, they began to broaden their idea of what it means to be a manager. As they became aware of and accepted both their agenda-setting and network-building responsibilities, they began to recognize just how right they had been during their first days on the job. Time management, ability to set priorities, and decisiveness were critical managerial skills. Now, however, most recognized that it was not simply a matter of ordering one's obligations and managing one's time and making decisions accordingly. The challenge they faced was more complex. First, they had to be able to set the agenda for their unit, to ensure that they were focusing on the things that were most important, "keeping focused on the forest, not the trees." Second, they had to manage trade-offs, a very delicate balancing act among their responsibilities, many of which were equally compelling:

> I am the chief negotiator. I've got to balance my people's needs with the company's needs.
>
> I've come to recognize my role in total. . . . It's a real challenge. The challenge is twofold. To balance corporate and business expectations (quota and tons of other measures) with people management, motivation, concern for the individual, and development. You can't let either slip. It is easy to do one or the other alone, but the trick is to do both.
>
> I've got to pay equal attention to the short term and long term. If either gets out of whack, I've got a problem. Without the short term, we won't get to the long term. If I don't plan for the long term, when we get there we won't make the short term.

Realizing that the managerial role required balancing fundamental tensions was one of the most difficult and important insights the managers made.[3] They had come to understand that overload, ambiguity, and conflict were inherent in the managerial role. They had to learn to live with imperfect solutions and with the knowledge that they could not be experts about everything. Their job was to manage the trade-offs.

Moreover, in my conversations with the new managers toward the end of the year, they began to talk about the lasting influence they would like to have on their units:[4] "I began to think about the implications of what my decisions would be two years from now when my replacement might be here. I don't want somebody to have to clean up my mess. I'm going to start putting together the right building blocks."

What did they want their legacy to be? They were even more ambitious in outlook than their superiors:

> In one of our first conversations, I think I said to you if I was supposed to be the captain of this ship, well this ship is in for a crash. Do you remember that? . . . Now, I have only

one objective, to make this the best unit in the company, and I want to do it in a way to make other people happy and satisfied: Are they feeling a sense of success and accomplishment? Are we making the numbers? Are we doing business in the most efficient and effective way? Doing the things that need to be done and doing them right, and not doing the things we need not do simply because it has been done that way for a hundred years? In the eyes of my peers, the other managers, and my boss, we're doing more than an acceptable job.

To meet the sales objectives first, that's foremost. Second to do it in a way that remains within the parameters of policy and practices of the corporation, as they relate to the customer. Third (there's not necessarily a significant difference in priorities) to manage my people in a way that allows them to work at 100 percent of their capability and to advance their career, and to get close to maximum fulfillment out of the job. And fourth—and I really think this is important—that I should work for changes in quality within the corporation.

It is hard to believe that the new manager who made these last remarks had only months earlier described himself as a "puppet in a puppet show."

ADOPTING A MANAGERIAL IDENTITY: THINKING LIKE A NETWORK BUILDER

My final interviews with the new managers revealed that for many, it had become second nature that they were "people managers." Compare one manager's definitions of the managerial role after a month on the job and after twelve months on the job.

After one month:

Seventy percent of my job is sales and sales leadership. If you say you went into management because you're tired of sales, you're wrong. I love sales. Ten percent is compliance, the dirty word. This is the most important part of your job or someone else will cost you your job if you're not doing the right thing, reviewing letters and new accounts carefully. Fifty percent is firefighting and solving problems. They've tried to resolve it at their level and could not, and so they've come to you because it is a big problem. You have to drop everything and attend to it. Five percent is human relations and counseling. Five percent is other administration and 5 percent is recruitment. Does that add up to 100 percent?

After fifteen months:

People development is my main mission in life: 50 percent people development, 30 percent sales and product leadership, 10 percent administration, and 10 percent compliance—you go to jail if you are not the policeman on the block.

When asked which skills were critical for management, most replied that strong technical and interpersonal skills were both required. Some even ventured that the latter were more critical.

By the end of the year the managers also better understood their place in the larger organization. More began to see the value of "politics," a lesson learned by experience, in this case, failure to achieve objectives:

It was really that first experience of getting in there. I got into a difficult account situation, where I needed a lot of area support, in different areas and in different facets. I knew what resources I needed and that they were available in the company. But I found I didn't have the credibility or experience on the job to get them. I'd call and say, "Gosh, this isn't getting done. Gosh darn it, I expected it to be done. It's your responsibility. I want it done by tomorrow." I didn't have the experience or the credibility to pull it off. These were bargaining situations. I said to my employees, "Well, we ought to use this resource to get to point B, then we'll bring in resources A and C and put these together and we ought to be able to do it in this time frame." I think I'd just make the calls and get it initiated. I couldn't pull it off even though I knew whom to call. I had to rely on one of my peer managers, who had been a manager for a lot of years. He made the call for me and got it done.

The job is to learn how to manage resources. You've got to be able to quickly identify where a resource is. The biggest crime you can make in a company like ours with so many resources is not using those resources because you don't know they are there. . . . You find out about them by getting to know people around the company and what they do. . . . The area office has 150 folks who are there to provide help. I didn't know they were there until my boss made me promise to call there at least twice a week.

If you are going to get something out of the region, you've got to know where the real help is, where the power plays are in the region. . . . You can read the manual and phone book and find out where the resources are, but you can learn the power things only by trial and error.

Furthermore, because all the managers had been through at least one business planning cycle, they were forced "to live with what happens when you don't look out for your own interests." Either their quotas had been set significantly higher than they thought appropriate, or they received the "short end of the stick" when resources were distributed: "Goals and standards will cascade from above. Unless you are well connected and can influence them, your point of view goes unheard at the top."

To succeed, most of the new managers acquiesced to their "political" responsibilities. They acknowledged that they should devote time and energy to developing relationships with those outside their unit. They began to schedule times and create opportunities to spend with their bosses and peers, admittedly with reluctance. Interestingly, although they came to appreciate how important politics internal to their organizations was, they failed to see fully its value outside the organization. With a few notable exceptions, they failed to become actively involved in their community to build up the office's reputation. More experienced managers in both research sites devoted much time to such activities, working hard to become "Mr. [company name]" or a "big name in the community." One experienced manager said that these responsibilities often began to consume his work life, even his social life. Perhaps they were so overwhelmed with all their other responsibilities that they were not able to see beyond them. Still, they had come a long way since their managerial debut. Their model of managerial work had been at once broadened and refined. It had been an arduous and painful journey:[5]

> Suddenly, I found myself saying, boy, I can't be responsible for getting all that revenue. I don't have the time. Suddenly you've got to go from yourself and say now I'm the manager, and what does a manager do? It takes a while thinking about it for it to really hit you . . . a manager gets things done through people. That's a very, very hard transition to make.

LESSONS FOR THE FUTURE

The managers had changed their perception of themselves and the world around them in a remarkably brief time. They had done so by learning from experience, by solving problems, from social situations. As they began to *act* like managers, they began to *become* managers.

They were moving from doer to people manager, from producer to businessperson. They stopped seeing themselves as the proverbial hedgehogs who knew a lot about and concentrated on one thing, and began thinking of themselves as foxes who knew something about and worked on a lot of things.

The transformation was by no means complete. Most now understood the facts of managerial life and put together many of the pieces of the managerial puzzle, but some still eluded them. Although they had accepted the role as people manager, most had yet to fully understand their leadership responsibilities. Although they had begun to appreciate their place in the organization, some were still not convinced that managing relationships with those outside their unit should be part of the job. And as they knew all too well, defining the managerial role was the easy part. *How* to do it (our subject in Part III) was the real challenge.

Moreover, most still reminisced fondly about their days as individual contributors; in fact, they began to idealize those times somewhat. And at times of crisis or when they felt overwhelmed (which was often) they would retreat into the comfort of their old identity until they gathered strength to go forward again. For most were just beginning to shift their sources of self-esteem (more on this subject in Chapter 6):

> Whenever I begin to panic I remember, I trick myself. . . . I say as a manager I'm still a salesperson and my primary job is to sell by working with the people in my office: to develop them and sell them on what I believe is right and what I believe the firm believes is right. I will work with them. I will develop them. I will market them. I'll be the best salesman there is.

NOTES

1. In both sites, cost-cutting had been identified as a managerial priority. Also, new families of products seen as key to future profits had been recently introduced.
2. Roethlisberger (1945), p. 283.
3. Sayles (1989) provided one of the most comprehensive and insightful descriptions of the dilemmas of managing paradox (pp. 294–296).
4. The order in which the new managers adopted their managerial roles was consistent with Mintzberg's (1973) observations about new managers:

> Lacking contacts and information at the beginning, the new manager concentrates on the liaison and monitor roles in an attempt to build up a web of contacts and a data base. The decisional roles cannot become fully operative until he has more information. When he does, he is likely to stress the entrepreneurial role for a time, as he attempts to put his distinct stamp on his organization (p. 129).

5. In Chapter 5 we will look at the stresses and emotional side of the journey.

II

Developing Interpersonal Judgment

Building effective relationships with their subordinates was unequivocally the most difficult task the new managers faced.[1] They were surprised to discover just how daunting it could be and how vulnerable they were:

> I thought if you had the product skills and answers, that was all you would need. You need interpersonal skills and attitude projection to be successful.
>
> The personnel side. No, let's not call it personnel, it is the art of managing people . . . that is probably the hardest part of the job to learn to do well. After all, you're promoted to the job because you've been successful in marketing.

In their nonmanagerial jobs, the managers surely had learned valuable lessons about managing work relationships; otherwise, it is hard to imagine that they could have been so successful as salespeople. Still, they had been promoted primarily for their technical competence, not their management or interpersonal skill. Getting things done through a significant number of other people takes a different order of skill from working with just two or three people. Moreover, learning to exercise formal authority and to create a productive, satisfied work force were new challenges.

The managers can be thought of as novices trying to practice the delicate craft of managing people without benefit of an apprenticeship. As we have seen, when they embarked on their new careers, they faced a surprisingly foreign and complex job and environment. Bombarded with new and confusing information and inadequately armed with rules for making sense of it and evaluating its relevance, they still had to make decisions and take action. As they coped with the human dilemmas that arose in managing subordinates, they relied upon a kind of "personal case law" to build up a judgment base or set of guiding principles.[2] They found it difficult to talk with precision about how and what they were learning about people. They talked about "hunches," "automatic thought processes for dealing with situations," and "intuition absorbed through experience." They actively experimented with and practiced different ways of handling the situations they encountered: "I was constantly testing my ideas on how to deal with people."

Most of the time, however, the managers depended upon trial and error. They were unaware that they were experimenting unless forced to reflect on their actions because of consequences that were unanticipated or undesirable: "Every day I discovered something else I didn't know about how people operate. It has been a [process] of learning from my mistakes."

Formal and informal feedback on how their subordinates perceived them was perhaps the most effective teacher, though it was devastating, for it was unexpectedly negative and often suggested that their intentions were misunderstood. Because they were at such a delicate stage in their careers, knowing all too well that they had much to learn, they were very susceptible to feedback. Finally, the managers relied heavily on experience, having recently been subordinates themselves, to figure out how to manage a particular situation (as we will see, sometimes this approach created more problems than it solved).

Despite some individual differences in the issues the managers found most trying as they learned interpersonal judgment, two lessons were at the core of their curriculum: how to exercise authority and how to manage individual subordinates' performance. Each is considered in turn in Chapters 4 and 5.

In these chapters we address the challenges of managing subordinates, but not those of managing peers or superiors. Needless to say, the management of peer and superior relationships can be as difficult as that of subordinates. As we have seen, though, peer and superior relationships were not the managers' highest priority; that went to subordinate relationships. These were, after all, the new or unique addition to their world. This narrative comes from the new managers' point of view; for them, developing interpersonal judgment meant managing down.

NOTES

1. What is an effective relationship? Gabarro (1987) proposes this definition:

> The pattern that characterizes effective relationships is that mutual expectations, trust, and influence not only grow over time but become more concrete, tested, and grounded. In those relationships described as being less than effective or satisfying (by one or both parties), expectations were vague, or differences in expectations were not worked out, and a solid basis of trust had not developed (p. 101).

Gabarro found that most work relationships were developed and stabilized (for better or worse) within a manager's first twelve months on the job.

Much evidence shows that interpersonal competence is a prerequisite for a successful managerial career. See Boyatzis (1982), Bray et al. (1974), Katz (1974), and Kotter (1982).

2. With all the complexities in human nature, behavior can never be fully understood and predicted. Hence, solving human problems in organizations is different from solving technical ones. Human problems are surrounded by great uncertainty in the nature of problems, implementation of solutions, and evaluation of outcomes. Hannaway (1989) elaborates on the challenges of making sense of such problems:

> [There are] . . . limits to the human capacity to process information and therefore there are limits on human cognition. Because of the limits, individuals search for information in a highly selective way

and operate within simplified models of the world. Decision-makers tend only to "satisfice" taking the first acceptable solution to a problem rather than searching for the optimal or best solution. . . . They typically are overloaded with information and underarmed with rules about what is relevant. In such situations, information biases have a field day. . . . To simplify, there are two stages in which biases occur either consciously or unconsciously. The first is information awareness and acquisition. The second stage is that of interpretation, when sense is made of the information that has been acquired (p. 14).

There are no clear-cut descriptions of "correct" behavior for managing people. There are, however, better and worse ways of handling human problems. Although people management is not a science, it has a system of unwritten rules and logic. This is the logic the new managers had to develop and refine. As they moved from simplified, naive models of the phenomena to more complex, sophisticated ones, their judgments about interpersonal models improved. My thinking about interpersonal competence and judgment was greatly influenced by Weick's (1974) conception of skills as "programmes," analogous to computer programs, as sets of inner rules and instructions governing behavior.

4

Exercising Authority

It took me three months to realize I had no effect on many of my people. It was like I had been talking to myself.

The new managers had to learn how to exercise their newly acquired authority. Ironically, to do so required that they develop the capacity to exercise power and influence effectively without relying simply on their formal authority or power of position. More specifically, they had to learn how to

- establish credibility
- build subordinate commitment
- lead the group

FROM RELIANCE ON FORMAL AUTHORITY TO ESTABLISHING CREDIBILITY

As they began in their new positions, the managers talked about getting off on the right foot, and felt that "a first impression is a lasting impression.'' Much thought and energy went into deciding how they should look and behave in the first days on the job:

> Because I'm new, they are still impressionable. They don't have any preconceived notions yet. It's an opportunity to define who I am for them.
>
> The first thirty days were critical. I had to demonstrate that I had ability. I kept looking for a big win, picking the right stock, stealing a big producer from the competition. I had to demonstrate that I worked hard. I stayed late nights and came in on weekends. I wanted them to know I wasn't just a crisis manager. It was hard to get relief from the pressure of it all.

The managers were surprised to find out how difficult it was to build credibility and trust. First impressions, though important, counted for only so much. They had embarked on a slow and arduous journey:

> I knew I was a good guy and I kind of expected people to accept me immediately for what I was, but you really had to earn it. Folks were very wary. As a new manager, you had to earn their respect.
>
> I finally realized I had to earn their respect when a fairly senior person said to me, ''You are trying too soon to be one of us. You are assuming you are a sales rep still and you can be one of the gang, but you are not. You have to understand that and accept that.'' Yet, other sales managers were one of the gang, and you say, Wait a minute—why is it different?

The managers soon recognized they had to prove that they deserved their subordinates' respect and trust. Indeed, they felt as if they were being scrutinized under a microscope.[1] The subordinates were clearly sizing them up, but they relied on stereotypes and even highly impressionistic information in judging managerial credibility.[2] One manager was horrified that his being divorced was grist for the mill: ''In the Midwest it matters if you are divorced. They [his subordinates] wondered if it meant I could not maintain strong relationships.''

Most managers found the scrutiny unnerving, particularly because they felt overwhelmed by their new positions. One manager described feeling insulted by a conversation he inadvertently overheard between two of his key subordinates:

> They had checked up on me`. . . and found I had only been a big producer, not a super producer. They couldn't be sure if my decisions were really backed by experience, although they had no real complaints about me. They were actually questioning my qualifications.

At first the managers appreciated only one criterion their subordinates used in evaluating them: Was the new manager competent? Although the managers primarily meant technically competent, they later recognized that their subordinates had a second, equally significant question: What were the managers' motives or intentions? After reflecting on numerous subordinate comments and reactions, one manager finally figured out that his subordinates "weren't so much worried if I could do the job," but rather they were "looking for clues that I was only out for [myself]":

> I guess the key underlying thing is: Is he a caring person and supportive? And does he have that sense of having been around a long time? Is he going to be here and has he chosen to be here?

Others reported:

> They knew I was a big producer in the institutional end and they were worried that I was probably going to miss the money and be very oriented toward my bonus and only manage the numbers. People will put up with a lot of mistakes so long as they feel you are sincere. You are not just there to ride them for two years and you are gone.
>
> One of the initial things that I tried to do I felt turned out to be very important. I learned everybody's name in the office in two days. That really impressed them that I was interested in knowing who they were as individuals, and I was. I also brought some wine and cheese in a basket to say that I really appreciated the welcoming that I received.

Just as they had started by thinking of managers as technical experts, not managers of people, the managers put more

99

effort into demonstrating their competence (especially technical competence) than into their commitment to their subordinates. Many of them therefore missed early opportunities for building good will among their subordinates, just when they needed it most. Inevitably, the managers made mistakes on the job. Whether or not the subordinates would forgive and forget strongly depended on whether or not they saw the manager as caring and supportive. A subordinate of the manager who had taken the time to learn her subordinates' names commented:

> She has been tremendously generous and she has demonstrated from the start that she will give support. She has given so much I suspect she dipped into her own personal funds. That has been very well received. She bought and paid for loyalty that will get her something later when she tries to create high expectations. She'll see it has paid off.

The managers had to learn what their subordinates looked for in judging managerial commitment. They discovered two factors that most subordinates weighted very heavily: how much time and resources the manager invested in subordinates and how the manager handled subordinates' mistakes. The managers could see that availability and active, one-on-one involvement with individual subordinates were critical in developing effective relationships:

> I hardly shut my door. The door is always open. When I'm talking to people and the phone starts ringing I just let it keep on ringing. I try to provide an atmosphere where I'm constantly available and I'm not your boss from a negative standpoint or to watch out for you or babysit for you. But no, I'm your boss from a positive standpoint. I'm here to help people contribute, and I'm here to contribute whatever is necessary to make you successful.

They saw that small things and personal touches made a difference, as in working side-by-side with their subordinates on special projects, working nights, and taking them out to dinner:

> I held a big party downtown for a broker who had been with the company twenty-eight years and who was retiring. I

gave him a nice gift. It just seemed like the thing to do. Well, people were very excited. Everybody talked about it for weeks; it seemed to them that I cared. People are very aware of those things.

"A terrific manager is a manager who has a lot of contact." One manager said, "My time is my most valuable and prized possession. I spend a lot of time just sitting and talking." The managers came to recognize that they must take others' feelings into account and be responsive to build credibility and trust:

> People have a difficult time telling you how they feel. Sometimes they have the urge to tell you and you have to be open to it. It means listening to somebody when they spout their frustrations, and you defuse it by letting them talk and get it out of their system.
>
> He stopped by my office every day and talked to me about his wife, who was having an affair with a neighbor. I started feeling like his therapist. I guess he was just so upset he couldn't help himself. He was always apologizing. You had to feel sorry for the guy.

At first, some of the managers resented the need to "stroke" their people and talk about personal matters. These activities were not a part of the job description. Indeed, they were so overworked and overwhelmed by the new position that finding the time to spend with subordinates was no mean feat. But in their quieter moments they recalled their own experiences as subordinates:

> I hated it when my manager closed the door, even if I did not want to go in there. I just didn't like the idea that the door was closed. Does that make sense? I just hated the idea that he had the audacity to close the door and that I would have to knock if I wanted to see him.

Many of the new managers also received feedback, both formal and informal, that they were not spending enough time with their subordinates. A peer of a new manager shared this experience: "She [a new manager] got back a bad summary. We were talking about it, what she was doing wrong. I said just go out and touch someone. She said she couldn't do it."

Moreover, as the managers realized that they depended on their subordinates to be effective on the job, they began to define building effective relationships as a critical aspect of their responsibility. They began to see that devoting time and energy to this endeavor bore fruit.

It became clear that their subordinates were especially sensitive to their way of responding to mistakes, when deciding whether or not the manager could be trusted. The subordinates seemed to expect them to hear their side of the story, be fair, and as much as possible protect them from negative consequences. Although they understood the subordinates' expectations, they found them difficult to meet. They could not help but feel that a subordinate's mistake reflected badly on the manager. The managers admitted that their first impulse was to become angry and punish the subordinate:

> He [a sales representative] really screwed up. He ordered and shipped the wrong keyboard. It would cost the branch a few thousand dollars to rectify. It was just an oversight. He should not have done it. I wanted to go through the ceiling and tell him I'd kill him if it happened again and take it out of his hide. It took all my willpower to remain cool and tell him not to let it happen again and that I could cover it in the budget when I knew my boss would not be happy.

> The difference is, as soon as they trust you and know where you are coming from, then you become more like one of the gang. It takes going through a couple of crises where you have a couple of options. You really can either blame the rep for everything that happens, and play Pontius Pilate and wash your hands of it, or you can dig in and say, "Okay, you made a mistake. A mistake happens and I am not worried about whom to blame it on. The question is, how do we fix it?" If you go through a few of those and there are really no reprisals, you are on your way.

> If they make a mistake, they expect me to go through that mistake with them, to do what needs to be done to correct it, to go to bat for them, but not to chastise or punish for mistakes that were made unknowingly, which I call legitimate mistakes.

Especially in the beginning the managers felt that their subordinates were actively testing them:

> The honeymoon was over. It is hard to know when and how to tell a broker not to do something. The bigger the broker the more important the judgment is. It takes time and work to build credibility. You can't do it overnight. But you can lose it overnight.
>
> You may have to confront them [the sales reps]. They won't come to you. They will miss sales meetings or be late a lot. You have to know when to say something. You have only so many chances to build credibility.
>
> They think the broker is king instead of the manager. I've got to show them I am willing to earn my money and to go through with things they don't like when necessary.

The managers described most of the tests as "thinly veiled or explicit challenges to their authority." The more insidious and seductive tests, though, were subordinates' efforts to befriend them: "They either try to give you all kinds of trouble or to befriend you." As this manager's comments reveal, it was often the manager who initiated the "friendship trap," not the subordinates:

> I think probably the first four or five months on the job, whenever a rep came in with a problem, maybe the first three months, I was too intent on having the reps like me, gaining credibility with them. When they came in with a problem I'd grab it and run with it so that they would like me.

This was a very important admission. Most new managers very much wanted to be liked. Research on salespeople indicates that they generally have an above-average need to be liked.[3] The managers in this study were no different. One said he had to "fight the burning desire to be accommodating and not make the tough decisions, so that they would like me."

Until the managers recognized this collusion with their subordinates—that the manager was a friend—they were unable to confront a fundamental managerial tension: the difference between being respected and being liked. Resolving this conflict was critical in fully accepting the responsibility in being a manager and developing credibility. The managers had to learn that building strong personal relationships with trust and confidence did not mean becoming a friend: "When I think about the exceptional sales managers I know, their people respect them and also like them. But the first piece is respect."

McClelland and Burnham found in their classic study of managerial motivation that the better managers have a higher need for power than they do affiliation.[4] Managers with high affiliation needs, trying to stay on good terms with everyone, indiscriminately made exceptions for individuals that their other subordinates often considered grossly unfair.

Finally, to build credibility and trust, the managers had to learn not to respond defensively to challenges and criticisms from subordinates. In the early months, this restraint was next to impossible for them to achieve. One new manager said he needed to "at least hold on to the illusion that [he] was the boss . . . and the boss is always right." By the end of the year, this manager was able to manage these challenges more effectively:

> There is a constant challenge, and if you look at the challenge as a personal threat, you are in trouble. If you look at the challenge as just that, a challenge—they are throwing you the gauntlet and the quickest thing you can do is just throw it back—without spilling blood. I see it more as a game now, this is an ego business. . . . I told them all in my one-on-one talks recently that if you come in and ask me for something the answer is yes, providing three things: first, you can sit in my chair and answer yes; that is, it makes good sense from my side of the desk. Second, it makes good sense from your side of the desk. And, third, if you put your stockholder hat on, it makes good sense. If two out of three are right, you get a yes. They seemed to accept it.

Another manager proudly reported in her seventh month how she remained calm when one of her subordinates came in and told her he disagreed with how she had distributed the accounts of a broker who had left:

A few months ago, I would have been tempted to say, it's none of your business. I am the boss. But this time I said he had a right to express his opinion and I had a right to do it differently than he suggested. Then I explained why I did it the way I did and that was that.

How did the managers learn to handle these challenges to their authority more gracefully without becoming defensive? For one thing, they came to realize that having a subordinate disagree with them about something did not mean a challenge to their authority. As they gained self-confidence, they understood that a subordinate might legitimately have a different point of view on an issue and was simply trying to express an opinion. Further, out of necessity, the managers became more "thick-skinned." As we will see in another chapter, much to their surprise and chagrin, the new managers were inundated with "negativity." To survive, they learned to cope with the stresses associated with negative feedback and emotions. One manager said that for self-protection she became immune to the negativity. But more important, only by giving up the myth of manager as expert and feeling more self-assured could they tolerate negative feedback from their subordinates. In fact, protecting their self-esteem was vital in developing the new managers' relationships.

FROM CONTROL TO COMMITMENT

A primary aim of the managers when they started in their new positions was learning how to exercise or gain control over their people. They were eager to exercise their formal authority and to implement their own ideas about how to run an effective organization.

As we have seen, most of the managers adopted a hands-on, autocratic approach to management. This approach was consistent with their initial notion of the managerial role: the manager as boss. They chose such a style not because they were eager to exercise power over people, but because they wanted to influence results.[5] Initially, they were unaware that

they were being very directive. Most described their management style as consultative, not authoritative. Looking back at
their first months on the job, though, they provided these less
than flattering descriptions of themselves:

> This was not a democracy. It was a kingdom, and I was
> the king who would handle all the problems.
>
> I wasn't good at managing. I am really a driver and so I
> was bossy like a first-grade teacher.
>
> Now I see that I started out as a drill sergeant. I was
> inflexible, just a lot of "how to's." This is the way you do
> this, this is the way you do that.

The managers soon discovered the limits of their formal
authority, however. They were giving directives, but very few
people seemed to be following their orders. Their subordinates
were testing them. And the managers were failing to meet the
challenges to their authority, for they were unable to "force"
their subordinates to fulfill their requests. One manager described exasperatedly how he began to feel uncomfortable in his
"huge paneled, elegant office, an office fit for a regional director
[a manager two levels above]." He began to feel like a fraud.
"I can't even guarantee that my secretary will do what she is
told."

The managers did not realize that they were confronting a
basic reality of managerial work: that management is as much a
position of dependence as a position of authority. They had to
learn to lead by persuasion and not by directive. When asked,
after eight months on the job, what advice he would give a new
manager, one manager remarked, after a hearty laugh, "Whatever you do, don't let the title of manager get to you, because
it's not much of a title. Remember you're the same person you
were before you took the job."

Another commented:

> Forget the authority. Get your ego out of the way and
> start convincing and not giving orders. I realized they [my
> subordinates] were never going to change their ways unless I
> *sold* them. Your responsibility is to motivate and guide, not
> direct people in selling our products. Your selling skills will

be more important than ever. Besides, half the time you don't know what the right thing to do is anyway. And so you can't tell them what to do.

You're not quitting sales, you're just changing your client base. You've got to sell ideas and your enthusiasm for them to build support. I quickly found out that knowing the right answer was much easier than selling it.

This manager said he had made a big step. He was on his way to understanding what his role was. He had learned that it was not to befriend his subordinates, nor to compete with or dominate them. Rather, a manager must motivate and develop subordinates toward the organization's objectives: "I began to see them [her subordinates] as clients, who I had to pull rather than push along."

Motivating Subordinates

For the managers, two of the more important revelations about building subordinates' commitment and motivation were the advantages in using a more participative style and relying upon positive rather than negative reinforcement.

Advantages of a more participative style. When the managers realized that their directives were not being followed, they began to experiment with ways of winning subordinates' compliance. One described how, almost by accident, he realized that when he provided the reason for his decisions, his subordinates were more receptive to implementing them. "Out of desperation," he found himself explaining in some detail why he thought it was important to enforce a new administrative procedure:

It was an unpopular procedure, time-consuming. But they seemed to accept that they had to do it once I explained why. I was able to broaden their perspective, I guess, by giving them the parent office's point of view.

As the managers had other such experiences, they became devotees of communication. By the sixth month many were describing people management as communication and saying communication skills were vital. Interestingly, they still emphasized speaking, not listening skills. By the end of the year, however, they identified listening too as critical. By then, most of them were able to accept subordinates' disagreement as simply that, and not a challenge to their authority. Consequently, they were more open to hearing subordinates' opinions:

> In my initial meeting I said here are the things I expect of you. Tell me what you expect of me. I thought I was being participative, but it was not two-way, really. I told them, then I listened a little bit. Now I listen more, and get immediate feedback on my decisions.

The managers discovered that when subordinates were permitted to offer their thoughts and reactions to decisions, they were much more likely to do as they were asked.

At first, the managers did not really understand why it helped to let their people talk things out. Many assumed it was a kind of cathartic effect: "If you let them blow off steam, they are ready to get on with it."

They later realized that it was something more. If the subordinates were consulted on a matter, they accepted some ownership of it. When they were allowed input on a decision, they felt some obligation and commitment to see it implemented. They also became aware of another benefit in listening to subordinates. They acquired valuable information about subordinates' feelings and insights: "When I stopped feeling that hearing employees' problems was a waste of time, I learned a lot from them that could be used to make better, more workable plans."

Although many of the managers were thus moving toward a more participative style, they had not moved very far. Indeed, they were no longer simply making decisions and announcing them. They were presenting ideas and inviting questions and sometimes even changing their decisions according to what they heard. Generally, though, they were not letting their subordinates make the decisions.

Advantages of positive reinforcement. When asked to define what they saw as their major sources of power over their subordinates, the managers first identified the power of their position (formal authority), and their ability to withhold or provide financial rewards. Soon discovering the limits on the first source of power, they began to rely heavily on the latter; they believed their subordinates were primarily motivated by money.

But the managers found themselves facing an interesting dilemma. Some of their key subordinates were already earning so much that money was no longer much of an incentive:

> If a guy wants to make a lot of money, have a big office, prestige, if he wants to be wealthy, then I can show him how.
>
> They make so much money [$100,000 and up] they're not hungry any more.
>
> I could not offer him [a big producer] enough money to get him to take on extra work. He was hot stuff in [a medium-sized midwestern town]. He owned one of the biggest houses in the best neighborhood, traveled all around the world, had a summer home. What did he need?

The new managers were perplexed. What did they have to offer these subordinates? They gradually realized that money was not the whole world to their subordinates. To their relief, they then recognized they had many more incentives, both tangible and intangible. They had resources (such as administrative support) and opportunities (participation in training programs) to offer. And they began to fully grasp the power of conveying appreciation and recognition:

> They [subordinates] like to be noticed, even if it is just by writing a letter or making a phone call. It is the subtleties, the little extra plus. If someone has a really good day, I call. That's important. I had a party today and used the discretionary income for it as a token of my approval. I got him a little holder for his business cards because he had a $3,000 day. It is just a reminder to him that he is very important to me. Not that he will behave differently right away, but it makes him feel good, and this is a tough business.
>
> Now, I try to make it a point to get out in the boardroom to recognize something or someone. Last night at five I handed out an award in the boardroom just to the individual. It was the first time in his career he had done $100,000, and I gave

> him a piece of glass and said I'd heard a rumor that somebody
> out here just crossed over $100,000 and I said congratulations,
> shook his hand, and walked away. It was not public in the
> sense that I gathered everybody around. But I knew and he
> did too. I have a philosophy of publicly praising and privately
> criticizing.

A critical lesson is revealed in this quotation: the advantages in using rewards rather than punishments in controlling subordinates' behavior. The managers learned the hard way that their subordinates were also motivated by the fear of failure and fear of humiliation. Most described themselves as going in "with the stick" when trying to motivate their people in the first months on the job; such an approach was consistent with their autocratic style. Most did not recognize that they were relying heavily upon intimidation as a strategy for influence. They saw themselves as just "helping [the subordinate] appreciate the likely consequences of his actions" and "motivating them to see [their] mistakes."

The managers soon became aware of some negative consequences in the punitive approach. They noticed that punished subordinates often felt humiliated or alienated, and some even quit, "out of the blue." They also became hostile, looking for opportunities to get even with the manager or venting their frustration by acting vindictively toward coworkers. Most of the managers came to see that "you can't shame people; you have to work on the positive side":

> You've got people walking around with incredible egos,
> making 100 to 300 K. You've got to be strong enough to stand
> up to them and persuade them not to be destructive in the
> office. You've got to do it without using your authority and
> power. You've got to go down without using the stick; you
> just can't punish them very much. Deep down they are really
> fairly insecure people under a lot of pressure to perform. They
> have to be committed to what management wants them to
> accomplish. It is best to lead by example and with support.
>
> Believe in your people; you've got to learn to teach them
> to believe in themselves and to even dream a little bit, and
> they can be better than they are. Stroke them daily. Keep the

kicks in the pants to a minimum. Keep the atmosphere very positive in the boardroom so that they see they have your total respect.

Although the managers would continue to rely on punishment at times, they were more aware of the risks:[6]

> I'm only human. I came down hard on her, because she was the weakest of all. I'm frustrated. I told her not to come back until she closed a deal. I didn't mean to raise my voice, but I was angry. She'd been practicing for three weeks and I couldn't believe she wasn't closing. I probably crossed that fine line of pushing too much. You've got to give feedback they can tolerate.

FROM MANAGING THE INDIVIDUAL TO LEADING THE GROUP

When the average person thinks about exercising authority, he or she immediately thinks about leadership. The managers, like the average person, acknowledged their leadership responsibilities. From their first days on the job, they sprinkled the word "leadership" throughout their conversations, announcing, for example, that they intended to lead the organization. Leadership seemed a catch-all phrase. They were not able to articulate with much confidence what they meant by it; they just knew it was important and that it was their job as manager to play the leadership role.

Without a doubt, leadership is one of the most studied and least understood notions. Two tenets, however, are implicit in all definitions of leadership. The first is the idea that leaders manage not simply by directive, but by persuasion, motivation, and empowerment; they identify and gain commitment to an exciting or challenging vision. The second is that leaders manage not only individual performance, but also group performance; as a way of exercising authority, they create the appropriate organizational context. Consider definitions by two renowned experts. Bennis describes leadership: a leader "knows what he wants, communicates those intentions successfully, empowers others, and knows when and how to stay on course and when to change." Kotter distinguishes between leadership and management: "management controls people by pushing them in the right direction, leadership motivates them by satisfying basic needs."[7] Kotter says that leaders set direction, align people, and motivate people, and managers plan and budget, organize and staff, and control and solve problems. In their research both men go to great lengths to demonstrate the attention and skill that leaders devote to creating a context or culture that will encourage subordinates to better their performance and commitment.

Before the managers could begin to understand what providing leadership meant, they had to grasp these fundamental ideas. We have seen how they learned the former. We now consider how they came to understand the second idea, the significance of managing group performance and context.

The new managers did not come to appreciate the distinction between managing the individual and managing the group until near the end of the year. For most of the year, they conceived of their people-management role as building the most effective relationships they could with *individual* subordinates. One manager said it was the "personal relationship that affected whether people worked hard or even stayed." No wonder the managers neglected managing their groups; that responsibility was not part of their awareness. How did they come to see the importance of managing the group? As with everything else, the realization came with experience—particularly the mistakes. The managers were perplexed to discover that actions directed at one subordinate often had unintended influence on other subordinates. In the examples they mentioned most often, they had made an exception for a subordinate:

> My biggest mistake so far. I really screwed up royally. I hired a guy from the competition because one of the regional objectives is that we hire a certain number of people from the competition and my bonus was in jeopardy. I got the guy cheap; he was from a really small firm and wanted the opportunity to work in the big leagues. Well, a guy had never been hired from the competition in the office before. To make it

112

worse, instead of money to entice him, I gave him a private office. I had made a big mistake. The people in the office said there was an unwritten rule that you had to have seniority in the office to be eligible for a private office. They were very upset for over a month. It took up most of my time talking and explaining my rationale to people. Four months later and it still hasn't completely blown over.

Almost all the managers described situations in which they thought they were just being flexible but ended up making exceptions that proved dangerously precedent setting:

> I was being nice; I didn't want to be completely tied to the book. I didn't want it to feel like I was just a rules-and-regulations person. Well, Mr. Nice made one exception to a rule and discovered he had created a monster. It spread through the grapevine and then everyone had to know if they could have the same treatment.

From such circumstances the managers found that their actions, though intended to address an immediate problem or issue, had broader effects. Soon they saw that they could take advantage of this phenomenon, which one manager called a "mystic new power": "Even my most insignificant decisions can have an impact on the atmosphere around here."

Soon they began to talk about being proactive in creating such effects. For at about the same time they were having this revelation, they could feel that they were managers, not doers. They began to define themselves as organizers or orchestrators. Further, they began to toy with the possibility of orchestrating the right atmosphere: "I finally realized that my responsibility consisted of bringing good people together with good people, creating the right environment, and getting out of the way." They had discovered that organizational culture could be a very efficient and effective tool for managerial control.

By the end of the year most managers were working to set the context within which their subordinates were working. Hoping to create a healthy organizational environment, they began working toward four objectives: defining the long-term goals or vision for the organization, setting high standards, creating an open and supportive climate, and (for just a few) building a cohesive team.

The new managers wholeheartedly accepted setting the organization's long-term goals, seeing this as a quintessential managerial task; it had originally attracted many of them to management. At first they directed all their attention to identifying the right strategy for the organization. The definition of leadership became "determining the vision." As they learned to appreciate communication and ownership, they set themselves to building subordinates' commitment to the strategy. One manager issued "A Manager's Pledge," laying out his goals for the office, beginning with the promise "To surround you with high-quality people who have a winning attitude."

The managers eventually found that the course was not set merely by pronouncement, however. In many ways their actions spoke louder than words:

> I'm the role model. I set the direction and pace of the office by the kinds of people I hire (you're only as good as the people you hire), the products I tell them to push, those I reward and punish, those who need help. From these activities they really get a handle on where I want them to go. It filters down.

As the managers saw the need to build commitment, they relied more on these indirect methods of control that influenced the entire group. They could "stretch" subordinate expectations and "ask for more" from them if they relied upon the "subtle pressure" of organizational culture and "symbolic gestures," not explicit requests:

> I can get away with general statements, like "I believe people should be as good as they can be and are as good as you allow them to be." But if I said it directly to one of my people, "I think you should be as good as you can be," he might take it as an implied criticism.
>
> If I am always upbeat and show drive and determination, they'll catch on to what is important to me.
>
> By controlling group behavior you can control individual behavior. People don't like to be on the outside; they want to fit in.

> You can't keep driving them. You can create a climate that they'll want to work in. Use subliminals to motivate them. Management is the art of getting people to do what you want them to do, without their knowing it.

The managers strove to build a culture of high standards, supportiveness, and openness. Their first priority was to create an atmosphere of ambitious goals and optimism:

> It should inspire them to be better than they are through subtle pressure; to be ambitious, with little tolerance for poor performance or mediocrity. We provide high-quality service. We always want to reach just beyond our potential.

> They should feel like they're in competition or in a war and they intend to break records and win it all.

> I want to push continual growth of people and of accounts. We won't rest on being half-million-dollar producers, we'll push to be one-million-dollar producers, to all do more business.

Many managers realized that if they were going to expect subordinates to give 110 percent, then they had to build a culture that was also supportive and open, recognizing the special stresses in the sales function:

> In this business you can have a bad day, bad week, bad month. It can be demoralizing. You've got to keep them on track. Once they get demoralized they start bitching and want to just get away from the office.

> Frustration levels get high. If they don't make quota, they don't eat. It is important to maintain an informal atmosphere, a position where the door is always open and I'm walking around and talking to everybody. People will know I'll be responsive to their needs.

> I have to create an environment where the fear is stripped out, so that they will be as creative and hardworking as possible. It has to be a trusting climate with a fix-it, problem-solving orientation. A nurturing environment where people emphasize growth and development. A place where people can be honest and speak what's on their mind.

By the end of the year the managers acknowledged how important it was to build a culture that could set the tone they believed most conducive to employees' satisfaction and performance.

Only a few managers, though, appreciated the merits of encouraging a team approach. The managers in the computer company emphasized teamwork somewhat more than their counterparts in the broker industry, for in selling complex systems a team approach was the norm. But the idea was relatively new to the financial services industry. Senior executives in these firms were trying to implement team-selling units consisting of a generalist or relationship manager working with a number of product specialists to meet client needs. The middle managers, and certainly the brokers, had yet to be convinced that such an approach was feasible and valuable. The experienced managers in both companies (who were selected for interviewing because senior management saw them as very effective), all advocated team building.[8] The handful of new managers who talked about team building spoke of assembling a happy family and a high-quality team:

> My name is Dave. They came up with the D team and I was Mr. D. We had electronic mail, and whenever I sent something out I had a standard note that went out to the D team, signed by Mr. D. Then we had a little contest and we gave away lobsters to the person who came up with the best replacement name for the team. I didn't want them always using my initial; I wanted them to see that the team was all of us, to turn it over to them for safekeeping.

This manager had "stumbled across" the tactic. It fit his personal preference to use humor at work and to have warm, informal relationships with his people. He was pleasantly surprised to learn how committed people could become to a group once they felt a part of it:

> They've become like my soldiers. They would walk through a wall for the good of the team. And now other reps in the branch are looking at us and how we cooperate and you can see they want to join in. We have pride in ourselves; that is what attracts them. And being part of a team helps them get through the peaks and valleys—they know they have supports out there.

This manager, unlike most of his counterparts, had come to see the power of appealing to people's need to belong to something larger than themselves. When asked if he could see his influence on his organization, this manager spoke fluidly about the unique personality of his group and his contribution to it. Still, in some ways this manager had yet to fully embrace the notion of building a team. Most of his energy was focused on creating subordinate esprit or a cohesive unit in which people felt emotionally committed to one another. He instituted few practices that encouraged his subordinates to work actively in a coordinated or collaborative fashion to accomplish a common task.[9]

An Elusive Role: Leading the Group

In summary, it was late in the year before the new managers began to appreciate one of the tenets of leadership: managing context. They could not understand this notion until they accepted the more fundamental idea of managing group performance, not simply individual performance. Although the notion of building an organization's culture seemed mysterious and difficult to control, many managers recognized it was worthy of effort. They had learned an essential lesson about the intricate connection between individual and group performance. They understood that an important management role was structuring situations so that the group knew the direction in which the organization was headed and the broad parameters within which they were to work. Most were perplexed, however, about how to fulfill this role proactively. Moreover, very few had taken the next step and seen that value of creating teams. In short, they had yet to embrace fully their responsibility for leadership. But some of the critical building blocks were in place.

CONCLUDING REMARKS

During their first year the managers became *aware* of some of the major principles in exercising authority: establishing credibility, building subordinates' commitment, and leading the group. Two factors that decidedly influenced their ability to internalize these lessons were refining their understanding of the managerial role and their increased self-confidence. To be effective in influencing their subordinates, they had to accept their role as manager of people and to confront their insecurity: "I had to get rid of that albatross called my ego, but still maintain self-assurance."

They still had much to learn about how to exercise power and influence; now that they understood some of the principles, they had to implement them. Exercising power and influence, especially without relying heavily on formal authority, is a challenge for even the most seasoned managers.

But a substantial foundation was laid. The managers now appreciated the need to build and nurture relationships with subordinates. They were gaining richer understanding of human nature and were becoming more sensitive to others' feelings. Their sources of power and strategies for gaining influence were more diverse.[10] They had moved from almost exclusive reliance on their position and track record as sources of power. They realized that they had to establish credibility and trust with their subordinates before they could influence them. They came to see that assertiveness (as in using incentives and pressures) was only one of many strategies for gaining influence, as they observed the value of achieving commitment from and not simply control over subordinates. The managers began to supplement "push" influence strategies (approaches in which an individual pushes against another to get him or her to change in some way) with "pull" (the individual attracts another to get him or her to change in some way). That is, they began to attempt, albeit at times with limited finesse, to build bridges or connections with subordinates or to motivate or inspire them to pursue mutually agreed-upon goals.

Finally, the managers were becoming aware that they must empower or share power with their subordinates. Early in the year the idea of sharing would have been anathema; as bosses, they were to be in complete control. By the end of the year the managers had refined their understanding of what it meant to be in control (more on this subject in Chapter 5). One manager described the technique as "managing and controlling your people without making it feel like you are managing and controlling them."

> What matters is your ability to motivate people, and that is kind of a nebulous term. When I say motivate I don't mean that you can get them to work up to a frenzy and you are constantly whipping them to a frenzy. I think it has to do with sincerity; you develop mutual trust and understanding, and the people really feel you are going flat out for their best interests and have their concerns at heart. And when they sense the trust and confidence, that you are out there for them, they really want to deliver back to you. Because if you develop it in any other way, sales management belies authority. You have the ability to hire and fire, but the moment you rely on that authority or imply it, I think the battle is lost.

The new managers still had much to learn about managerial control. They had not really moved far on the continuum from boss-centered leadership to subordinate-centered leadership, as Tannenbaum and Schmidt describe these methods.[11] Those authors describe a range of managerial actions based on the degree of authority used by the boss and the amount of freedom available to subordinates in reaching decisions: at one end the manager makes the decision and announces it; at the other the manager permits subordinates to function within limits defined by the superior. Most of the managers still saw themselves as the ones who should initiate and determine their subordinates' functions. The subordinates were welcome to provide input and assume power only at the manager's will. In other words, the managers were not aware of all their options in exercising their authority and control.

More tools could be added to their repertoire, including those of leadership. Leadership was a subject that had suffered benign neglect among the managers. As we have seen, only at the end of the year did they begin to appreciate one of the basic ingredients of leadership: managing group performance and context. Although most had come to understand how important it was to provide leadership, none claimed to know the behavioral or action elements in fulfilling this function. These findings are consistent with those of Kotter, who writes that most companies are overmanaged and underled.[12] Unfortunately, evidence is growing that leadership is ever more indispensable to business success in today's world of change and increased competition.

But we still have heard only part of the story about how the new managers developed interpersonal judgment. Next, we consider what they learned about managing subordinates' performance.

NOTES

1. Gabarro (1987) identified four stages in building trust and influence: orientation or impression formation, exploration beyond initial impressions, testing and defining the interpersonal contract, and stabilization (pp. 113–114). Hannaway (1989) reports that in her work on management successions, subordinates typically spent "many hours hanging onto his or her [the manager's] every word and action, trying to interpret it" (p. 116).

2. Weick (1974) delineates the kind of information relied upon in establishing an individual's credibility:

> Credibility assumes great importance in manager–subordinate interactions given managers' heavy reliance upon verbal information and the fact that managers have neither the time nor the resources to check the validity of instant communication. . . . A final implication of the "live action" analysis is that . . . nonverbal communication and communicator credibility may be more important . . . than we realized. If managers rely so heavily on verbal information, then that verbal information invariably arrives with an extra verbal overlay. If anyone is affected by this "additional" information, it should be people who value and use face-to-face contact, namely managers (p. 114).

3. See Flamholz and Randle (1987), p. 135.

4. McClelland and Burnham (1976) write:

> In short, as we expected, affiliative managers make so many ad hominem and ad hoc decisions that they almost totally abandon orderly procedures. Their disregard for procedure leaves employees feeling weak, irresponsible, and without a sense of what might happen next, of where they stand in relation to the manager, or even of what they ought to be doing (p. 165).

5. Cox and Cooper (1988) observe the same in their study of executives. Their desire for power and influence "did not seem in any way related to possessing or being in a position of power over people" (p. 59). They tended to speak of

the pleasure they felt from knowing they were in a position to influence the company's success.

6. The new managers were in good company. The use of negative sanctions is prevalent in organizational life, as Whetton and Cameron (1984) describe:

> For many agents of socialization (parents, teachers, managers), punishment is used far more frequently than positive reinforcement to modify behavior. In a work situation, for example, many supervisors just assume that employees fully understand what is expected of them and are self-motivated to achieve high performance. They define their role as that of a sheepdog, circling the perimeter of the group, nipping at the heels of those who begin to stray. They establish a fairly broad range of acceptable behaviors and then limit their interactions with employees to barking at those who exceed the parameters (p. 327).

7. My conceptualization of leadership was influenced most heavily by that of Bennis (1989), Bennis and Nanus (1985), Kotter (1989), and Zaleznik (1977).

8. The experienced managers did, however, comment that team building was not easy in their companies. The evaluation and reward systems recognized individual, not group performance.

9. Hackman (1990), a leading group theorist, stresses that the notion of teams implies more than cohesiveness; it suggests proactive collaboration or synergistic activity toward a common goal.

10. For instance, Cohen and Bradford (1990) and Kotter (1982) find that diversifying power bases is critical to managerial success. With it comes greater likelihood that managers will have access to the appropriate power base and influence strategy for any circumstances.

11. Tannebaum and Schmidt (1973), p. 3.

12. Kotter (1988).

5

Managing Subordinates' Performance

The second set of lessons about interpersonal judgment the new managers had to learn was how to manage individual subordinates' performance. In management textbooks, it is the most extensively covered topic, and includes evaluating performance, diagnosing performance problems, setting expectations, delegating, coaching and developing, providing feedback on performance, and linking performance to rewards and punishments. The new managers had much to learn about each of these subjects, but they found some management performance tasks more challenging than others. Basic tenets of individual performance management often eluded them. In these pages, we observe as the new managers develop and refine their interpersonal judgment in four areas: accepting subordinates' diversity,[1] responding to that diversity, managing the problem subordinate, and delegation and control.

To put the managers' experience in context, we briefly look

at their subordinates. In some ways the managers were faced with an especially difficult supervisory task. Their initial preoccupation with their roles as boss and expert and their hands-on and directive style conflicted inherently with their subordinates' motivations. Salespeople are notorious for their great need for autonomy and independence.[2] They are often described as counterdependent—that is, resistant to authority. The stereotype of brokers especially is that they are "lone wolves with big egos." Salespeople are known for being very outspoken, impatient, and tenacious, never giving up and constantly "moving the question." Compared to people in other functional areas, they feel little compunction about challenging or questioning a superior.

Salespeople require goals set for them with maximal clarity and hold high expectations for recognition for their accomplishments. They are mainly driven by and accustomed to straightforward feedback (money), directly contingent upon their ability and effort. Finally, salespeople are generally seen as more loyal to their accounts than to their companies. In fact, the salespeople in this study were very mobile; they were constantly receiving lucrative offers to join competitors. These were the people with whom the new managers had to build effective relationships.

ACCEPTING SUBORDINATES' DIVERSITY

One of the first tasks the managers took up was evaluating their subordinates:

> I spent the first ninety days meeting with every one of the brokers for either dinner or breakfast. Open-ended, the meetings ran an average of two to three hours per individual. It was a general question-and-answer session and I hope they talked more than I did. A theme and some specifics would evolve. I had said to myself I'm not going there with a bad attitude. I'm not going to prejudge the office. I'm going to give everybody the benefit of the doubt.
>
> You have to assess the situation in light of everybody

who is out there. Who are your winners and who are your losers? You have to learn your strong performers and where you have to do a little surgery.

Like everything else, the managers found it more difficult and time-consuming to assess their subordinates than they had imagined. They were not sure, one manager said, "what evidence to dismiss and what evidence to take seriously." They lamented that it would probably take months, not weeks, to get to know everyone's strengths and weaknesses.

A major insight for the managers was that everybody was not like them. In fact, they were dumbfounded by their subordinates' diversity in talent, motivation, and temperament.

> The people you manage tend to be a whole spectrum. You are a manager because you were a good sales rep. If there are one or two of "you" in your unit, you are probably lucky. You have the whole range of people who are very marginal or poor performers, who have no business being there, all the way up to people who can operate on their own.

They were dismayed to discover that some of their subordinates were not very capable or committed to their jobs:

> You start out thinking that people have a fairly simple psychological makeup—they're drivers, motivated to new ideas, aggressive, understand what is going on, and are capable of getting a lot of their own feedback. Ha, I wish! Everybody has their own ground you've got to work from.
>
> I think the biggest surprise is when you are in a career path for management, you tend to associate with other people who are career-pathed for management. You are looking at people who have aspirations and want to move in certain directions. You land in a branch managing people who don't share those aspirations. That's not good, that's not bad necessarily, but that's a surprise. You don't have people who are motivated the same way you are. Theoretically, you understand that; all the textbooks tell you. It just makes sense that people are different, but when you get there, you say, Wow, how could this be?
>
> I've got several people who are really happy being reps, and they're enjoying themselves. Many of them are solid citi-

zens. They're not going to break any records and that is how they want to be. I've got a couple who are pretty close to being like me, and so it's a gamut.

The managers were disconcerted by this diversity. They had assumed they could use themselves as models in understanding how to manage their subordinates. Many recited, "Do unto others as you would have others do unto you" as the management principle they would follow. They found out, however, that everyone did not want to be treated as they would. Worse yet, they found that what one subordinate appreciated, another hated. Reviewing opinion survey data he received, a manager was perplexed by these questions:

> Thirty percent say they are satisfied with the amount of direction I give them, 30 percent are neutral, and 30 percent want more direction. I am not sure what I am to make of this. What am I supposed to do about it?

This manager went on to ask if I knew how valid such opinion surveys were. "It must be a mistake," he insisted. When I returned just four months later, he made these remarks:

> I started out making what must be a common mistake. I tried to treat everybody like they were the same—turn them all into clones of myself, instead of figuring out what would be comfortable for them. You can't make people do it your way. They can't or they don't want to. You have to let them do it their way as long as they are going in the right direction. That is the most important lesson I've learned.

After getting over the shock of the survey results, he had taken the time to discuss his feedback with his subordinates. From their comments, many quite straightforward ("They held no punches."), the manager came to see that each had different expectations of him. Another new manager came to the same conclusion after receiving feedback from her boss that many of her subordinates had been dropping hints that they thought she was trying to "mold them in her own image."

> They resented that I tried to make them just like me. But that is really what I want them to be. I want to say, "This is the way you dress. This is the way you talk." This is the way

you do this; this is the way you do that. But I have to resist trying to make them surrogates of me. I'm trying to look at everybody in a different angle now.

In other words, the managers realized they would have to treat each subordinate as an individual:

> I may not be the best role model for a particular individual. I've got to focus on getting to know everybody—their personality, what makes them tick, what turns them off and on—so that I won't say the wrong things and get the best results out of them. Who is intellectual, who is motivated by logic, by emotional appeal? Who needs to get a kick in the pants once in a while, who needs more strokes. Some people stay late. Some come in early. Some avoid conflict. Some rant and rave.

> It's analytical. The first principle—every individual is an individual and needs to be treated that way, particularly if you're asking them to do a professional job, and they are professionals. They feel that way, act that way, get paid that way, and are that way. It's fundamental to our business. In doing that you have to spend the time to get to what really makes this person tick. You learn to take a look at an individual, analyze their needs and wants, analyze the business requirement, and then try to figure out how to motivate that person and get the achievement that you want. It sounds very mechanical, but it isn't, because people aren't machines.

> You have to realize that spectrum and your job isn't focused with the good people because you just have to motivate them and keep them going and be there when they need you, because they don't want you in their hair. You get rid of the bottom and focus on the middle group to try to move them up.

At first, the managers found the notion that they should treat people differently inconsistent with another strongly held belief: they should treat people fairly. They came to see, however, that in fact, "to treat people fairly is to treat them differently." In the second half of the year almost every manager made that statement to me, almost verbatim. It was a relief for them to understand this management principle:

> What do I wish I'd done differently? I tended to treat people more as equals than I should have—equal time, equal

help. . . . They don't need or want the same things. . . . But then I was just trying to get my arms around what I was supposed to do. Now, I have a different philosophy, a philosophy that is fair, but not equal.

RESPONDING TO SUBORDINATES' DIVERSITY

The managers realized that they would have to adapt their management style to fit each subordinate. They began to see that they would have to develop different approaches and skills for handling relationships with different kinds of people. The task would be much more difficult than anticipated: "There isn't one right answer for this people management stuff." In the latter part of the year, the new managers began to emphasize being flexible, which, one manager said, was easier said than done:

> Another thing a manager needs is to be able to get along with and understand different types of people. And what motivates different types of people? If there are clashes, well of course they need to know how to adapt to them if they are not naturally suited to each other, and they need to know how to communicate despite clashes.

To be effective, the managers understood, they had to set appropriate expectations for their subordinates: "If you have responsibility for people, you have to establish principles on what you expect from them and what they can expect from you."

Indeed, one of the most important organizational tasks managers face is developing and working through shared expectations about roles, goals, and priorities with their subordinates. With time, these expectations should become more specific and concrete. But the dilemma the managers faced was that they did not even know what expectations were appropriate for their subordinates, much less how to negotiate social contracts with them. With experience, the managers understood that they would have to set different expectations for individual subordinates; again, they saw the danger in using themselves as a model:

Expectations are very high for your employees when you first come in, which I think is probably true with anybody coming into any job where management is involved. You've got to come in with your tail wagging, kind of like a puppy. . . . Expectations being too high—that can have its positives, but you've got to come up with realistic stretch expectations that suit the individual.

In the same vein, the managers did not know how they should manage their time and energy, considering their diverse subordinates. They considered the advantages and disadvantages of different approaches:

Do I let the cream rise to the top or treat each hire as an investment and try to raise each one?

It is like having a basketball team, with five people on the floor at once. You always have your stars: two equals underneath, three at the next level, and nine people on the bench. If you look at how you should spend your time—not much time with the number-one person. Spend time with the bench; the people on the floor have pretty good skills or they wouldn't be on the floor. And you're going to need a good bench when you get to the sixth or seventh game.

By the end of the year the managers had not decided which of these approaches was more effective, however; they spent a disproportionate amount of time with the less experienced and problem subordinates. To illustrate in some detail how the new managers learned to respond to subordinates' diversity, we'll look at their relationships with the less-experienced, more-experienced, and problem subordinate.

Managing the Less-Experienced Subordinate

Starting out, most of the new managers found it more comfortable to work with the less-experienced subordinates. They felt they understood their needs and were confident that they had critical technical competencies to share with them. Clearly, they also felt more like the boss and in control when working with them. Many commented on how very responsive the inexperienced subordinates were. One particularly insightful manager suggested that he found the less-experienced subordinates easier to work with because they depended on him as much as he on them. He sheepishly admitted how much he enjoyed feeling in command when working with the inexperienced subordinate. He pointed out that "It was such a rare experience!" And he chuckled, "They're as bad off as I am, maybe worse."

When asked to describe what sales representatives with less experience required, the managers made these observations:

> From the new employee's standpoint, the sales manager is the first manager the employee has with the company, and they have to present the whole image of what the company is. They have to understand the company, their job. They have to understand what is really important and what isn't important in the multitude of things happening around them. They need a lot of guidance. It is incumbent upon you as a mentor to give them a lot of the breadth and view of the company they need.
>
> What does he need from the manager? Support, guidance, training, how to get new clients, and how to get into the cycles—really specific suggestions. I need to give him ideas about where to go, how to target different groups, and help him develop a script that will fit who he is. And help him with a way of meeting people face-to-face, if he is better at that than with the phone. It is important that a manager pick up on the good particularly and show them how to use it. You've got to be accessible always, have very open rapport with them.
>
> Younger people want your ideas about new approaches, your involvement, your suggestions. They need your help about everything from prospecting to how to get along with their administrative assistant.

As these quotations reveal, the new managers were well aware from the start that their inexperienced subordinates greatly needed support and coaching and development. They emphasized the technical knowledge and skills they had to impart to these people. They spent much of their time meeting individually with and holding group training sessions for them (weekly sessions on how to prospect, make a cold call, and close). And most soon recognized, generally within the first three months, that the subordinates needed help not only with the specific mechanics of the job, but also with how to think about what they hoped to accomplish in the future:

> They need guidance in their marketing activities, guidance in their careers, guidance in the business world.
> They expect me to prepare them for this job and their next job opportunity.

With few exceptions, though, the new managers took more time to give equal weight to the emotional support their less-experienced subordinates required:

> When I went out on call with the rep to see the CEO [of a small company], I saw how nervous he was. He had asked me along, I think, because he was scared. . . . We had gone over his script over and over and he knew it cold, but he almost clammed up. I got him started and then he was all right.
> They know the right thing to do often, but they can't make the decision. They don't want to have to. For instance, they cling to customers even though they know nothing is coming and it is a waste of time. They're afraid to end it on their own.

Again, the managers remarked that they did not really understand why they should be surprised that the young people were nervous. When they thought back on their first experiences as sales representatives, they recalled their insecurity all too vividly. But one said "That seems like eons ago."

In talking to the new managers' subordinates, it became clear that those with less experience were more pleased with the new managers than those with more experience. The less-experienced employees shared a common complaint about the new managers, however: they had "trouble letting them go."

The managers were obsessive about whether they were giving any of their subordinates enough attention, especially those with brief time on the job. In the first half of the year when I asked the new managers the biggest mistake they made with their younger sales representatives, they remarked, "undermanaging them":

> Sometimes you'd think I had the sink-or-swim philosophy. The younger people generally have more energy—go, go, go. In that situation you have to make sure that they're go, go, going, in the right direction. If they're going in the wrong direction, you have to pull them back and fix it.
>
> I worry that I send them out before I have taught them to swim. I let them drown because I don't have the time to give them. I'm too busy.

By the latter half of the year, however, the managers identified their most common mistake in managing the less-experienced subordinate as overmanagement:

> The problem I saw happening with the trainee was that I was not backing off soon enough and continuing to do it [training about the mechanics of the job] for too long a time. Finally, the trainee all but said, "Hey, back off."
>
> She asked me why I was still going on customer calls with her. Didn't I trust her? She made me stop and think. I had been having trouble figuring out what calls I should go on with the middle group. I have to stop and think, what would I have wanted at this point?
>
> It was time to let them make their own decisions and for me to let them come to me for support. They are self-starters and want to own their territory and to walk on their own two feet. They're ready for the responsibility.

How had the managers come to this realization? They noticed that as time went on their less-experienced subordinates began to avoid them: "I began to feel that I was forcing myself on them." When this indirect feedback did not produce results, the subordinates became more outspoken, using both formal and informal channels:

> If I see something wrong, I go address it right away versus waiting until the next morning. I feel better and I thought people round me felt better. It is really hard for me not to jump on the problem once I see it. I came in with a motherly

> attitude. I had lots of new reps and I wanted them to be suc-
> cessful. This was their first territory and I wanted to help them.
> I was smothering them. They were strong enough to come in
> one day and tell me, "You are putting your arms around us a
> little too hard." I had to swallow hard.
>
> My boss had been hinting for nine months that I wouldn't
> let people solve their own problems. I couldn't see it until I
> got the numbers [the opinion survey]. When they came in with
> a problem, I grabbed it and ran with it, and they resented that.

The managers also had to live with unanticipated consequences of their way of handling the problems and mistakes of
less-experienced subordinates. Notice the images that come to
mind as they discuss themselves:

> You're a manager, and all of a sudden you're God. I
> mean, you got this job because you were really good as a rep
> and now you have the reps reporting to you. You feel as if
> you've got to tell them how to do their job instead of realizing,
> "Hey, these people *are* doing their job." Soon, they give the
> job back to you.
>
> I was very responsive to any problem they had, any ques-
> tion. I fixed any mistake. Mommy and daddy are always here
> to help you, whenever you hurt yourselves. Well, the only
> way they're going to learn to live for themselves is if mommy
> and daddy let them learn for themselves. By being so respon-
> sive to people, I was hurting them as well as helping them.
> Mommy, fix this for me. Okay, I'll fix it for you, darling. And
> so you fix it, but the child never learns how to solve problems
> for himself.

The managers were beginning to appreciate the long-term
effects of their actions on their subordinates, and in this instance, they were frustrated to discover that they had created
more work for themselves:

> I thought I knew best how to run every territory. I could
> see the solution to every problem. The folks on the floor will
> let you do everything. I was getting stuck with all their prob-
> lems; I was letting them throw the monkey on my back. Before
> I knew it, it felt like I had ten accounts to run on my own.
>
> I hadn't made them stand on their own two feet, ever.

> Now, they weren't ready for the responsibility, but they [should have] been. I think of it as if I had been tutoring, too much step-by-step work, instead of coaching. They weren't becoming independent thinkers. And now I have new trainees to work with and just don't have the time for them.

Even though the managers recognized the error of their ways, many had trouble throughout the year breaking the habit of solving subordinates' problems. They were still struggling with the doer syndrome; they still believed "deep in their hearts" that when push came to shove they had to solve problems personally if the problems were going to be solved.[3] Besides, they found it emotionally satisfying to slip back into a role at which they felt quite competent (a mostly unconscious impulse) and were intent upon gaining credibility.

By the end of the year, however, most realized that their behavior was unacceptable and, with some ambivalence, began to work hard at eliminating unwelcome and unnecessary management intervention. They began to see that to help subordinates grow and develop they had to allow them to make and live with their own mistakes. It was the managers' responsibility to manage the organization's overall risk and to protect subordinates from making excessively costly mistakes:

> The only way to learn is through the crucible of experience, and the job of the manager is to make sure that his people feel they have the latitude to take a risk and . . . the freedom to make some mistakes. The manager's job is to make sure they don't make the big mistake, one that threatens the company or their career. As I say to my folks who work for me now, "When was the last time you went and studied after you made an A?"

> I had to learn when it was best not to interfere, when to let a rep handle a client account on his own, when to let my people fight it out among themselves. Now, when they bring a problem to me, I start by asking, "What have you done about this?" If they haven't done any thinking, I send them away and tell them to come back when they have some ideas. It is far better to be out there making some mistakes. It means you're out there doing something and not sitting back doing nothing and being safe.

The new managers came to see that their role was not to take on the problems of their less-experienced subordinates, but rather to give them guidance or the resources to solve them:

> If they have got a problem, I help them fix it by helping them with the thought processes to come up with the solution to the problem. We have strategy sessions.

Managing the More-Experienced Subordinate

A delicate challenge the new managers faced was managing the more-experienced subordinate, one of the topics they discussed most frequently with me.[4] One manager even wrote a poem about it, to try to work out why he felt so mixed up about it. They described as very tricky and catastrophic their early relationships with their more-experienced subordinates, many of whom seemed to agree with their assessment.

A number of factors contributed to this difficulty. The managers did not feel in control of the more-experienced subordinates, particularly the successful ones. Ironically, the people upon whom they felt most dependent, their big producers, were just the ones they felt least control over. The managers generally were younger and had less experience as producers than some of their more-experienced subordinates, and were not sure if they were more technically competent. They did not know what they really had to offer. Moreover, they saw their primary source of leverage—financial rewards—as less effective with the big producer. They experienced the senior representatives as always challenging their authority; those representatives of course were much more likely to volunteer suggestions, and to disagree with or question the managers' decisions.

Throughout the first year the managers attempted to determine their role toward these key subordinates. The veteran subordinates voiced two primary complaints about the managers: that they gave the subordinates too little respect and autonomy, and they gave them too little or the wrong kind of attention.

Early in the year the managers complained, often bitterly,

135

that the more-experienced subordinates were constantly challenging their authority; and in the beginning, as described in Chapter 4, they interpreted almost all subordinates' suggestions and disagreements as challenges to their authority. With their insecurity about their new role and their organization's culture, in which the star producer was held in the highest regard, the managers did not know if they could "win these battles." They worried that the experienced subordinate would go over their head and gain support from their superiors. Sometimes this fear was legitimate, especially in the securities firm. In fact, the more-experienced subordinates sometimes were acting, in part, out of animosity. They were often taken aback at how eager the new managers were to "change things, to introduce their own procedures as quickly as possible without getting to know the situation or soliciting their advice":

> I have seen some young guys come along and they are of the mindset that they will change this; that is why they brought me in, as an element of change, an agent of change. I've been with a customer maybe seven or ten years. I've been in the business twenty-five years. You'd think they'd listen to my opinion. They'll get change all right—changed right off the job. Another thing is that we will be here when they leave. They'll be on a fast track going nowhere if they're not careful. And we will still be here when they go.

Also, for even the most enlightened, it took time to adjust to having a younger boss "telling you what to do."[5] And of course the managers were doing just that with their rather autocratic style.[6] At the start of the year, then, the seeds were sown for rocky relationships. Moreover, most managers were clearly intimidated. Understandably, they reacted defensively. At worse they adopted the attitude, "I'll show you who's boss," which only created a cycle of conflict, or they chose to avoid conflict altogether and never confronted even inappropriate behavior by subordinates.

The subordinates with more experience complained that the new managers were overmanaging them. They were incensed about the encroachment on their independence:

136

There are two reasons I do this job: I'm well paid and I have my freedom. Do not overmanage me. Accept my opinion. Hear my strategy. Offer some suggestions and then leave me alone. Here is my quota, go to it. Don't put daily pressure on me, just look long term whether I've made my quota.

I'm a million-dollar producer because I want to be. I tried to explain to him to let me do my business and leave me alone. I've been in the top five for the last six years, making over $200,000. But he still treats me like a trainee—"Here's what I think you should do."

Now, I'm one of the biggest and cleanest producers in the office. But I am still subject to the mundane office kinds of things. I need to get the same kinds of approval as a new broker. I think that is dumb. A manager should be comfortable with me and not require me to come in and tell him why I'm selling a client a mutual fund. He should tell the operations people to go ahead and assume that he has approved what I am doing. It's a judgment call that he doesn't know how to make, and so he is wasting my time and his time.

Much of this indignation was justified. The managers had not yet learned how to adapt their style to fit the subordinate's abilities and experience (of course, not all the experienced subordinates were competent and committed to their job). And even when they realized the necessity for doing so, as described earlier, they were often unwilling or unable to do so. Said one experienced subordinate:

Recently, we had a sales manager in here who would literally rehearse you when you made a customer call, to the point of putting words in your mouth, "This is what you say." Now that might be good for trainees, who really have never experienced this, but anybody who's qualified, on quota, doesn't need to have words put in their mouth, unless they come asking for help. The manager agreed with me when I told him all this, but damn it, the next day he was at it again.

As described in Chapter 4, when the new managers better understood the principles behind exercising authority, they began to adopt a less-directive approach and ask for subordinates' input. Their relationships with the senior subordinates—if they were not beyond repair—improved dramatically. By the second half of the year, most managers appreciated the more-experienced subordinates' need for more independence:

> Now, I'm at a stage where I hold them as quasi-equals who can come in and sit down and talk. I let them come in and put their strategy on the table—"Tell me what you want to do. Let me see where you are going. Help me understand this" is the way the conversation goes.

> It took me seven months to really understand that I have an individual who is a good performer. He can solve problems; he's got years of experience. I'm not going to spend much time with that person. I can give that person a lot of freedom. When I tell him to do something, I can say this is the result I want; I don't have to go into all the details. Now, with the young people not only do I have to tell them the end result but I'd better tell them the steps on how to get there.

The second complaint the subordinates with more experience had about the new managers is evident in this quotation: the managers gave them too little attention. According to one experienced subordinate:

> Managers are taught to concentrate their attention and an inordinate amount of time on those relatively new people who produce very little of the business. They spend most of their time on the two-years-and-under crowd. What a waste. Those who have spent a number of years with the firm don't get the attention. That's where the action is. They could be getting us resources to do our jobs smarter—secretarial support, computers. They spend the time getting space for some new person who more than likely will leave. They don't respond to my needs. They don't even know my frustrations. And we're the bread and butter of the firm.

It seems paradoxical that the managers were both overmanaging the subordinates with more experience and neglecting them. The managers were devoting attention to the wrong issues in their interactions with veteran subordinates. They were spending their time advising and coaching the more-experienced managers on what and how to sell. Instead, they should have been providing them with a sense of their strategic vision and goals for the organization, recognizing their achievements, garnering resources for them to do their jobs, and preparing them for the future:

> I've learned that I'm in management and not direct sales. A manager really cannot influence the daily activity of what's going on, particularly when you have senior people. You have to let them go out and do their job and not get in their way. Be helpful and supportive, assisting them when you can, and monitoring only to the extent they go off in directions that may not be consistent with what you want. These guys are hungry and they're good people. They're going to go out and do what is needed to get the job done. The big ones are going to come; they will feed themselves and call me when they need me.
>
> Management in the case when they are high producers—the average for those guys sitting over there is $425,000 a man—they don't need the same type of management the zero-to-two-year new broker needs. I should have seen that earlier. They need management by leadership of example. They have to be focused from time to time on the direction of the firm and the segments that are going to be the future of this business. And when they have a problem, they need to be able to come to me and get it resolved.
>
> The older brokers want my support getting recognition and resources. They want me to help make their lives trouble free so that they can stick to their knitting. They're not looking for guidance per se; they want cooperation—in dealing with the regional office, knowing where to get something done.

In the early months the new managers neglected their responsibility for helping the subordinates with more experience stay current and prepared for the future:

> You have a very large body of our sales force who consider themselves traditional investment-management people. And they are not embracing some of the new strategy of insurance, real estate, tax minimization, and banking. And so when I talk to a young person I have a captive audience. I can tell that and look them straight in the eye and know that they have an opportunity that is unprecedented. What I have with a senior broker is an individual set in his ways trying to maximize his income in a shrinking environment, and unless he is

willing to expand his product and segment base, he is in trouble. It's a waste to talk to that kind of guy. With one or two exceptions he is going to do his business the same way until we throw him out the door.

Both the computer and financial services industries were undergoing rapid change. The organizations in this study were implementing new strategies and introducing major restructuring. The managers seemed to assume that the more-experienced subordinates were inherently resistant to change and unable to learn to behave in new ways. They described them as set in their ways; they were always reciting the cliché, "You can't teach an old dog new tricks." And as they reminded me, they had to have priorities. In their mind continually developing their senior people was not a high priority; they had real, more pressing, problems to solve instead.

Most of the senior subordinates complained that the managers did not encourage them to keep up to date and informed of the latest developments: "Even a person with my experience can grow. They should be constantly pushing me to make sure I'm on the cutting edge and stretching myself. Otherwise I'll get complacent or bored."

Admittedly, these subordinates had to show some personal initiative to upgrade their skills. Few of the managers, however, arranged developmental opportunities—training or otherwise—for the more-experienced subordinates. Those who did so received high praise:

> He asked me to be a team leader. He was really surprised that I said yes. No one had asked me before, and it was fun. Each of the senior brokers has been assigned some young people to mentor. It keeps us fresh.

By the end of the year the managers were beginning to generate creative ideas like the one described below for keeping the more-experienced subordinate motivated and current. They recognized the need to design developmental experiences that would allow the subordinates with more experience to "keep their pride intact." Said a new manager:

I realized that some of the seniors wouldn't come to me for advice if their life depended on it. I had to come up with some way to teach them about the new marketing strategy without causing them to lose face. . . . On Wednesdays I held a meeting that was mandatory for "two and unders." I was getting great attendance and they loved it. The only thing I did was shut out those who wanted to come otherwise for fear that they would be classified as no better than those new in the business. I didn't say anything. One week I stopped having the Wednesday meeting and instead had a Thursday meeting, which I just called our new regular Thursday sales meeting. The size of the group doubled. Some of our biggest producers were there. They had heard I had been telling the two and unders about my meetings with the bigwigs in corporate. I went through some statistics that showed why we had to change our business. Some even took notes.

MANAGING THE PROBLEM SUBORDINATE

When asked to identify what was most stressful about their jobs, most new managers replied without hesitation that it was the problem subordinate:

I understand the people management piece of it so much better now [ten months on the job] and I understand what my deficiencies are. It's very hard for me to grapple with the nonstellar performer. It is the stress of expectations. Is it a reflection on me?

Some said it very simply and graphically: "dealing with turkeys." As we saw, the new managers were generally surprised that some of their subordinates lacked ability or motivation. They were especially unnerved by the number of experienced subordinates who fell into this category. In part, the managers had been naive and idealistic; one said that they were expecting great things of every individual. Another commented that his "egocentrism" led him to believe erroneously that everyone would be as committed as he to making his organization work. On the other hand, managers lower in an organizational hierarchy are more likely to encounter problem subordinates than managers higher up; the incompetent, unmotivated, or those who simply do not fit the company culture are usually let go before they move very far up the organizational ladder:

> People had warned me that this job was notorious for being the worst in the company. It's the front line, where you find most performance challenges, more than in any other job, because the performance problems have not been weeded out.

Working with the problem subordinate was overwhelming and frustrating; new managers kept "grossly underestimating" the amount of time and energy—intellectual and emotional—needed to manage the problem employee:

> I'd like to take a big club and beat him to death. But I can't do that. I've got to be really creative and make sure I stay on top of things so they don't fall apart. I'm never sure how to do it. I have to check up on him and persuade him to be sure he lets me sign off on things, to keep me informed. When what I want to do is jump up and down and scream and holler that I'm fed up.

They had to learn how to diagnose performance problems, give feedback to problem employees, and decide on and implement actions to improve their performance or remove them from their positions. Also, because they had strong emotions about managing the problem employee, an important part of the task was learning to manage their own emotions.

The managers discovered that it was not easy to diagnose problems in performance. They had to distinguish between problems because of a lack of ability from those of a lack of motivation. This was not a simple determination to make:

> After six months I knew who my winners and losers were. Herring had to go; Perkins was a question. Herring didn't care. He was coming in at nine o'clock and going out at four and not coming to training meetings. It was obvious he should be fired. Except when he did work, he got results. He probably has the touch. Perkins works his heart out. First in in the morning and last out at night. He got the best scores in

the training program. But he just doesn't fit in. This business is not for him. It's not working for him and I can't figure out how to make it work. How much longer should I give it?

Who or what was at fault when subordinates made mistakes or performed poorly? Was it the subordinate or the nature of their business? The new managers understood that subordinates' account portfolios varied considerably; some were simply easier to manage than others. Also luck was seen as significant in the sales business. Finally, the managers had difficulty confronting the possibility that, in part, they might be the source of the problem. Perhaps a new manager had set an unrealistic quota for a subordinate because of his or her limited experience in setting quotas. Worse yet, maybe a manager had inadvertently been rewarding the subordinate for inappropriate behavior or had not given the needed assistance:

> One individual, who produced 20 percent of the business, was creating 40 percent of the operation's mistakes in the office. I was sending him a mixed message, because if people were producing the same, they got the same support—same size office, amount of secretarial support. He was actually being rewarded for not doing things properly. And I was afraid to really confront him. I stood the pressure for a very long time before I said anything; I couldn't afford to have him walk out.

> I wasn't very patient. Maybe I should have given her another chance. Figuratively, it was like I just grasped her and shook her up and said; "Why don't you do it my way?" I should have set up parameters and time frames and worked with her. People change slowly, but they change. Don't expect any really abrupt change.

The new managers often felt at a loss in trying to figure out what or how their problem employees thought. They had no experience to help them empathize with the problem employee; the managers had been star producers for whom the job had come naturally:

> I have no emotional feel for these people. What does it feel like to have performance problems? Why don't they like

to work hard? Why do they want to tell lies and cheat the company? And why on earth do some want to steal?

To their distress, the managers found that inept subordinates often did not themselves understand what assistance they might need: "He doesn't know what he needs; he only knows what he likes." Because they were not very good listeners, managers came to realize that they often missed the full implications of the little information the subordinates provided.

Learning to provide performance feedback was a critical skill for managing all subordinates, but especially the problem employee: "How do I provide feedback that is specific enough to be helpful? How do I provide candid feedback in a way that does not make the person defensive?"

The new managers came to see that their lack of listening skill was interfering with their ability to give feedback to their subordinates; the feedback should be an interchange, not simply "tell, tell, tell":

> The first couple of meetings were useless. I can see that now, they were talk-at, talk-down—ego sessions I call them now.

A manager described the long-term effect of one conversation he had with a problem employee:

> It was early in the game, and I didn't understand the sensitivities of the past, what the history had been. So I mishandled myself. This person had problems with previous management and I didn't understand that. In retrospect, I know I sounded awfully heavy-handed, not intending to do that at all, but assuming that his reaction to management would be the same as my reaction had always been. But I've never shared the experiences he had, and so if I could live those few moments over again, I think I would definitely try again. I suggested to him that I wanted to meet his customer one-on-one. He just flew off the handle. What I meant to say was that his account had been managed by too many people and I wanted the customer to understand that now he would be the focal point. I never got that point out. I'm still repairing that. Our rapport is poor.

Giving feedback meant being prepared to confront and manage conflict. Because most wished to avoid conflict, they held news back too long, thereby cheating their subordinates out of a chance to learn and improve their performance:

> I had a manager once who was one of the nicest persons you could ever work for. But now I see he was totally useless to learn from. He never beat anybody up. When people make mistakes they carry the weight on their shoulders, saying, "Did anybody notice? Is this bad? Is this good? Am I going to get a five on my next appraisal rating because I screwed this up?" They want that negative because you take the monkey off their back. You know about it and it is out in the open. You got upset, blew off steam. It isn't as bad as you expected. It's done. But if you never provide any negative feedback and if you never counsel people on mistakes, there is no forum for learning.
>
> If they are going to be saved, I have to do the assessment earlier and give it to them right away so that we can strategize. I've got to get them on a different course of action as soon as possible.

The new manager who described the nice manager admitted that, in his first months, he too avoided conflict, "unless it was absolutely necessary." He wanted his subordinates to like him. This manager was finally forced to overcome his reluctance when he had to severely discipline a subordinate who broke one of the cardinal company rules.

By the end of the year all the managers had disciplined or punished a subordinate; most had to demote or fire an employee. They found it much more difficult to be decisive about their people management than about the technical decisions; they just did not feel as confident about the former decisions. When they had to make a decision as final as firing someone, they were understandably unnerved. It was among the most dreaded acts. They resisted taking such "responsibility for someone's job, someone's life." They hated the emotions they experienced:

> I had a person working for me who had no business being a sales rep. He was probably the most likable, nice person in

the world. Everybody loved him. Customers loved him, but he wasn't selling. His idea was, you go out and do everything right for the customer and when he is ready to order something, he will write you a letter and order it. You could never get across to him that if it is justified next year, and the customer feels he is going to get a return for it next year, why won't he do it this year and start getting that return in benefits this year? To him you were trying to push things on the customer. The guy would work incredible hours. But he belonged in a support position, not in marketing. As a manager you carry this on your shoulders—oh, God, I have to address this guy—and you practice it and rehearse it and you say, When am I going to do it? Finally, you bite the bullet and you sit down and say, "Look [name of rep], I don't think marketing is right for you." I did all the basics, came out from behind my desk. . . . At the end of the conversation, he thanked me profusely for telling him. It blew my mind. He'd been waiting for someone to let him off the hook. . . . I felt like vomiting afterward. I didn't eat all day. I rarely get that upset, but I still felt I had failed him.

Finally, as is apparent from this quotation, the managers discovered that firing took skill. You had to be as constructive as possible, to mention only the most significant problems ("They don't want you to pick out everything they screwed up."), and at all costs, to allow the person to leave with dignity. To do otherwise would be needlessly cruel.

The managers reported that firing a subordinate taught them to be even more selective in hiring. It was especially traumatic if the manager had to fire someone he or she had hired. Because of the relatively short time I spent with them, this event was rare, but by the end of the year they had come to define hiring as a critical management skill:

It takes time to realize the importance of the hiring function. Now, I expend considerable time and thought on recruiting and interviewing. I'm trying to develop a fairly systematic approach. It can never be scientific. In the end you have to make a judgment call about whether the person can cut it or not.

DELEGATION AND CONTROL:
THE NEW-MANAGER NEMESIS

Learning to delegate was perhaps the most difficult challenge the managers faced in managing subordinates' performance.[7] A consistent theme throughout their interactions with subordinates, both experienced and inexperienced, was how to achieve that critical, fine balance between delegation and managerial control. The managers had to decide upon just the right length of rope to give subordinates: too short and they would feel overcontrolled, too long and they would feel neglected and unsupported.

Although delegation is one of the most fundamental management processes in organizations, most of the managers soon recognized that their skill in delegation left much to be desired. They did not fully recognize, however, the extent of the problem, which was partly related to their feeling dependent on these same subordinates. In fact, when asked to describe their management style after three to four months on the job, most described themselves as doing a moderate quantity to a great deal of delegating. They saw themselves as having a consultative decision-making style, using relatively loose follow-up, and being very open to persuasion. Some even worried that they delegated too much: "If I've got a weakness, I delegate too much. I give total responsibility to people and expect them to handle it." This manager's subordinates told a different story. They saw the manager as giving little direction about what she really wanted, but telling them more than enough about how they should do "it, whatever *it* was."

Reflecting on their first year in the job, however, the managers realized how poor they had been at delegating, which most identified as "the hardest part of the transition." We can discern three primary inhibitors to becoming effective delegators. First, as we have seen, they had to learn what it meant to be a manager of people, not the task. When they started in their new positions, most had not yet recognized this distinction. We observed the slow and often painful learning they went through to find that being a manager meant to work through others: "You know the training that we joked about, it's weaning them off the technical side and getting them over to the management side, so that they stop trying to tell you how to do your job."

The second inhibitor was the new managers' personal preferences. One said that delegation went against her nature. Another made this astute observation:

> I had to put fifteen years of experience behind me. For three months at least I behaved just like a producer. I think almost all new managers must do it initially. Whether they make it depends on how long it takes them to realize and step back.

Even though they were wearing themselves out trying to remain technical experts, the managers found it easier to rely upon habit and what they knew. Their technical knowledge had always stood them in good stead: Why abandon it now, when they felt so insecure? Besides, the technical aspects of their work had always been stimulating and rewarding:

> I'm competitive and victory is sweet. You have to be close to the action, directly at the table, in the driver's seat, to really feel it. It is different if you are just counseling the driver and passing him various tools to help drive the bus. You miss the smells of success.

In fact, the third inhibiting factor was personal insecurity. The common opinion is that managers are reluctant to delegate because they do not want to share or reduce their power. For the new managers, reluctance came from a more fundamental insecurity: delegation was a threat to their self-identity and self-esteem. As they fully appreciated that being a manager meant placing their destiny in others' hands, many panicked. One manager reported how he sweated profusely during his first month on the job every time he thought how others "could bring him down." In one of our last conversations he made this observation:

> Most of the new managers have talent. The problem that develops is—one of the scary things is—this job demands that you rely on somebody else to get it done. Forever and ever

before you were the master of your fate. It was the ultimate because you had no one to blame but yourself and no one to take credit but yourself. And now whether you get the numbers you are rated on and paid on and everything on, you have no direct control. . . . You know someone is supposed to do something and you don't hear anything back and comes the day that it is due and you still have not heard anything from anyone, but you assume they have not done it and you immediately get upset. Your immediate reaction is that the next time you see that person, you really light into him and say, "Look, that thing was due today. By God, where is it?" I would say 95 percent of the time they've already done it. You have to trust that they want to do the job well and that when you delegate something it will be done.

The managers had good reason to feel insecure. They had not yet learned how to manage their subordinates, and hence were not sure they had the people management expertise necessary to get their subordinates to produce. Delegation truly involved interpersonal judgment, taking calculated risks on whom to trust. The managers did not know whom to trust. Making these determinations required assessing subordinates by three criteria: competence, personal integrity, and motivation to assume greater responsibility.[8] They did not know *how* to determine whom they could count on. They were not inclined to give people the benefit of the doubt, until proven guilty. Until they felt more confident about their ability to assess subordinates' ability and motivation, they considered it too risky to delegate important tasks:[9]

When you are confident and sure of yourself as a judge of human character, then you can afford to be trusting. There are a lot of gray areas where it is hard to decide until you have more information and experience. Before that you have a genetic desire to inspect everything, to tear everything apart. It's the insecurity thing.

How did the managers eventually come to delegate more? Mostly because circumstances forced them to; in time, they realized their jobs were simply too big to handle alone.[10] As the months passed they found it more difficult to keep their technical knowledge and skills on the cutting edge. They did not even have time to read through all the new product announcements, much less figure out the best strategies for selling them. They found it disconcerting that they were beginning to feel rusty after such a short time. Further, as described earlier, adding insult to injury, in their first months they had created additional work for themselves. Because they had not delegated properly, their inexperienced subordinates were not acting as independently as they might—they still demanded much of the managers' time. And because the managers did not ask for much assistance from their more-experienced subordinates, they had cheated themselves of some potential allies and resources. With all these pressures, the managers began to reassess their actions. When they realized the full scope of their new positions—their predicament—they were willing to accept the risks of delegation. One manager stated that it was a "simple cost-benefit analysis; I couldn't do everything I was in charge of." It took this manager eight to ten months "to really break away from his reps."

For others, the move to more delegation was more abrupt. Managers who took extended vacations (three weeks or more) or who were put on special assignment (on a task force) had to come to grips sooner with their insecurities about delegation. To do so in this manner was traumatic. One of the vacationers reminisced that neither he nor his wife enjoyed the vacation they had planned for years. Others were forced to change because they received clear feedback that their subordinates wanted more authority and responsibility. Many reported uncomfortable confrontations with their subordinates:

> He said he had tried to be nice and ask in small ways for a little more independence. . . . But I was so thick-headed. . . . He shouted at me, "If you really want to be the rep for this account, *you* make the phone call. Just take the account; now that you've told me exactly what to do." I asked, "You don't have to be so nasty about it," but deep down inside I knew he was right.

When they thought about it, the managers were not surprised by these confrontations; they could not really be angry about them. If they had been in their subordinates' shoes, they would have behaved in the same way. Toward the end of the year the managers reframed the delegation problem—instead of whether or not to delegate, the issue became *how* to delegate:

> I've got to be more hands-off and work through the talents of my people. The individual owns the account and the problems that come with it. When a problem comes up I can quickly identify what resource should be used. I can direct the *responsibility* back to the rep. I rarely put on my sales hat any more. My job is to train and develop the reps the best I can.

Once the managers understood the importance and advantages of delegation (particularly a more manageable workload and developmental experiences for their subordinates), they still had to learn how to delegate. At first they went to extremes, swinging from too little delegation to too much: "It tended to be all or nothing." As they received complaints about this seesawing, they began to refine their delegating behavior. They had two primary questions: what to delegate to whom and when to follow up or intervene. The first dilemma has been discussed: the managers gradually learned that their subordinates varied extensively in skill and motivation. They came to see that different subordinates should be treated differently. Some should be delegated a great deal of responsibility and others should not. Eventually, the managers even realized that in time people could grow and change: "People mature. There is one guy I am spending a lot less time with, and I'm delegating more as I see he is starting to improve more and more. As they come up to speed, I get involved on an exception basis." Mainly by trial and error, the managers' judgment in delegating the right amount and types of responsibilities to each subordinate improved.

The question of what to delegate was fundamental, relating to the managers' understanding of the managerial role. Of course, they did not experience it in this way. For them it was the more concrete matter of solving a problem, figuring out what to delegate to a subordinate. From listening carefully to their ideas about delegation, it seemed clear that they were weighing the balance between managerial control and prerogative and subordinates' rights. Professionals expect to and should be given substantial operational autonomy, but the managers in the beginning obviously had great difficulty distinguishing between operational and administrative autonomy.[11] They were busy interfering with what should have been their subordinates' operational authority; instead they neglected their strategic and administrative responsibilities.

In time, however, the managers did begin to discern the difference between administrative and operational autonomy; they began to understand the two essential principles of delegation: the need to provide the strategic and administrative constraints within which subordinates should operate, and the need to monitor and follow up performance based on those parameters:

> You can't just let them [subordinates] go. You have to develop a system of controls or it will just come crashing down. You have to have ways of checking and rechecking upon a person's progress—to make sure their plans fit with the unit's goals and are being carried out in the right direction.

Although the managers devised no hard-and-fast rules about when they should intervene, they did have a yardstick for making the judgment: whether or not the subordinate's actions were consistent with broader organizational objectives. But, as we have seen, not until the end of their first year were the managers prepared to even face up to their responsibilities to manage not only individual but also group performance. Only when they began to devote more attention to managing group performance did they define the parameters within which their subordinates would work.

CONCLUDING REMARKS

We have been on a long journey, watching the new managers struggle with the many challenges in managing the individual subordinate: from evaluating subordinates' performance to linking performance with rewards and punishments. To reiterate, the critical lessons for the new managers to learn was accepting subordinates' diversity, responding to that diversity, managing the problem employee, and delegation and control. Eventually they began to create personal maps for diagnosing the human problems they encountered and rules of thumb for resolving them, as they worked day by day with their subordinates. The managers had to develop both their knowledge and skill in both analysis and implementation. They made more progress on the former than the latter. They discovered just how complex an analytic task they faced when they began to recognize how diverse their subordinates were. The first step in managing that diversity was being able to discern key differences.

Exactly how to manage that diversity, the challenges of implementation, was a dilemma. Once again the managers were confronted with the need to manage paradox. It seemed they were struggling to balance three sets of tensions: treating subordinates fairly, but as individuals; holding subordinates accountable, yet tolerating their mistakes and deficiencies; and maintaining control, yet providing autonomy. Balancing these tensions required finely honed knowledge and skill that the new managers had only begun to acquire. Perhaps their struggles with delegation, a fundamental managerial skill, best exemplified how much they had left to learn.

The new managers had begun the year with the assumption that an effective manager behaved consistently. But their experience showed them that which management researchers have found time and again: an effective manager is versatile and adapts his or her approach to the demands that come up in specific situations.[12] Although they were coming to understand this managerial principle, they still did not know how to live up to it.

NOTES

1. For many, the phrase "managing diversity" has come to mean managing people of different gender, ethnic, racial, or religious backgrounds. In this

current context, I mean diversity in subordinate talent, motivation, and temperament. We had too few individuals of different gender, ethnic, or racial backgrounds to make systematic observations about how the new managers responded to and managed such differences.

2. See Strumm (1985) or Webster (1983).

3. Flamholz and Randall (1987) found this kind of behavior in the new managers they studied.

4. See Flamholz and Randall (1987) or McCall et al. (1988). In their research, all found that new managers encountered special difficulties in working with more-experienced subordinates.

5. The relatively older new managers seemed to have less difficulty establishing credibility with their senior people. One forty-year-old new manager stated that he had less baggage to bring to the relationship.

6. New managers who had a more participative style from the beginning appeared to have better relationships with their more-experienced subordinates than those who had a more autocratic style.

7. Many have argued that one of the fatal flaws a manager can have is unwillingness or inability to delegate. Gabarro (1987) discusses the dangers of the Lone-Ranger approach (p. 72). Whetten and Cameron (1983) identify the unwillingness or inability to delegate as one of the major causes for managerial ineffectiveness.

8. For example, Leana (1986) found that managers relied upon these three criteria in granting different degrees of role latitude to subordinates (p. 757).

9. Weick (1974) writes: "Delegation may be problematic because the manager is a flawed and mobile databank, not because he's on a power trip" (p. 112).

10. In the McCall et al. (1988) study of managerial development, the demands of sheer scale (responsibility for more people, dollars, functions, products, markets, and sites) were leading developmental forces. Leana (1986) discovered that workload was the only variable that was a significant predictor of differences among supervisors in amounts of authority delegated (p. 772). She concluded that situational constraints rather than personal predispositions had a greater influence on supervisors' delegatory behavior.

11. Raelin (1989) provides a useful conceptualization of autonomy. Using Talcott Parsons's work, he categorizes three types of autonomy: strategic or institutional, administrative, and operational:

> Strategic autonomy entails the freedom to select the goals and policies guiding the organization. The agents responsible for this level of autonomy are responsible for distinguishing the corporate mission and mediating between their organization and the society of which it is a part. Administrative autonomy constitutes the responsibility for managing the activities of a unit within the organization and coordinating the tasks of that unit with other units in the organization . . . the agents also contribute to corporate policy by reacting to the direction of the organization articulated at the strategic level. Operational autonomy, meanwhile, is having the freedom, once the goal or problem has been set, to attack it by means determined by oneself within administrative and strategic constraints (pp. 216–217).

12. See Skinner and Sasser (1977).

III

Confronting the Personal Side of Management

The new managers were caught off guard by the stark transition from producer to manager, especially the transformation it required. They did not at first appreciate how profound their career choice was. For in accepting promotion to manager, unbeknownst to the new managers, they did more than consent to new job responsibilities. They made an initial commitment to form a new professional and personal identity, oriented toward managing people, not technical tasks. The managers soon discovered that the task learning (acquiring competencies and building key relationships) was only part of the story.[1] The personal learning—that is, adopting attitudes and a psychological perspective consistent with their new role—was even more demanding. With their first year on the job came much personal learning and change. In this part of the book, we observe as the new managers work on themselves, the heart of the process of becoming a manager.

The managers were surprised by the amount of personal learning they did. A number of them said they had never been very introspective or focused on their internal development, favoring as one stated, "action over thinking." Many believed at first that adults in fact could not change. But of necessity, they began to work on themselves as they adapted to managerial work and their new network of relationships. They had much to adapt to, for the move to management required numerous changes: a change in their way of presenting themselves, a change in others' ways of treating them, and new sets of people with whom they had to interact. Barley, a leading career theorist, writes that the managerial role should not be "conceived of as predetermined rights and privileges that [can] be donned and doffed as easily as a well-tailored suit of clothes."[2] Instead, as we saw in Part I, for each new manager it emerged through an ongoing process of negotiation with their new partners: subordinates, superiors, peers, and customers. Through the negotiations, the managers learned not only what management was really all about, but also they changed themselves. They developed new behaviors and attitudes to accommodate the expectations of these constituencies and the realities of managerial work.

In Chapter 6, we chart the new managers' voyage of self-discovery. They had been attracted to the promise they thought management offered, only to learn that they held many misconceptions about the work and themselves. We consider their initial motivation for management and then follow as they evolve a new professional identity and managerial character. In Chapter 7, we focus not simply on what happened to the new managers, but rather on how it felt. This distinction is critical for understanding the managers' experiences. As we have seen, how they felt affected how they thought about and behaved on the job. They had to learn how to cope with the traumatic mental change they were undergoing and with the stresses inherent in the managerial role. Evidence is growing that how resilient managers remain in the face of organizational demands and adversities may be as important to their careers' success as their specific achievements at work.[3] We cannot neglect the emotional effects of becoming a manager, as those responsible for managerial development often do.[4]

NOTES

1. The categories of task and personal learning are suggested by Hall (1986).
2. Barley (1989) elaborates on the notion of status passage to understand important career transitions (p. 50).
3. Wood and Bandura (1989) make this observation about managerial research:

> Cognitive approaches to decision making are further limited because they usually ignore the impact that affective, motivational, and other self-referent influences have on one's information acquisition, evaluation, and choice. In naturally occurring decision environments, interactions between situational demands and self-referent factors can exert a powerful influence on the decision-making process. For example, in studies of organizational decision making, perceived threats and setbacks have been shown to reduce managers' willingness to seek new information or to incorporate it into their choices (Tjosvold, 1984), to strengthen their commitment to past courses of action (Brockner and Rubin, 1985), and to narrow their focus, or to foster a retrospective focus, in their search behavior (Conlon and Parks, 1987; Janis and Mann, 1977) (p. 369).

4. Some notable exceptions include the work of Bennis (1989), Flamholz and Randall (1987), Hall (1986), Hirschhorn (1988), Kaplan (1989; 1990), Schein (1978), and Zaleznik and Kets de Vries (1975).

6

Gaining Self-Knowledge

Although the new managers did not at first appreciate the full ramifications of their decision to become a manager, they knew the choice was significant. All admitted that the decision to accept promotion created some anxiety and ambivalence. They pondered two questions: "Will I like management?" and "Will I be good at management?" The answers would come only with experience.[1] As the year progressed and they could see a new professional self-concept forming, they found themselves asking an even more unsettling question: "Who am I becoming?" They were learning about themselves, one said, not only as "a manager, but also as a person." Therefore, we end by discussing the development of the managerial character.

WHY DID I BECOME A MANAGER?

Why the new managers chose to pursue a managerial career was one of the first issues they considered in our earliest conversations. In fact, they brought up the question before I could do so because it was uppermost in their minds. They seemed more unsure about whether they would like management than whether they would be good at it.

Almost all began by listing the wrong reasons for becoming a manager: "You can't do it because you're tired of selling, you're tired of being on commission, or you're bored or tired of working so hard." Many reluctantly admitted that they had been attracted to management because they were growing tired of their technical work:

> Candidly speaking, I had done it all, seen it all, and was ready for a change. I was afraid I was getting burned out, losing that edge. Of course, I didn't tell this to the personnel people. They would never have considered me.

Although such frustrations made many managers receptive to considering a managerial career, the reasons that ultimately led them to make the choice lay elsewhere. The primary reason was the opportunity to assume more authority and responsibility than their technical positions would ever afford, and in the long term to make more money.[2] In short, they wanted to be the boss, to exercise power and influence. They craved the opportunity to "show others the right way to do the job, to straighten out the inefficient practices" around them:

> I was tired of having somebody else coming in and telling me what to do. I had some ideas about what it takes to be successful and, rather than someone hindering my chances I said, "Why not take it over yourself? Why not run the whole show?"
>
> I've always wondered what it would be like to be in charge and get people to do things the right way.

They wanted to contribute to the organization's success and be recognized for doing so. They saw the promotion to management, and the associated money, prestige, and status, as desirable symbols of achievement and success. About two-thirds of them aspired to move up in the executive ranks, and the others wished to remain first-line managers with ever more successful, larger units:[3]

> This is a stepping-stone for me. I want to move into corporate someday. But it is important that you pay your dues.

> It's [sales manager] a credential I want to have under my belt that will pay off later. You get your stripe, then you move on.

> If I could be here [in the same branch] for the rest of my life, I could do it. I like the area [California]. It's a good community to raise a family in. There is a lot of opportunity to grow; people with money are still moving in. Eventually, this area should be able to support one or two satellite offices.

> If the opportunity presented itself, I would love to go higher in the firm, but I am not obsessed with it. The higher you go, the more political it gets. I could be happy staying here where you have more command and control over what goes on around you.

The managers' motivations appeared to be ones consistent with traditional assumptions about the appropriate reasons for pursuing a managerial career. Others have found that the most effective managers are those primarily motivated by a strong need for socialized power.[4] That is, their need to influence others is oriented not toward self-aggrandizement but toward achieving the organization's goals.

A handful of the managers had embarked upon their sales positions with such an intention:

> I caught on [to sales] fast, but deep down I was never a salesperson. That was a difference I always felt. There are people who truly love sales. I knew one sales rep who, if you gave him a flip chart and a magic marker, it was like opening heaven's door. He went into a world of his own. He loved to have an audience, to have customers to make presentations to, and to close the deal. He was excellent at it and loved it. I always respected him. I could pull it off too, but my heart just wasn't in it as much. . . . On the other hand, I enjoyed the contact with people. I felt comfortable with people, could communicate well with people, and I was very supportive of them [customers, other reps, support people]. I got excited

and enjoyed watching things go well. I also got upset when they did not go well. I guess I always wanted management. My father and brother are both managers in *Fortune* 500 companies. They encouraged me to get my feet wet in sales first so that I'd really understand the customer.

This manager was unusual, however. Most others had decided to pursue a managerial career only after years of experience as a producer. Many had first been invited to be management candidates and then decided to seek the promotion:

> I had never thought of management, a renegade like me. But my boss talked to me about looking into it. He said it offered many exciting opportunities that I should at least take a look at. [The company] was always desperate for management talent. And if you were good, you could have it all.

This invitation from his boss had instigated a career choice that this new manager had never consciously considered. Like him, most of the managers were still enamored of sales; hence, their ambivalence about the decision to become managers. Although they enjoyed working in their field of specialty, a career in management was appealing. In their minds, they were sacrificing some of the satisfactions of technical work for more authority, status, and pay. Perhaps they were open to pursuing a new career path because of their developmental stage. According to most theories of adult development, these managers were at the stage in which they were establishing and consolidating their career. Levinson, perhaps the most influential writer on this subject, sees ages thirty-two to forty as the time when men (most managers in this study were men) are trying to complete the goals of settling down and becoming a respected member of their world. At this time they define the direction in which they will strive in the future.[5]

After a few months on the job, as the managers came to understand managerial work, they began to appreciate more what they had given up. Relying upon their sales experience for comparison, they evaluated their new role, finding what they really liked about work and how the managerial role fell short. They could see how much they enjoyed actually selling and missed its intellectual challenge and glamor. They discovered how much they preferred very explicit goals to measure themselves against and the gratification they got from instant, predictable feedback:

> At any point in my day, I could calculate just how much money I had made. How much I made was mostly under my control; if I worked hard and worked smart, I got more dollars. There was a direct connection.
>
> Before it was all objective. You brought in this amount of dollars, you get this percentage. Now, it's all subjective. They [senior managers] can't even communicate it to you so that you can understand exactly what standards you'll be measured against.
>
> You can just say, "I had a small degree of positive influence" sometimes. You never really feel like you have accomplished anything tangible. Before I could break my work down into parts, there was a beginning and end. At the end of the day, I could see what I had done. Now, I never seem to get any closure.

Almost as dramatic as the loss of personal or private recognition of their achievements was the loss of public recognition. As star producers they were used to receiving public accolades and acknowledgment of their achievements. Most of the reward and incentive systems (award ceremonies, placards, trips) in the organizations were designed for the producers, not the managers:

> You certainly don't get the recognition you used to get as a rep. Because as a rep, the boss was always coming in and patting you on the back and saying what a great job you did. And you always got in front at branch meetings and got rewards and everything. As a manager, you're giving out all the recognition. You hardly even get the pat on the back. That's a big piece I've picked up from an adaptation standpoint—the loss of recognition.
>
> In management you're trying to provide an environment for your own people to excel. If you go after recognition for the manager, then maybe you're trying to get a part of yourself that will cost or jeopardize your employees. A lot of the recognition has to be kept at the rep level.

In both companies the big producers were held in the highest esteem, considered the "backbone of the organization," the "company nerve center in touch with the all-important customer," the people doing the essential and "sexiest" work. As discussed in Chapter 1, managers were often seen as "self-absorbed bureaucrats" who got in the way of the salespeople's single-minded drive to make money for the company and themselves. Managers' motives were often suspect; they often found it necessary to disavow the "wrong motivations." They did not want applied to them the old dictum, "those who can, do, those who can't, teach (or manage)." Indeed, many of their old peers questioned their decision to become managers. They had lost, in a relative sense, some prestige, and they had lost a fundamental source of recognition.[6]

And finally, in terms of losses, the managers came to see just how much they valued autonomy and control. To the question, "What did you like most about being a sales representative?" a new manager replied:

> I'd say just the success. The fact that you got immediate feedback on how well you did. You were, for the most part, in control of your own destiny, your own success. You know the money was a nice piece, but it was the challenge of finding out how well you did next to other people's results.
>
> I'm no longer an independent spirit. When I gave up my book [portfolio of clients] I lost my security blanket. And to think I did it willingly!

They had erroneously assumed these needs could be met in a managerial position. Hence, they failed to recognize the inconsistency between their espoused motivations for management and how they derived satisfaction from work. After a short time in their new positions, the managers understood the incongruity all too well; reality shock had set in.

DO I HAVE WHAT IT TAKES?

As the new managers spent time on the job and realized how ill-prepared they were for their new responsibilities, their doubts shifted from, "Will I like management?" to "Will I be good at it?" Although they had to learn if they were suited for management and about their managerial interests and talents, they faced a first, more fundamental challenge: how to assess their personal impact on their organizations.

Assessing Personal Impact

The new managers soon understood that managers must make critical decisions from incomplete and flawed information and must live with imperfect solutions. As individual contributors they had been accustomed to explicit, tangible measures of performance, and they were used to being held accountable primarily for one outcome, the sales quota. As managers they were now evaluated by many criteria and were responsible for both short- and long-term objectives. Every managerial decision required trade-offs among competing interests. It was difficult to know what criteria and evidence to rely upon in evaluating their performance:

> I'm evaluated on a morass of touchy-feely things besides quota. Many of them seem in direct conflict with making quota. Anyway, even if you make quota, you don't know what you had to do with it. Maybe you're in a good business cycle.
>
> I can never really give myself an "A." Somebody is always dissatisfied or something is always left undone. You just can't do it all. You have to learn that you can only do your best and your best may not be good enough. That's hard for an achiever like me to swallow—to accept that I can't always deliver what people want. You just can't please all the people.
>
> You can't get to the perfect solution. You've just got to find the workable solution. You never know if you could have done better. What could I have done differently? How could I have helped? What did I do wrong? I've come to realize there's only so much that I can do, and ultimately that's all I'm going to do.
>
> I may not see the results of my efforts this week [the manager had spent the last few days on planning] until next year. With that kind of time horizon, how can I know how much my planning contributed to the outcome?

The managers also soon recognized the special difficulties in solving human problems in an organization and how hard it was to ascertain their contribution to the organization's success now that they worked through others. Furthermore, they were learning that human problems were rarely responsive to the quick fix: "they [took] coddling and patience." They had to learn how to evaluate their effectiveness: which criteria were appropriate, what evidence to rely upon, how to establish cause-and-effect linkages. For much of the first year, they were preoccupied with assessing their influence on specific individuals, especially subordinates:

> You can never get solid proof that what you did made a difference. You can't prove cause and effect. And so many factors come into play that you don't have control over. Maybe you just got lucky. You've got to take it on faith.
>
> The company doesn't give you much guidance. They're not good at measuring the work you do with people, the coaching and support. It is pretty nebulous, and it doesn't always show up so clearly on whether you make quota. You could have worked your butt off helping a rep and you finally got the rep doing everything right. Then they don't make the sale because a competitor introduces a new product that fits the customer's needs better, the day before you think you are going to close the deal.

Toward the end of the year, when the managers began to devote time and attention to managing the group, they set out to assess their effect on the organization as a whole, on organizational climate or culture. Ascertaining their influence on such an amorphous phenomena turned out to be even more complicated than seeing how they affected individuals.

The managers eventually learned to cope with the ambiguity in measuring their performance. They began to see the advantage of gathering varied information from different sources to deal with the ambiguity, cultivating both formal and informal sources of information (more on this subject in Chapter 8). They relied on others' feedback—subordinates, peers, bosses, and customers. They would synthesize the points of view, hunting desperately for convergent validity. Finally, they paid attention to their own behavior, analyzing with some precision how they had handled situations. Because they were so often surprised by people's reaction to them and conscious of their subordinates' attention, most were acutely self-aware and introspective:

> I paid attention to the littlest detail. I was so self-conscious. You have to manage yourself, what you wear, how you speak, what your personal habits are. Because the first thing you understand is that everybody is watching you, everything, every day. If you walk past one of them and forget to say hello, they'll remember.

With experience, they began to have faith in their judgments in making evaluations, though the picture was often incomplete and cloudy:

> What evidence do I use to tell if I'm managing people well? The number-one evidence is turnover. The other is a low morale situation or a series of customers' complaints. You often hear it from outside the office. If the broker is unhappy then the operations person is unhappy. If the operations person is unhappy then the corporate operations people are going to hear about it. Then you're going to hear through the grapevine, first as hints, that [the branch] is not a good place to work. But the glaring measure is when a group of brokers walk out, including some good ones. Management is typically the reason people walk out, but it is not 100 percent by any stretch of the imagination. It's not a perfect measure, either, but it will have to do.

> Often I can't explain why something worked. It just did. If you can't explain it, then you can't be sure you can create it again. For example, with him [a problem employee], I was successful the first time. He changed what he was doing. But it took me maybe three or four other times of dealing with [problem employees] for me to realize in any detail what I was doing and to be sure that it was really my methodology that was making the difference. It got to the point that I sometimes felt like I was running a test—if I do this, they'd do that.

In his eleventh month, one of the managers remarked:

> I think I can see my stamp on my folks. I use humor a lot; now they do, too. It's funny to see how you affect people.

There are these bits and pieces of evidence that you can put together like a puzzle. I'd be interested in hearing what they tell you my impact has been. . . . As a manager you achieve results gradually, over months and maybe even years. They are not always visible or concrete, but they're real.

The managers gradually became aware of the confidence and strength it took to look toward the big picture, not instant gratification and be paid for "50 percent subjective things." ."

Discovering Managerial Weaknesses

As chronicled in Part II, the managers soon realized they had much to learn about managing subordinates. Managing was not simply doing more of the work they did as producers. The transition reflected a qualitative, rather than a quantitative, shift and they lacked much of the required knowledge and many skills that an effective manager needs. Worse still, behaviors and attitudes that had been assets (such as their hands-on aggressive approach to sales and reliance on immediate feedback and reward) to them as salespeople were now liabilities. Slowly but surely they saw each unnerving revelation, and they asked themselves how they could ever succeed. They liked managerial work less than they expected. It seemed who they were was the antithesis of who they needed to be. They did not have the competencies they needed to be managers. Moreover, as they began to appreciate more fully what it meant to be a manager of people, their performance anxiety grew, for many assumed that interpersonal competence could not be learned; it was "inborn":

> Either you have it or you don't. Your personality and how you get along with people is set by the time you are an adult. You're not going to change much.
>
> Leaders are born, not made. You can't develop people skills. It is something innate. You can't get them in the classroom.
>
> Management is an art, not a science. What if I'm not an artist?

The new managers were at a crossroads.

168

WHO AM I BECOMING?

Fortunately, the new managers could change and most did, admittedly with reluctance and much "backsliding."[7] One manager said of his self-concept that it was a year of "confirmation, elaboration, and revelation." Yes, revelation, because the managers matured and changed throughout the year, as they constructed an integrated managerial identity for themselves. In fact, most began to acquire not only managerial knowledge and skills, but also managerial interests and a managerial temperament. We will watch next as the new managers revisit their motivation to manage and make discoveries about new sides of themselves, their managerial strengths, and their managerial styles.

Revisiting the Motivation to Manage

As we have seen, the first months of management were a time of many surprises, most negative but some pleasant. After they began to feel more comfortable on the job, having acquired some managerial skills and regained some self-confidence, the managers discovered things they liked about the job. By the second half of the year, most began to recognize the satisfactions they could derive from having an influence on the whole organization and managing people:

> When I'm out on the floor walking around and asking people what they are working on, I've begun to notice that people are more businesslike. And they are laughing more. People seem more comfortable now, and I think I've had something to do with that. At least my people tell me I do. Their last boss wasn't around much; he had made his money and was out on the golf course a lot—like an early retirement. It's fascinating to see you have impact. It really feels good.
>
> This has been a time in my life that has taught me what I like and what I don't like. I don't like the politics of the job. I like having a positive impact on people, an impact on their salaries and career opportunities.

169

They were especially pleased to discover that creativity was involved in managing people, in figuring out how to motivate each subordinate. Many were surprised, relieved, and even "thrilled" to learn how fulfilling coaching and development could be:

> I like training people, helping them become more successful in production. It gives me the best feeling to see somebody do something well after I have helped them. I get excited. If I can take a young person in here who is having some problems getting started and maybe teach him some things that will help him feel good about himself and start doing what needs to be done for the client, I enjoy that. I didn't know how much fun it could be helping other people make production instead of doing my own.

> She [a sales representative] thinks differently now because of me. I enjoy explaining things to her more than I did to clients. I always got involved with clients and spent time trying to educate them about financial management. I can see my influence on how she looks at customer situations now. She even uses my words, phrases things the way I do, like when you notice that your kid is starting to walk like you and use your gestures.

> I helped him [a young salesperson] fulfill a dream. He can afford that European vacation this year thanks to my support.

As the new managers grew to appreciate their new role, most found aspects of the work like these satisfying and rewarding. Even by the end of the year, though, most still held a very strong technical and functional career anchor,[8] and although none considered returning to production, they grieved for what they had lost: "I've cut the cord; there is no going back. I've had to reset my goals now that I am a manager. It hasn't been easy; I still miss being close to the action."

But by the end of the year most had begun the pivotal task of shifting their source of self-esteem. In fact, one manager could not believe what he was saying when I observed, "It sounds as if you like being a manager":

> Gee, I hadn't thought about it in a while. [He stopped to laugh.] Sure, the success of the troops became the success of

the office and became my success—and I don't just mean in earning me money. My success—and I know I was by no means the most successful manager—is the result of my people and the environment. But I did my best to feed them both. I realize now that when I accepted the position of branch manager that it is truly an exciting vocation. It truly is awesome, even at this level; it can be terribly challenging and terribly exciting.

Another manager remarked:

What satisfies me about the job? Well, you do get feedback. Every month you can see how much your team has generated and you can see which people have developed and maybe even been promoted. You know you are doing something that is important to the company, something that needs to be done—both making money and helping people grow and move—both aspects bring their own satisfactions.

Discovering New Sides of the Self

The promotion to management had startled the managers into facing themselves and coming to grips with their own limitations. They had to confront unpleasant realities about themselves as they received feedback from others about how they were perceived:

I saw my style as very aggressive, demanding, interested, and involved. They [his subordinates] saw me as a dictator, a tyrant on their backs.
I was just being myself. But after three weeks on the job it was coming back to me that people thought I was harsh, harsh. I needed to soften.
What an eye-opener. People were trying to tell me I was too indecisive. I made them nervous because I seemed timid. No one had ever called me timid before.

Despite their intentions, the managers found they were not having the desired effect on others. The expression "eye-opener" came up regularly in our conversations. A major preoccupation was reconciling people's perception of them with their own self-image. They became very defensive at times and discounted feedback they were receiving. But again, because they were so eager to succeed as managers and knew "deep down" that they had much to learn, most were remarkably receptive to even the most threatening observations.

Even more distressing than the feedback were the "foibles" they uncovered on their own. The managers were discovering new sides of themselves that had never been expressed because they had been untested. Many were "horrified" to learn how they responded to the stresses of management. They had always thought of themselves as having much self-confidence and a "healthy ego." Many pointed out that sales was a stressful occupation:

> This business [stocks and bonds] is a high-risk business. You can be wiped out by things beyond your control—the volatility of the market. As a broker, I was dealing with emotion. Every decision I made involved three emotions: greed, fear, and risk. You know some people would kill their mother for money or give up their health. You've got to be strong to handle all that risk.

The new managers' reactions to the stress of being promoted suggested, however, that their egos were not as healthy as imagined. One manager asked, "What happened to my self-assurance?" Another discovered that he was literally afraid to engage in the kinds of interpersonal conflicts he now faced regularly with his subordinates:

> I don't react well in conflict situations. I back off. It really hurts me to have people get mad at me. I can't even look the person in the eye without starting to sweat. I always thought it took a lot of backbone and thick skin to be a salesperson, all the rejection. Now, I find myself acting like a jellyfish with people who supposedly work for me. I'm a big man, but as big as I am, I don't have much confidence.

Another manager in his late thirties declared, "There are days when I walk in here and I'm scared to death."

In fact, the managers most often discovered new sides of themselves in managing conflicts with subordinates. A manager

172

in his early forties described a scene in which he screamed at one of his subordinates. As he spoke he was still visibly shaken:

> I let her have it. I ranted and raved for I don't know how long. In one part of my mind, I knew everybody could hear my outburst. But it was as if I was out of control, I was so angry. . . . But I've never been a shouter at work or at home. I have a reputation for being calm, coolheaded, and somewhat softspoken. But hell, I've never had anybody else in control of my destiny before.

Another manager painted a similar scenario:

> I had never, ever, unless when I was a child, yelled at anyone outside my family. And I literally got into a shouting contest with somebody the first month of the job. My physical reactions were just amazing. To watch my body and feel it do things it had never done before was just amazing. But I walked away from that saying, "Holy Toledo, that is something new and different." It was a real eye-opener.

As the managers became more comfortable on the job and learned to cope with managerial stresses, they were relieved to see that these "Dr. Jekyll and Mr. Hyde acts" began to dissipate.

A number had decided to model themselves on the behaviors and demeanor of a favorite boss or company hero—a very reasonable strategy. This tactic was easier said than performed, however:

> He [a favorite boss] had been a role model, really a father figure to me. I tried to think to myself, "What would he do in my situation?" I even dressed like him, to look like an authority figure. I could figure out what he would do, but I couldn't do it. I wasn't him. I didn't have his personal charm and ease with people, and so I came off as a phoney.
>
> [My favorite boss] always kept people up. You enjoyed coming to the office, because he always had fun up his sleeve. I wanted to create that kind of atmosphere. But guess what I found out? I really don't have much of a sense of humor and I'm not spontaneous like him. If you have to work at making something funny, it falls flat. I had to come up with another

way that fit who I am to create the right office atmosphere. I could keep his concepts, but I had to put my own words and form around them.

It was terribly disappointing for the new managers that they could not emulate those they admired because they did not have their personal qualities or skill. But as implied in the last quotation, they slowly found that to be successful as managers, they had to discover and capitalize on their unique managerial styles.

Discovering Managerial Strengths

Of course, the new managers were able to learn. They gave up their deeply held habits and attitudes reluctantly, often taking two steps back in order to take one forward, but they moved forward nonetheless. For them it was difficult to detect progress at any specific time. It was an unconscious, evolutionary progression, with an occasional revolutionary change of which they became quite conscious. But by about the ninth month, most (some more than others) began to feel that they were getting a handle on their jobs. They recognized they had far more to learn, but felt they were on the right track.

At about that time, the managers also began to feel their own managerial strengths and style. They uncovered personal aptitudes they could exploit. One manager discovered he was particularly "good at handling temperamental people." His peers had even begun calling him for advice because he really understood problem subordinates and could work with them. They discovered other assets as well:

> A real strong suit is my enthusiasm. That I care. That I listen. I'm very sensitive to them [subordinates]. I lead by example in what I do in the office, the time I spend there, the effort I put forth. They know I will only ask of them what I ask of myself. They try to help me because they know I try to help them.
>
> I seem to be really good at giving feedback to people. I let them know what they're doing, the bad and the good. A lot of people are uncomfortable praising others; they give the

good points short shrift. Not me, I take the time to tell [my subordinates] what they're doing right. They seem to be able to hear the bad better, too. I hear all the time how fair they think I am.

My strength—I don't need to be liked. They know I just want to get the job done. I don't have to play any games to protect my ego and so I give it to them straight. They like my predictability.

I was worried that my youth was going to be my biggest problem. I didn't have as much business experience as a lot of the other new managers. It turned out my youth is my strength. At least in this office, my freshness was welcomed. I'm not a crusty old guy who has been with the business forever. I'm not set in my ways and am open to listening to their ideas. They perceive me as very sensitive, eager to do the right thing. But they know I'll step up to an issue. Once we take care of a problem they won't hear about it for months after.

As many observed, it was easier for them to learn about their weaknesses than their strengths:

I guess we learn more from our mistakes than our successes. If something works, we don't want to bother a good thing—"don't fix it, if it ain't broke" mentality. You don't even want to think about it. Besides, you're busy. You don't have any luxury time to sit around patting yourself on the back.

But as these managers discovered, learning one's strengths was a very empowering experience. They could depend on these qualities to help them compensate for some of their weaknesses.

Discovering Their Managerial Style

Generally by the middle of their first year, after they had gotten over the shock of moving to management, the managers became aware of patterns in their behavior; they discerned their managerial styles or preferred ways of interacting. In descriptions of their styles, three characteristics were most often discussed: task- versus people-oriented; authoritative versus participative; and less often, formal versus informal. These are, of course, three of the most commonly considered issues in the literature on management style. As we saw, for their first months on the job the managers showed a clear predilection for a more task-oriented and authoritative style. One might even label this the "new manager style." As the year unfolded and they began to understand their role and feel more secure, their "true" styles became visible. In fact, they showed some variation along these two dimensions:

> I think it is the nature of the job, and, as you get involved in the job, your personality changes. Some managers become very people-directed and others are more sales- and customer-directed. You rarely see that people are perfectly balanced on these. I'm leaning toward the people side now, which surprises me. I always loved the customer contact so much as a broker.

> It turns out I'm more laid back than I thought I would be. I like to give people lots of independence and just check on them every once in a while.

> I'm real hands-on. Now, I see that as a problem because I won't want to delegate when I should. I'll have to fight it. But I'm always going to need to be involved in the detail more than [my last sales manager] was. He was like the band conductor who never wanted to play the drums again. I'm more like the drum major. I want to be out on the playing field.

> Managers have various styles. I had been trying to copy the way [his favorite boss] did things. But we don't have the same styles. My style is that I am involved. I like to feel, touch, and understand what is going on. I want to get to be buddy-like with my folks. Others don't need that. They're more reserved and are comfortable understanding things intuitively. They feel comfortable sitting behind a desk. I wouldn't even have a desk if I didn't have to. See, I have a round table in here where I do most of my meetings, or else you'll find me out there walking around.

The managers came to feel they ought to have a style that fit who they were:

> I tried to adopt a style at first that was a bit of a masquerade. It got me into trouble because I was always confused. I

needed to find something that I was more comfortable with, so that I wouldn't be perceived as one thing, but know inside that I was another.

The jury is still out on my results. But at least now, I've become a known entity to myself. Things feel more natural. I know what my problems are. There is a lot I do wrong, but now I'm being me. I'm comfortable in my skin and the troops have picked up on the self-confidence that feeling gives me.

By the end of the year the managers were not able to talk confidently about their styles, which were still evolving. And none of them had even begun to think about shaping their environment to better fit who they were—a strategy many effective, experienced managers rely upon. It was as if they had spent the first year simply gaining insight into who they were and acquiring basic managerial skills and attitudes.

ACQUIRING THE MANAGERIAL CHARACTER

Along the way, as the managers were learning what it meant to be a manager and the lessons of interpersonal judgment, they were also developing the managerial character—personal qualities or attitudes essential to effectively manage people. Managerial experts have written about the emotional competencies required to be a manager.[9] From interviews I was able to identify the prime qualities the managers saw as part of managerial character: self-confidence, willingness to accept responsibility, patience, empathy, and ability to live with imperfect solutions.[10] Most said such factors of temperament were critical in making the transition successfully. Some even evaluated themselves periodically on such criteria, fretting that they would not be able to change. One stated that "By now, I am who I am." Indeed, an individual's character is mostly a function of his or her early history, including genetic factors, socioeconomic background, and relationships with others, especially parents.[11]

For the new managers, self-confidence formed the core of the managerial character. Without self-confidence it was difficult to see how one would take on the remaining qualities in the managerial character. Looking back over the year, they were struck by how much their behavior was determined by their feeling about themselves: "I am paid on so many subjective things now. I had to learn to be strong and confident about what I was doing, even though I knew I would make *many* mistakes in this subjective, nebulous job."

As the year progressed and the managers' interpersonal judgment improved, we saw how they gained self-confidence. With this increased self-assurance they could be less defensive and more open in their interactions; it freed them to delegate work to their subordinates:

> I had to trust my intuition and be willing to confront people. It took strength to enter into the fray; there were so many uncertainties and conflicts. Many times I wanted to run off scared, the risks seemed so high.

If they did not feel self-confident, they found themselves shirking the immense responsibilities of the new position:

> I was the guy running the show. I had to be ready to share the credit and take the heat. At first, when I had to ask my people to do something I knew they wouldn't like, I would blame it on my boss. Stupid and cowardly—what can I say? I didn't want to be the bad guy.

It was the new managers' responsibility to their subordinates, not the organization, that most oppressed them:

> [Discussing the decision on whether to fire a subordinate] You're making a million-dollar decision for the company when you consider the life span of the employee, and that is a tough decision. But what really makes it tough is that you get to know the person fairly well and you know he has a wife and two children and owns a home and has debt like the rest of us. You are saying, "Look, you aren't cutting it." And you are assaulting their self-image and threatening their whole life-style.
>
> I had to accept responsibility for my people's lives and future prospects. That they were in my hands was hard to swallow.

As they were forced to engage in intense and demanding interpersonal interactions, the managers grew the calluses necessary to cope with them. Firing employees above all taught them to adopt a tough and unsentimental attitude. They were rightfully worried that in time this "thick skin" might shield them from emotion. They had to maintain their humanity if they were to be effective people managers.

The managers knew from the start that they were not especially patient; salespeople are inclined to prefer action and the short run. That tendency was an asset for them as producers, but as managers was a liability. They grew to understand that "coming on like gangbusters" was not always the best idea. They also saw why subordinates had been taken aback by the speed with which the managers tried to introduce new policies and practices. Asked at the end of the year how he would advise other new managers, one replied:

> I guess I would have to say, Sit back and listen. A momentum was building before you came; if it was damaged, it's damaged, and you're not going to fix it in a month. If it's undamaged, it probably won't get damaged in that short a time. Take the time to sit back and listen and establish a routine for yourself. Take it as slow as possible. I think people approach the job the same way I did. "I'm just so excited about it. I'm ecstatic about it. I'm going to just get in there and do all these things." That attitude is nice, but it is wrong.

A second manager came to a similar conclusion:

> Take ninety days to see what you have. It takes that long to get behind the numbers and see if your winners are really winners and your losers really losers (they could have lousy territories). Hold off interviewing for the first ninety days; you won't even know what you should be looking for. Say to yourself, I'll take ninety days to see what I have here. You also need that time to figure out the politics in the place; who talks to whom, what is your best entrée to the grapevine.

Similarly, the managers learned that acting impulsively was wrong for a manager, because everybody was paying attention to him or her. Because they had to live with the consequences of their actions, they were less likely to "shoot from the hip":

> Tread carefully. Do a lot of listening. When you're asked for an opinion, give the appearance of reflecting before you come back with the opinion. If people think you are too spontaneous, they don't think you have put enough thought into it. I learned this trick from another manager. Before he answered a question, he would pick up a cigarette. He would force himself to take at least the time it took to light the cigarette and set it in the ashtray to review the alternatives.

Having the patience to listen and being a good listener were defined as critical mangerial tools:

> You are going to hear a lot of half-truths. You've got to listen carefully to tell what is real.
>
> I wasn't the best listener, and I paid for it. On the one side, I was naive and took almost everything people said as gospel. I should have asked more questions, probed to understand exactly what it was they were trying to achieve. I had some interesting scenarios that were built in the first three months by people jockeying for position and trying to appear that they were the best and could do no wrong.
>
> I was surprised to find that one of my biggest weaknesses was that I didn't listen. I make up my mind before people come in and so I don't really let them speak their mind. . . . I'm still not really good at it, but I've admitted it to my people and told them to learn to yell louder.

A skill related to patience and listening was the ability to empathize. The new managers, over the year, realized how limiting it was to use themselves as models for predicting how others would interpret stituations or respond to their actions. They had greatly improved their ability to understand another person's point of view. Empathy was crucial for managing diversity among subordinates. If the managers were to find an approach suited to a subordinate, they had to understand that person's perspective: "You have to be able to climb into their shoes. You can't stay on your side of the desk. You have to have the ability to crawl inside them to figure out what motivates them."

A stereotype about salespeople is that they are highly emphatic; because they are able to "read" others, they can invent sales strategies that appeal to a client's needs. But one of the managers made this interesting observation about the difference between understanding a client and a subordinate:

> With clients you have to decide quickly, in one or two meetings of twenty minutes or so, what you think of them. You make quick, almost snap, judgments. You're constantly reading people. You can't judge so quickly when trying to read your own people. You need to really get to know what they're like, because you'll have to trust them. It can't be superficial.

By the end of the year the managers were learning to live with ambiguity, for managing people meant living with imperfect solutions. Human problems in organizations were not like technical problems. They found no clearly right and wrong answers in dealing with people. Every decision or action led to a suboptimal solution from any one perspective. Management involved balancing or synthesizing many conflicting objectives (such as managerial control and development of subordinates). Fundamentally, one manager said,

> Most managers want to think with either their head or their heart. To be really good you have to think with both. If you think with your head, you'll be dominant, aggressive, boom, boom, boom. The person who thinks with the heart is Miss Milquetoast—nice, nice, nice. The head person loves confrontation. The heart person hates it. Run it like a business—think with your head. But realize you're dealing with people—think with your heart. It's a balancing act, and you don't want to slip too far off in any direction.

This manager is on his way to adopting what Sayles, an authority on management and leadership, calls a "creatively integrative" approach to management—realizing that organizational life is not black or white, but rather consists of many shades of gray.[12]

When asked to reflect at year's end on their personal growth, the new managers were pleasantly surprised by how much they had developed. They were justifiably proud of their accomplishment: "I can't guarantee that I can deliver results from my people, but I *know* I've become a better person."

Becoming managers had given most of the new managers a chance to discover inner strengths, the qualities of the managerial character. As Kaplan, among others, comments, as adults confront new challenges and new roles, some change in personality and character is not only possible but is often required for survival.[13]

CONCLUDING REMARKS

Many studies tell us that, to be effective, a manager must have a balanced view of his or her motivations, abilities, and limitations. From the challenges and hardships they encountered, the new managers gained invaluable insight into who they were and what they were capable of. They acquired a more comprehensive and balanced view of both their motivation and their ability. Many discovered the intrinsic satisfactions (such as the fulfillment that comes of developing people and solving complex problems) associated with managerial work. At the beginning of the year they had been aware primarily of the extrinsic rewards (additional pay, status). They later found out about both managerial deficiencies and strengths. The former at first grossly outweighed the latter. But as they acquired managerial competence, the balance began to shift. As we have seen in this and earlier chapters, the managers learned a great deal in a very short time.

All the managers could point to things they had come to know about themselves and ways in which they had matured. And most were beginning to be transformed so that they would feel, value, and think more like a manager. The fundamental shift in their self-concepts was well under way. Some compared becoming a manager to such seminal experiences as getting married or having a child. Anthropologists describe such experiences as "status passages," ritualized occasions when an individual's being is transformed in the eyes of the culture.

The new managers still had much to do. In the years to

come they had much to learn about themselves; their managerial identity was just beginning to take hold. They still mourned the loss of their old identity. They would need more time and experience to discover if they would truly feel comfortable with their new identity and if they possessed the managerial character. Each still had to find too the managerial style that best suited him or her and work to shape the environment to meet their talents and needs. Of course, even very experienced managers do not always achieve such integration between professional identity and role. Perhaps if we understood more about the complexities of major career transitions, like the one researched here, we could help more managers do so (in Chapter 9, we return to this issue).

NOTES

1. Schein (1987) makes this observation:

> The difficulty is particularly acute in the occupation of "management," because of the difficulty of simulating some of the key skills and abilities. Until one actually feels the responsibility of committing large sums of money, of hiring and firing people, of saying "no" to a valued subordinate, one cannot tell whether one will be able to do it, or, even more important, whether one will like doing it (p. 158).

The early years in an occupation are a crucial time for learning, both about the occupation and about oneself in relation to the work's demands. People often come to a job with many misconceptions about the work and themselves. With experience on the job, testing, and feedback, we can gain critical insight into the work and our interests and aptitudes. Moreover, as Schein documented in a classic study of career development, as our lives progress and we have the opportunity to make career choices, our self-concept matures. Self-concept refers to individuals' assumptions about their areas of competence, motives, and values. With experience, an individual's self-concept moves from being vague and impressionistic to being more refined and grounded in reality. With this self-concept, we make career choices that are consistent with our perceptions of ourselves:

> Dominant themes emerge: a critical skill or ability that one really wants to exercise, an important need one has discovered, a crucial value that dominates one's orientation toward life (p. 185).

2. Some of the new managers actually took a reduction in pay when they first became managers. In both companies the star producer could make more than

the new manager. Only the exceptional star producer, however, made more than the manager with more years.

3. The managers in the computer company were more eager to move into the senior ranks than those in the financial services firms.

4. See McClelland and Burnham (1976).

5. For example, Levinson et al. (1978) observed:

> In this period a man has two major tasks: (a) He tries to *establish a niche* [author's emphasis] in society; to anchor his life more firmly, develop competence in a chosen craft, become a valued member of a valued world. (b) He works at *making it* [author's emphasis]: striving to advance, to progress on a timetable. I use the term "making it" broadly to include all efforts to build a better life for oneself and to be affirmed by the tribe (p. 59).

6. For example, Freedman (1972) observed an analogous phenomenon in his work on physicians who became administrators. Their peers saw their administrative responsibilities as unprofessional and of limited value.

7. Career transitions are times of increased personal awareness and change. Although there has been considerable controversy over the nature and extent of adult development, there is growing evidence that major career transitions are linked to changes in people's identities. In an intriguing empirical study of job change and the adjustment, Nicholson and West (1988) came to this conclusion:

> Our view is broad, embracing both the minor and the fundamental parameters of identity. It can be supposed, for example, that through job change people may acquire any or all of the following: new behaviors and habits, different ways of relating to other people, fresh attitudes and values, altered intellectual or cognitive capacities, and re-formed personality traits or dispositions (p. 117).

They conclude that the job changes including altered social relationships, such as functional promotions within the organization, were linked with personality change. Nicholson and West contend that psychologists have underrated the responsiveness of the self to the environment and its proactive capacity to create change.

Klerman (1969) came to a similar conclusion in his work on physicians who were becoming administrators: "promotion may thus lead to enduring changes in ego structure, self-image, and professional identity" (p. 412).

8. Schein (1987) describes the career anchor of technical and functional competence as one in which a person's sense of identity is built around the content of their work, the technical or functional skill in which they excel. Most careers start out being technical or functional. In the early phases the individual is expected to develop a specialty (p. 160).

9. See Kaplan (1990) and Hall (1986).

10. Their list looks remarkably like those of researchers who have studied this subject. Schein (1987) defined it as emotional competence and McCall et al. (1988) labeled it executive temperament. They identified six characteristics: "being tough when necessary; self-confidence; coping with situations beyond

your control; persevering through adversity; coping with ambiguous situations; and use (and abuse) of power'' (p. 84).

11. See Zaleznik and Kets de Vries (1975) and Levinson (1968).

12. Sayles (1989) identified five levels of managerial cognitive development: rigid, simplistic; adversarial; supersales-oriented; compromising; and creatively integrative (p. 267).

13. Kaplan (1990).

7

Coping with the Stresses and Emotions

I never knew a promotion could be so painful.

We end this chronicle of the new managers' transformation tasks by discussing stress and emotion, for the sentiment in the epigraph expresses a theme in their experience. They were anxious about how much they would like and how well they would perform the new job. Mostly they looked forward to the promotion with excitement and optimism. Like many who have strong needs for achievement and personal growth, the managers actively welcomed the stresses brought by change and increased challenge as an opportunity for personal development. As they soon discovered, however, the stresses were greater and more debilitating than they had imagined.

Most managers reported some psychological or physical symptoms that they attributed to the transition. It was clearly a time of emotional upheaval, as revealed by a number of uncomfortable disclosures. Many commented that they were reluctant to mention the extent of their upset, even to their spouses. Some spoke of insomnia, low-grade headaches, back pain, and increased arguments:

> The pressure was intense for the first six months of the job. What a pressure cooker! I could feel it here [the manager rubbed the back of his neck]. Some days it felt like my head would burst. At the end of the day I had to get out of the building and run it off. I ran and ran.
>
> From the first week I started suffering from insomnia. I woke up every two hours or so even though I was so exhausted. It felt like I was in a crisis, a trial by fire.
>
> I've been losing weight. In some ways, it's good. I've been wanting to get rid of this excess baggage [indicating his paunch]. I can't keep anything down. My wife is getting worried; I've even been leaving dessert.
>
> My wife complains that I'm not there for her these days and she and the kids are trying to adjust to life in the Midwest, which is almost like moving to a foreign land. [The manager and his family had relocated from a New York suburb.] It is so much more conservative. I'll admit I'm preoccupied and snappy all the time. I've got to worry about whether I'm going to make it; if not, we'll be moving again.

An early, major order of business was learning to cope with the stresses and intense emotions of becoming a manager. The two sources of stress were those associated with the transformation itself and those inherent in their new role. The former began to subside as the managers progressed through the year; the latter, however, would remain. At the end of this chapter, we will briefly consider how these stresses affected managers' lives outside work.

STRESSES OF TRANSFORMATION

A growing literature deals with the stresses in career transitions. One aim in this research was to identify the aspects of job changing that are especially threatening and how people cope with them. In fact, most people find changing jobs stressful. They report some anxiety and frustration; that is, feelings that their responses to new demands are inadequate. When the individual instigates the career move, the stresses and anxieties are generally viewed as short-lived and tolerable, a prerequisite for getting the rewards and benefits. Most people are energized and motivated by low to moderate amounts of stress. Much evidence shows, however, that excessive anxiety and frustration inhibit adjustment and cause underachievement.[1]

Although they had elected to become managers, many initially found the stresses of the transition to be overwhelming and bewildering. Interestingly, Nicholson and West, studying job change, found that "the *most* [their emphasis] stressful job changes are those which involve an upward status move and no change of employer."[2] The managers in this study found the discontinuity between being an individual contributor and being a manager much greater than anticipated: "the change is so stark."[3] As we have seen, they experienced much performance anxiety. For the first time in their careers, many of them faced the possibility of failure. The pressures to perform were immense and their careers were on the line:

> They expect me to hit the ground running. I want to do the job well, but I'm so afraid that I'll fail. It's the biggest fear I've ever had and I know I won't be graceful about it if I do.
> It is important to me to be good at what I do. I have to feel that I'm making a difference. These days sometimes I feel like I shouldn't accept my paycheck.
> The company has lost a dynamite marketing rep and gained a weak manager.

The new managers wondered how, or if, they would ever master the new position. They were humbled to discover how ill-prepared they were. Argyris describes how difficult high achievers find it to cope with the fear of failure.[4] He finds they never develop a tolerance for the feelings of shame and guilt that accompany failure or the skills to deal with them.

The managers not only struggled with anxiety about their performance, but they also grappled with what it felt like to be undergoing a change of identity. They reported feelings of marginality, of being betwixt and between. They found "changing from" as traumatic as "changing to." As portrayed in Chapter 6, the promotion to manager was a mixed blessing because it forced the managers out of the specialty with which they identified. They lost their sense of mastery and of who they were.[5]

Paradoxically, as the managers gained insight into their new role and who they were, the transition became more stressful. It might be expected that with learning would come predictability, generally a major reducer of stress. But one manager said, "Ignorance is bliss. Once I knew what I had gotten myself into, I knew just how much trouble I was in." The managers did come to see that acquiring managerial competence actually meant sacrificing some of their technical competence. As they learned to delegate, their technical knowledge and ability grew obsolescent. As documented in Chapter 6, the transformation to manager meant losing not only a sense of mastery and control, but also concrete feedback, instant gratification, recognition, and autonomy. Only as they acquired some of the critical management skills and attitudes, hence the belief that they could control some of the "predictable chaos" of being a manager, did the stresses of transformation finally begin to subside. The stresses inherent in the managerial role remained, though.

STRESSES IN THE MANAGERIAL JOB

The managers eventually realized that many stresses would not be short-lived, but were here to stay. These pressures were built into the managerial job and could exhaust and paralyze if not confronted. To be effective managers, they had to learn how to cope with them and the attendant emotions.[6] This adaptation entailed developing the managerial character outlined in Chapter 6. The managers had to attain the "emotional competence" that Schein describes. He explains why learning to cope with managerial stresses lay at the core of the transformation to manager:

> The most difficult aspect of the general manager's job is to keep functioning day after day without giving up, getting an ulcer, or having a nervous breakdown. The essence of the general manager's job is to absorb the emotional strains of uncertainty, interpersonal conflict, and responsibility. It is this

190

aspect of the job that often repels the technically/functionally anchored individual but excites and motivates the managerially anchored individual. This is what makes the job meaningful and exciting.[7]

The managers had to learn to cope with four stresses: role strain, negativity, isolation, and the burden of leadership responsibility. We consider each of these in turn.

Role Strain

A number of sources of role strain are built into the managerial role: overload, ambiguity, and conflict. In Chapter 2 we saw how the new managers discovered and reacted to these characteristics, and in the literature we find many examples of their adverse effects. When they act in concert, the individual soon begins to feel stretched to the limit. The new managers did find that their new positions made excessive demands. They had too much work to do in too little time with imperfect information and limited resources. They were responsible for "too many things," some of which seemed contradictory (such as increasing revenues but holding down costs). And they had to answer to too many people: subordinates, customers, superiors, and peers:

> The dilemma of the first-line manager is that you have reps reporting to you who pull you in a dozen directions. And you have the second line of management coming down on you. You've got all the people-management and staff responsibilities, but still you have all the tactical things with customers, marketing strategies, and all.

The managers came to appreciate the tremendous investment of time and energy management took: "It's no wonder the top managers in this firm are workaholics." Most claimed they were working at least sixty hours a week. They spent time in the evenings and on weekends to catch up with unfinished chores:

> I've been running 200 percent. I couldn't be much busier. I've been pumping iron and taking vitamins to try to keep in

shape. To keep that mental edge, I've got to maintain the physical one. My father [a senior executive in a large company] had a heart attack. Now, I see why. I'm going to have to find some time to get away soon, or things will be in shambles. I'm getting sluggish.

I get up at 6:00 and I'm in here by 7:30. I stay until 8:00 or 8:30 every night. There is no time for life outside [the company].

At first the managers thought adjusting to the managerial demands was a matter of acquiring managerial skills and that it was "a time management proposition"; "it's a big job to get your arms around." In fact, time management was crucial, but it did not solve the problem. The new managers had to learn to live with the pace, brevity, and interruptions.

A lot of days, I'm in here early and out late. Still, I accomplish *nothing* that I was supposed to accomplish. I have so many interruptions and have to keep shifting my priorities. By the end of the day I feel drained, with nothing to show for all my work.

They had to learn to live with imperfection. Their time could not be neatly planned and controlled. And as described in Chapter 2, they had to realize that all managerial decisions were imperfect, requiring compromises among competing interests. They also had to learn how to handle their ignorance. They could not possibly be experts on the many issues they confronted in a day. They had to weigh options and make trade-offs with limited and perhaps inadequate evidence: "The desire to be right is a stumbling block in a way. You've got to make timely decisions, so you have to suboptimize most times." These were the strains and realities of managerial work.

Negativity

The managers were surprised to discover what they uniformly referred to as the "negativity" associated with being a manager:

I think the biggest surprises are the problems. Maybe I had never seen it before. Maybe I was protected by my management when I was in sales. Maybe I had delusions of grandeur. I don't really know, I just know how disillusioning and frustrating it is to be hit with problems and conflicts all day and not be able to solve them very cleanly.

It seems like everybody just stops by your desk, if they find themselves walking by, and point out something that is wrong. "Let me tell you something that really pisses people off about you." "I can't get this done or that done." It's a constant flow. "My typewriter doesn't work." "I think he [a fellow broker] is churning his account; you could get fired for that." When someone walks in and shuts the door, you say, "Oh boy, here it comes. What is it this time?"

You get shell shock from the negativity aspect. People just keep coming in with their problems. I'm amazed at the negativity on the job, Eighty percent or so of the time people are coming in to see you for negative reasons: they're trying to throw the problem in your lap or they want your help solving it. Let's see what the new kid on the block can do.

The new managers at first experienced negativity on the job as "a conspiracy against [them]," "egomaniac marketing types trying to test [them]." In time, they realized that the culprit was just managerial work.

As discussed earlier, the managers had to learn that their subordinates were not all as motivated or competent as they themselves had been as salespeople. Thus, a major managerial responsibility was dealing with the problem employee. And managing the problem employee inspired negative emotions in both the manager and the subordinate: fear, anxiety, frustration, and anger:

> I'm enthusiastic and idealistic. I have a strong work ethic. I have a high degree of integrity. My biggest weakness was my lack of sympathy or tolerance for incompetence. I didn't respond well to the negative traits people had. I'd write them off a little bit, as whiners or stupid.
>
> Sales have been off this quarter, and so the reps are not happy. They have personal problems because they do not have the cash flow. They're working long hours, but they're not

making money. They are complaining, looking for a scapegoat, and always asking for more support. They need more of your time—strokes—because they want to do well and are embarrassed. But you can't give them sales recognition or money because they aren't meeting quota. Still, you've got to figure out how to stroke them and at the same time say, "Hell, it's not working. Have you tried this?" You get the crap from the bottom and squeezed from the top sometimes.

The managers also had to learn not to classify all subordinates who came to them with problems as problem employees; "they [subordinates] don't seem very resourceful." If managers and subordinates were doing their jobs correctly, subordinates should, in fact, come to the manager only with problems they could not solve alone. By the time a problem reached a manager, it would by definition be very delicate or recalcitrant:

They [subordinates] should be coming to me for exceptions, not for the routine. That's their job. That means only the big hummers land on my desk.

Fifty percent of this job is going to be firefighting and problem solving. That is the way it is. They [subordinates] have tried to solve a problem at their level and can't. Once it comes to you it is a big problem and you have to drop everything and attend to it.

Isolation

I'm no longer one of the boys. No one asks me out for lunch. No one gossips with me. I'm alone.

Although most managers described themselves as craving independence and self-reliance, they also reported that they were gregarious; they enjoyed interacting with others. Customer contact and warm relationships with colleagues had been important sources of satisfaction for many of them. As managers they found themselves isolated. A major challenge was coping with loneliness.

A sense of isolation often follows a career transition. Barnes points out that the roots of the isolation run deep.[8] During times of transition, people feel lost as they find themselves without a clear reference group by which to identify appropriate values and norms. Barnes unerringly describes the transition to management. Much has been written about the first-line manager's especially intense feelings of anomie and isolation:

> A significant source of this anxiety is that the technologist is being taken off the top of the heap and put on the bottom of another heap. Instead of being the superstar technologist, he now is the newest supervisor who does not know the ropes. The whole heap is now piled on top of him. This dilemma is known as the "heap reversal theory." It creates feelings of alienation, loneliness, and uncertainty about whether switching to management was a wise decision in the first place.[9]

The new managers were well aware of the "heap reversal theory":

> I'm in a different fraternity now. I know that I'm now part of the management team. But I don't feel like a manager. I still feel like one of those guys [pointed out to the boardroom]. I feel like I'm in no-man's land.
>
> Even the geography bothers me. I'm uncomfortable sitting on this side of the desk. I'd rather be out on the floor where I'm used to being. All of a sudden I'm in a different position.

These feelings were particularly acute for the branch managers in the securities firms. As the only branch manager in their unit and physically separated from their new peer group, they were indeed "out on a rowboat alone in the middle of the ocean."

Making decisions that were unpopular with their subordinates, the managers felt even more isolated. They had lost their nice-guy image simply because of their authority:

> I detect animosity and threat. I guess I have to expect that, now that I'm the boss; I felt that way about my boss to a certain extent. But it still hurts that people don't trust me; that they don't feel comfortable even shooting the breeze with me. They won't talk to you about what they really think. They're always censoring. You can see them dancing around you. It is the first time I've felt that people distrust me.

For the two who had become sales managers in the branch office where they had been producers, the sense of loneliness was coupled with a strong sense of personal rejection. People who had been peers now seemed to avoid them.

However much they hated the loneliness, in some ways the new managers exacerbated the problem by their behavior. Many experienced "strong impulses to build a fence around [themselves]" to give them some "space" between themselves and the job's negativity:

> For self-protection—I just didn't want to hear any more bad news—I would tell my secretary to hold my calls, go into my office, and shut the door and take a breather from all the tension.
>
> In some ways I didn't want to get attached, too friendly. The rejection would only hurt more then.

In fact, as we saw in Chapter 4, the managers had to learn to detach themselves from their subordinates, for they had to be able to make the unpleasant but proper decisions. The managers also compounded their dilemma. They had many ties in the larger organization, friends and past coworkers from whom they could seek support and companionship. Many were unwilling to do so, however, especially in the first months. They feared their anxiety about their new positions would "seep out."

> I'm really not too excited about talking to my old buddies. They think I'm having a grand old time. If they knew the truth, they'd think I was weak or maybe even a fraud. I got promoted too fast or something. For the time being, I'm keeping my own counsel.

Their insecurities too often robbed the managers of invaluable support, just when they needed it most. But they were not as alone as they imagined: we return to supportive relationships in Chapter 8.

Burdens of Leadership

The managers were learning about the burdens of leadership, the stress of being the person with ultimate authority and responsibility. The strain, the negativity, the isolation all came with the territory. Management was a "perpetual preoccupation, impossible to escape," no matter how hard they tried. In the interviews, three themes stood out: managing risk, being a role model, and having power over people's lives.

Managing risk. The managers came to understand that management was a job of managing risks—business risks and people risks. Making important decisions under such imperfect conditions required confidence, strong will, and being comfortable with exercising power and influence:[10]

> You have to be willing to put your ego on the line if you're going to work through people. You have to be willing to be in the forefront. You might be verbally or emotionally abused, but you have to be the opposite of a wallflower and still do it with tact and style.

> Every day you put yourself on the line. You try to do the right thing. You may work hard to develop a rep; you think it's a good investment of your time. And she turns around and leaves the firm anyway or is just a slob and can't catch on. Or, what about compliance? Someone else does something wrong, but you lose your job. Like when you have the Boy Scout troop at your house and you know someone is peeing in the pool, but you don't know which one. Well, the firm expects you to figure it out and take care of it, even though it's nearly impossible. That's my biggest frustration, but I have to learn to live with it.

And a woman manager described her challenge:

> I've had to build my confidence. It is still difficult at times. I think one of the perceptions for myself was, Here I am, this woman who always believed that I should be with a family and home and children and a husband, the kit 'n caboodle. All of a sudden I am faced with making decisions for a lot of people. I am standing up in front of a group of men and telling them that they should be doing this or that or the other. That has been something to learn to deal with. It is a process of development, which is getting better and better. I'm growing into my manager shoes.

The majority of new managers did grow and mature. They came to accept many of their limitations, ignorance, and mistakes. Almost all scaled down expectations of themselves that were unrealistic. They became more comfortable with exercising power and influence. Toward the end of the year, one manager made this statement about himself:

> Now, I'm a firm believer in making a decision and getting on with doing something. I can't allow for paralysis by analysis. I found out I could sit and study something forever and never get anywhere. It's easier to change the direction of a rolling ball than of a ball that's sitting still. If you make a decision and start going down the path and say, "Hey, that's wrong. I blew this one; this is what we've got to do to fix it and get back on course." It's much easier to do that than it is to be back at the starting line and try to get going that way. I'm more decisive and willing to admit I'm wrong.
>
> It is far better to be proactive in doing something and make mistakes than do nothing and be safe. I've learned to live with the risks of visibility on this job.
>
> I'm not on top of the products like I used to be. Now I see my reps don't expect me to make a technical product call. I know it is not to my detriment to admit I don't know. I'm not reluctant to ask questions that might reveal my ignorance. I thought I had to be larger than life; now I know folks want you just to be "real people."
>
> My motto: Be up front and admit mistakes and bad decisions. They won't diminish your power in the office if you do it right. Remember, they very seldom put you in jail. They can only fire you, and that is not the end of the world.

The managers were gaining confidence in their ability to take calculated risks as well as handle the emotions of living with those risks.

Being a role model. The managers soon discovered their management responsibilities as role models. Their actions touched people with lasting consequences. They could no longer afford to bend the rules or "work in the gray areas" as when they were producers. The need for prudence was not what they found most burdensome, however. The demand they found most difficult was the need to manage their emotions. In the office, they must appear enthusiastic and optimistic. Subordinates looked to them for confidence, especially in trying times:

You can't be pessimistic on the job. The amount of your enthusiasm translates directly into how your people feel and how much effort they put into the job. I am accused of coming in with a smile and a cheery disposition almost every morning. They grumble about that. But if I don't seem happy about myself and the job, it makes them nervous. They start asking me if the ship is rapidly disintegrating. They don't want me to be bigger than life, but they don't expect to see me in the doldrums, either.

The managers had to be careful in expressing anger, anxiety, and frustration, portraying maturity and professionalism and a sense of serenity:

When I was a broker and I had a bad day, I'd let everybody know it. I'm a very emotional person and I couldn't hide my frustration easily. People would commiserate with me, "Yeah, yeah, it's a bad time. The market is going crazy." And I'd start to feel better. Now, I see a different expression in their faces. You can actually see how upset it makes them in their faces: "Should we have confidence in you?"

Be like a duck—on the surface calm and serene and underneath paddle like hell.

Their subordinates looked to the managers for cues on how to behave when they were under stress:

If they see you ranting and raving, then they think that is an okay way to behave when they're frustrated; it can quickly get out of hand. You have to teach them through your behavior what it means to be a professional. You can't take things personally all the time and just let out your feelings. You've got to model for them how to handle conflicts like a professional—get the issues out on the table and look at them objectively; don't be a prima donna.

The managers came to appreciate over time just how far-reaching their actions were:

The way I smile or frown when I'm walking around affects everybody in the office and in turn affects their spouses and kids.

Having power over people's lives. As the managers learned how much power and influence they had over their subordinates' work and their lives, their responsibilities weighed heavily:

> Making judgments about people, people's lives. I lay awake at night. It's tough to make a decision that is going to affect a person's whole career.
>
> I was looking at a picture of myself, taken a year or so ago. I didn't have all these gray hairs.

The managers found two kinds of people decisions most difficult. The first was taking disciplinary action of any sort. In Chapter 5, we saw how unsettling and sobering it was for managers to have to fire a subordinate: "It's terrible when you care about people. You know he has a young daughter. He has plans. But you've given him every warning, and he is still not cutting it."

The managers had devoted a great deal of time and effort to working with the subordinates they eventually fired, and had gotten to know them intimately: "I became his psychiatrist, in a way; his personal problems and work problems were so intertwined." The managers took subordinates' failures personally. They took subordinates' departures of all sorts as emotional experiences:

> The difficulty comes when the truly unexpected happens. Someone you've grown to like and respect decides to leave. The personal hurt when somebody wants to go elsewhere; you didn't do something right.
>
> It takes a piece right out of you, even when you know it's a good opportunity for them. They can't pass it up. You can't help thinking, "Why can't I provide them with a chance like that?"

The second kind of decision the managers found most stressful involved balancing individual and group interests:

> I couldn't give him what he wanted [a very successful broker with only two years on the job had asked for additional secretarial support]. It wasn't an unreasonable request. His secretary was overworked. But I had to think about the effect

on the group. Others too could have used more help and were as deserving in a lot of ways. But if you give it to one person, you don't have it to give to someone else. You've got to keep the big picture in mind.

The managers had never been forced to consider that individual and group interests could be in direct conflict. Again, they were required to make trade-offs that clearly implicated a "flesh and blood" person.

As stated in Chapter 1, the managers embarked on their new careers focusing on the rights and privileges of management. They learned all too well that rights and privileges brought even more duties and responsibilities.

New Managers' Personal Lives

How did their promotion change the new managers' personal lives? They spoke little about life outside the organization despite my efforts to engage them in conversation about it. They did not "feel like they had a life outside."

For the first half of the year the managers were, in fact, intent on mastering their new roles. Many reported neglecting their family life: "The company culture is that work performance comes first; no excuses. You have to work at a high level no matter what pressure you feel at home."

They expressed their guilt at "abandoning the family just when they need me most." All but two managers had relocated when promoted. Although their spouses had agreed to the move, most had been unhappy to do so.

Not only did the new managers feel they neglected their family lives, they ignored their need for leisure and relaxation. One manager described himself as a "speck engulfed by work" and drew this diagram of "self, family, and the job":

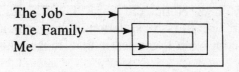

The managers had very little time to enjoy themselves in the early months. Most came to realize that leading such an imbalanced life led to dire consequences. They needed "time to stop and smell the roses." Some did force themselves to take time off from work. A few had been exercising religiously for many years. Despite frequently disrupted schedules, they took advantage of any opportunity to exercise.

The promotion to management affected both their professional and personal self-concepts. Many were surprised to find themselves reappraising their values and personal and professional commitments; "What is really important to me?" "What counts in life?" By the end of the year the managers were beginning to sort out their professional and personal goals. Choosing to become a manager was, one stated, "a life decision":

> I've got to maintain a balance between my personal life and my work life—achievement and happiness. Nothing can really be more important to me than my family, my little boy. I can't just squeeze them in in my spare time. . . . After this interview I think I'll go home. My son has a little-league game that I told him I wouldn't make. Why can't I? What's so important here?

Not without apprehension, the manager chose to go home and see the family. Research suggests that it is not easy for managers to acknowledge their own needs and figure out how to balance their personal and professional obligations.[11]

CONCLUDING REMARKS

By the end of the year the new managers had not mastered their new role, but most felt they could make it, some with more confidence than others. They still had their really bad days, one of them said, when they wondered yet again if they would ever feel on top of things. Notice the word "feel." Studies show that those who perceive stressful situations as opportunities that can be mastered cope with them better than those who view them as threats.[12] Indeed, we have seen time and again the interplay between the new managers' emotions and behavior. When the managers felt insecure or defensive, they regressed to the familiar and comfortable role of producer.

It had been a year of hardship and self-doubt, but for the most part the new managers had persevered. The stresses of transformation were beginning to subside. Of course the stresses inherent in the managerial role persisted, but most no longer felt debilitated by them. As we saw in discussing managerial character, many were pleased to discover internal resources they never knew they had. The confidence they gained by enduring and coping with the year's many stresses was immeasurable. "This year has left me with the strength of maturity. I've found out what I am made of."

The managers were learning how to cope with situations beyond their control, a foundation for their future career. McCall et al. found that experienced executives' early experiences at work played a critical role in their later career development:

> Successfully meeting their first challenges at work gave some of these future executives a shot of self-confidence. Even if they weren't five years of keeping an oil field running without blowing it up, early jobs could result in a strong sense of self that helped them approach much tougher assignments later in their careers with a can-do spirit.[13]

Why do people choose to become managers, to lead others? Management is a tough job to do well even under the best circumstances because of the demands and personal commitment required. Most managers in this study were acquiring the foundation to meet these challenges. For, as described in the Introduction, this has been a story about success, of human resiliency and capacity to learn. Their superiors felt all but three of the new managers had done a solid job in their first year. Just how effective and successful they would be as managers in the long term, only time would tell.

NOTES

1. See Sutton and Kahn (1987) and Feldman and Brett (1983), who summarized the work on stress and job change:

> If increased uncertainty and change are key variables that create stress in new jobs, then increased predictability and control are the key goals of coping strategies. When people feel they have little hope of reducing uncertainty or reasserting control, they are much more likely to develop feelings of helplessness and depression. . . . Most employees also want to be able to reestablish routines that are predictable, regain their confidence about performing well on their new jobs, and reaffirm their sense of personal control in the work setting (p. 289).

2. Nicholson and West (1988), p. 105.
3. Benedict (1989) introduced role discontinuity to describe the lack of order and sequence in the cultural role training of the life cycle. She attributed the stress of adolescence in the United States in part to the lack of role training. In cultures that provided training for responsibility and sexuality, she said, adolescence was a less tumultuous time.
4. Argyris (1991), p. 104.
5. Klerman and Levinson (1969) documented the emotions associated with "letting go" in his work on physician administrators:

> During this period, the Director-designate is engaged in what we shall call the *work of transition*. There are many other periods that have this quality of transition, of being at the boundary between two sharply contrasting life conditions. . . . The anticipation of performance and achievement is problematic during both stages. To a certain extent, the Director-designate is "playing at being the Director," just as the adolescent is "playing at being a man." The similarities are heightened by the fact that the adult man at about age forty is likely to be engaged in a personal developmental transition. . . . In all these transitions, the psychological work involves dynamics of loss and grief. One is required to give up important persons, group memberships, and modes of living. At the same time, new relationships and group memberships are being established and new commitments are being made (p. 423).

As found in my study, the new managers in Klerman's work showed symptoms of psychological difficulty:

> After an initial period of activity and exhilaration, Dr. P. noticed a period of depression with weight loss, fatigue, and poor sleep (p. 423).

6. Levinson (1987), a top leadership theorist and consultant, contended that the successful leader must learn how to manage his or her strongest emotions: aggression, affection, and dependency (p. 57).

7. Schein (1987), p. 167.
8. Barnes (1981), p. 18.
9. Badawy (1982), p. 71.
10. Having to make decisions in imperfect conditions probably was not as difficult for the managers in this study as it would be for a scientist or engineer making the transition. Medcoff (1985) observes:

> Given points out that technologists find it hard to make decisions when evidence is incomplete. They do not want to take the risks. Koplow also cites an excessive need for evidence when decisions must be made quickly. Managers must be prepared to make decisions frequently on the basis of inadequate evidence. This is counter to the training of scientists and engineers in which perfection and certainty are given high priority (p. 18).

11. See Kofodimos (1990).
12. For more on this issue, see Hill and Elias (1990), Kobasa (1979), and Lazarus and Feldman (1984).
13. McCall et al. (1988), p. 23.

IV

Managing the Transformation

The portrait of the transformational tasks the new managers confronted during the year is complete. Because they have been permitted to paint their own picture, we have come to appreciate the challenges they faced principally from their point of view. We now have a more textured understanding of what makes the promotion to management so difficult and why some with exceptional records as producers often fail to make the transition.

We next consider the implications of the new managers' tale: What can be done to help individuals make the move into management? Again, we begin by letting the managers speak for themselves. They remind us that you become a manager mainly by on-the-job learning. By grappling with real problems and facing real consequences they learned when they had to; that is, when confronted with circumstances they did not understand or did not know how to handle. By trial and error, observation and interpretation, and introspection they made sense of and learned from their experiences. The managers saw the year as primarily a personal sojourn, one they had to travel themselves: "No one can do it for you. And there are no short cuts. You have to live it."

They did have help along the way however. In Chapter 8, they share their insights about the resources on which they relied. These resources derived primarily from past and current experiences that were not deliberately planned for learning.

In Chapter 9, we explore ways in which the work of becoming a manager can be facilitated. Taking the new managers' experiences, we make recommendations for refocusing efforts in management development. Because the move to management requires transformation, though, no easy answers or quick fixes are provided. Instead, I suggest guidelines to help new managers *learn* how to learn from their experiences. Implications for practice are discussed for the managerial candidate and new manager and for those responsible for management development.

8

Critical Resources
for the First Year

I don't know how much you really can teach a person [about management]. It's like teaching someone how to ride a bike. You can go through the motions. You can understand perfectly well what it is you need to do—that you need to get on the bike, hold on to the handlebars, move your feet so that you turn the pedals just so, and go down the road to that tree over there. But that still doesn't teach you how to balance. How do you teach somebody that? I'm not sure. You can give them theory, you can give them a good feel for it, and work on the individual skills. But until they get on the bike and start riding it and fall down a couple of times themselves, they just can't know it.

As implied in this quotation, the new managers did have teachers who helped them learn how to be managers. In this chapter we consider the teachers—or, more accurately, resources—the new managers relied upon to help them cope with and master the challenges of the transformation. These resources comprised lessons from their careers and relationships they had established. We consider each in turn: career history (experiences as a producer), network of relationships, and formal training.[1]

CAREER HISTORY

The new managers' experience supplied the knowledge from which they acted and the framework from which they learned about their new circumstances. The specialized knowledge and skills they had gained about the business and the organization were critical assets they called upon to help them meet the year's many demands. These assets, mostly technical and functional "judgment and maturity," could be acquired only with experience:

> They [senior management] are thinking about hiring MBAs right out of school to be sales managers. And if they put them through a six-month training program they can learn enough about the business. I don't think so. You need intimate knowledge of the business, because it's about judgment that you absorb through experience. Besides, you need to feel confident about something. You don't know how to do the people side, and so at least you need to know the business side. Without the track record you won't have credibility with your people.

In his work on general managers, Kotter came to an analogous conclusion about the merits of internal promotion over external hiring to obtain executive talent:

> . . . Going for an outsider may be risky; an outsider may be very talented and may have an outstanding track record, but he will rarely have some of the characteristics that are absolutely needed to perform well. Specifically, he will rarely have a detailed knowledge of the business and organization and good, solid relationships with the large number of people upon whom the job makes him dependent. Under certain circumstances, a talented outsider can develop this knowledge and these relationships quickly enough to survive and do well; but most of the time, one probably cannot.[2]

Moreover, managers with more or varied experiences as producers (such as products, markets, and market conditions) argued that they had a distinct advantage:

> It's my heritage [that he had been a producer for ten years]. It gives me credibility with the reps. They say, "He has experience with both the up and down swings of the economy" versus "How can this guy tell me what to do?" They know I've probably seen it before. When they come for advice they feel they can trust me. This is especially important with the senior people.
>
> This gray hair lets everybody know that I've had a chance to mature—like a good wine. I know there is some substance here and they [his subordinates] know there is some substance here. There is no [technical] problem that is going to come up that I don't know how to grab on to and do something about.

Their years as producers had laid a solid technical grounding, upon which they were able to build managerial knowledge and skills and a managerial identity. Experience as producers provided three distinct but related resources for the new managers: technical expertise (specific to their particular organizational setting), critical for resolving the myriad technical problems that arose during the year; a source of self-confidence at a time when they were suffering with bouts of self-doubt; and credibility upon which they could build additional sources of power and influence.

The managers also relied heavily upon experiences that had provided opportunities to develop human and conceptual skills. These experiences included assignments such as product coordinator, overseer of sales meetings, trainer of inexperienced salespeople, and task-force member. The managers defined these experiences as opportunities to "play at management." A manager who in his last year as a broker had been put in charge of training new brokers considered the experience a turning point in his career. He attributed his decision to pursue a managerial career mainly to this experience. Not only had he honed his human and conceptual skills, he had discovered the satisfactions derived from such work:

It was a real challenge to figure out how to teach them what they needed to know. I really had to understand what selling was all about and then how to communicate it. When they made a good cold call or closed a deal, I was as excited as if I had done it myself.

Another manager, given coordinator responsibility for a large account team, felt that his transition to management was less "traumatic" than that of some of his cohorts because he was "used to dealing with lots of personalities and trying to get them to march to the same drummer." Managers who had been assigned to task forces or project work similarly saw these positions as helping develop their managerial competence and identity. The experiences helped them "think like a businessperson" and put decisions into broader contexts. McCall et al. found that project and task-force assignments were potent developmental experiences[3] with two major types of learning. They helped man-managers gain insight into the points of view of people in other functional areas and helped them become quick studies in unfamiliar territory.

The managers with more extensive experience working with the corporate or regional office also felt they had a richer and broader understanding of the managerial role. They found it easier to "take the organizational point of view." Indeed, they frequently referred to these experiences when trying to make sense of corporate policies or directives or in interpreting requests and complaints from their constituencies:

I've sat on their [the regional office] side of the table or should I say at the same table with them. I know where they are coming from—what their big headaches are with the branch.

The administrative guy was always worrying about the budget, the expense plan, while I was worrying about bringing in the revenues and servicing the customer. How much did that client dinner cost? Do you have to send the whole team to the site whenever there is a problem? Now that I'm the boss I'm the one whose butt is on the line if we are over budget.

The new managers in the securities firm seemed to have

more difficulty than their counterparts in the computer company in defining their place in the broader organization and distinguishing between thinking tactically and thinking strategically. In the computer company a conscious effort was made to expose potential managerial candidates to the corporate or regional offices and to senior executives. They "got to see how the senior guys think," gaining insights in corporate strategy and culture:

> They parade a lot of senior management through here and there is a tremendous opportunity to observe and to judge the good ones and the weak ones. I volunteered to pick them up at the airport and play host if their advance publicity was good. I got to eavesdrop on their informal conversations and often attend their presentations or meetings or whatever. I just watched the VP. How does he talk? How does he deal with people? What does he wear? I learned by observing the littlest details about what it takes to be successful around here.
>
> At the corporate office I got to watch fourteen managers very closely—intimately. I got a macro view of the world, not just the branch view.

But perhaps more important, because of the producer's task in the computer company (institutional sales and team selling approach), the new managers had more firsthand experience working with individuals from different functional areas and hierarchic levels of the company. They had had both the forum and the need to develop interpersonal skills (especially in empathy, influence, and negotiation) and conceptual facility (making sense of ambiguous and conflicting information and priorities, and living with imperfect solutions). Recall that the new managers in the computer company appeared to appreciate sooner than their securities firm counterparts the need to manage group as well as individual performance.

The producers in the securities firm were more autonomous. The sales task (primarily retail sales) did not require the producer to interact extensively with peers or superiors in the same or different functions. The new managers in the securities firm found the dependence associated with management more unsettling than did the new managers in the computer firm. They were "accustomed to working alone and being [their] own boss." Interestingly, the managers in the computer company found that being an authority figure with the final responsibility and accountability more unnerving than did those in the securities firm. The securities managers felt they were used to "stepping up to the plate," for they had always seen themselves as "entrepreneurs." In other words, experience influenced not only the knowledge and skills, but the attitudes toward work that the new managers brought to their new assignment.

NETWORK OF RELATIONSHIPS

If on-the-job experience was the quintessential teacher for the new managers, the second most important teacher was observing and interacting with coworkers: past and current bosses, past and current associates (principally peers). From these experiences the managers acquired not only important competencies, but also important values and attitudes, and instrumental and psychosocial support.[4]

Previous Bosses

The new managers relied heavily upon the vicarious learning gained from experiences with former bosses. When faced with a decision about a specific circumstance or when choosing a managerial style and philosophy, they reflected on these experiences. Exposure to a variety of past bosses seemed a great resource for the managers. McCall et al. found in their work that learning was hit-or-miss,[5] and, diverse experience proved valuable:

> You pick up bits and pieces from past managers. You look at how your bosses ran things and see a lot of different management styles. I like this and I like that. You try it out and sometimes totally rework it into your own style. Some things work and some things don't.
> I think that's why I have been really fortunate, being in the business as a sales rep as long as I was. Unlike some people who were reps for only two or three years and with

only one unit, I've been in a lot of branches. I've seen a lot of environments and a lot of managers. My style is an assimilation of the styles of my past managers, a composite of my experience. Two stand out in my mind. One got into things with you and helped you think through situations. He was an ally rather than someone who just gave you a raise or dealt with your upset customers. The second was the one who talked me into going into management. She helped me when I was going to have to miss an important retreat [at which he would have been exposed to senior management] and visited the customer [in another state] for me. She was sending a message that she was willing to help people. I still speak to her a lot.

The new managers commented that former bosses served as both positive and negative models. They recognized that all their past superiors had their strengths and weaknesses:

I remembered how controlling my boss was. He would never let me have control of my expenses. Oh, how I missed that. When I got a new boss who gave me the control, I was finally able to do my job. I had to ask myself, "Why aren't you giving them [his subordinates] more say about expenses?"

Well, [my third manager] was a guy who was technically very strong. But I think he was tremendously weak in personal relationships and his office morale was bad. I mean bad. He was tough and not as approachable as I think he should have been. I think about him a lot, though, when I am faced with technical problems. How would he handle them? And if I'm behind closed doors too much I think about what effect that had on me working for [my third manager].

The first manager that I had for quite some time was a very good planner and I learned from him the importance of planning and organization. My second manager was a person who should never have been a manager, and I think a lot of people recognized that. The last manager I had is now an assistant for one of the divisional vice presidents. He was the one who was most interesting, because we learned from each other. That is when I learned that it's a two-way street and there are certain things that you can learn from different people and vice versa. The one person I would call a role model that I have now, I don't condone everything he does or all his methodologies. But I hope I have the ability to develop the business sense he has and to be able to focus on an issue, to go through it in a very logical, business-like manner, and throw out the alternatives and make a decision. You look back and see that there is more than one way to skin a cat.

I won't say there is one mentor whom I really look up to and say, "Gosh, I want to emulate that fella." A couple of folks I've been around have some very good qualities. I've worked under bosses who were incredibly successful, but who had different philosophies. One crunched numbers; they were very important to him. The other believed you use money to enhance the business to get people to do the very best job for you. The other one thought the most important thing was good communications and rapport. He had superb presence in front of people. He got people excited and wanting to do things. You get to see all those different styles, their advantages and disadvantages. And so you can pick and choose and try to get the right mixture or balance.

From these quotations, we find that new managers learned different lessons from different bosses. What they learned depended upon whom they had encountered. As described in Chapter 5, they learned that they had to adopt styles and approaches that fit their personal competence, style, and values. Variety seemed to increase the probability that they had encountered a boss whose style and tactics they could emulate.[6]

Although the managers depended upon both positive and negative models from their past to help them cope with challenges in the first year on the job, it was the bosses they admired whom they reflected on most:

To learn from someone whom I admire and respect— how they think, how they act, how they deal with situations— those were the golden opportunities.

Good people and how they did their thing, how they got to where they were. The things they did that were right versus the things they did wrong, that again is hindsight. That is the luxury of observation. I don't recall for example sitting there and learning something. But I probably did. I do recall judging whether that person was good or bad. If a guy was a good bull-slinger, I could be conned, but by and large I was pretty good at judging. And when I found somebody who was really good I would try to probe why they were so good. I wouldn't ask them directly. Through observation I tried to find out what made them what they were. I tried to get into the mind of the manager to see the process he went through to make decisions. Occasionally, I asked them directly if it seemed appropriate.

He taught me a lot. It is hard to break down just what. He had an air about him that was highly professional and he conducted himself in a really first-class manner. He kept a distance between himself and his sales force. He taught me that. I don't believe in that really, keeping the fear there. But he taught me a lot about how the head man should carry himself.

Managers who had worked for one of the company legends—managers highly respected in the company—felt particularly blessed:

He was a master, one of the brightest and most perceptive people I've ever met. He had a tremendous reputation, one that he had earned. And I had the chance to learn from him. I was smart enough to realize that I didn't know everything and so I watched him carefully. And when I could I asked him questions.

I can't be him [a company legend who was a past boss]. If I had to be him I'd be in big trouble. He was one of the great men. I was so young when I worked for him that at the time I didn't appreciate what an opportunity I had. But I think back to him and aspire to steal some of his traits from him. I'd like to someday be able to communicate like him, to have his empathy. I'd like to think that with practice I might come close.

As part of this study, I interviewed some of the "company legends." Very few fully appreciated their profound influence on their junior colleagues. And certainly none viewed themselves as mentors to the new managers in this study.[7] Also, every legend devoted much time and energy to building their groups into high-performance teams. The managers who had worked with one of these senior people better appreciated the challenges of managing group performance, and not simply individual performance:

Working in his office was like working with your family. It was an exceptional atmosphere that I wanted to create (I wasn't sure how to do it) in my own branch.

I saw for myself what you gain when you build esprit de corps among your salespeople. That's how you can become a number-one branch in your region.

He forced team play in his unit. He expected you to have excellent peer relationships and to help people who depend upon you. We didn't have the problems, conflicts, and constant complaining that other units had.

The managers looked toward past bosses as models or for vicarious learning, and at least half of them had past bosses who, though not mentors, had engaged in mentoring behavior toward them. Long apprentice–teacher relationships were rare. Only two of the new managers reported that they had a mentor upon whom they relied to help them through the year. Previous bosses who proved to be the best resources had displayed three characteristics: they had set high standards, had made themselves available, and orchestrated developmental experiences.[8] Because of these qualities the new managers *trusted* these individuals for both professional and personal support. These were the people who became their advisers, counselors, and confidants. Curiously, most of these individuals had been the new managers' first bosses when they joined the company. It seemed they were people the new managers had a history with, bosses who were "more like friends, in a way, than just bosses":

I turn to him for help now. He was the best boss I ever had. He set the bar high, more than any other manager I had. I trust him from my own experience. He handled me the way I wanted to be treated. He wasn't just interested in testing me, he cared about me. He helped me grow.

My first manager used to give me his philosophies, and I use them now. He calls me once in a while or I call him. One of the things he said is, never manage out of fear. You have to make a decision, be fair, and listen to and support your people. You make them feel good and look good and they'll do anything for you. Why is he my main role model and confidant? He was so honest and up front with me. If I needed him to fight a battle for me, he would fight it. If I wanted to do something and he had his doubts about it, he would say, "Go back and think about it. And if you've thought it out, we will go for it."

These former bosses were oriented toward their subordinates' career development. They provided the help that Hall refers to as "supportive autonomy": "The combination of autonomy and the supervisor's availability and willingness to work as a coach when the young person wants help may be the best combination for learning."[9]

They were delegators who allowed their subordinates to participate in big decisions and, when appropriate, make such decisions alone:

> He let the power flow away from him. He didn't think he was good. He never got defensive; he was sensitive to you. As you knew more, he loosened up more. You were always learning. Sometimes he'd do these random inspections, to catch you on the details, but you knew it was no big deal, really. He just wanted to keep you on your toes.
>
> The critical issue is the responsibility he gave me. He let me put [a deal] together alone and carry it through without having to check with him or the team coordinator. He involved us in budgeting and hiring decisions, even though those weren't in our job descriptions.
>
> He was very challenging. He would never let you bring problems to him until you could prove that you had been working on the issues as hard and as smart as you could. And that you had gone to your peers to see if they could help you.

They also held their subordinates accountable for their decisions and actions, giving them timely and candid feedback about their performance:

> He gave me almost complete flexibility about spending money and buying resources. But I knew at the end of the quarter he was going to ask me what kind of revenues I had generated from doing that thing and this thing, and he was going to hold me accountable for every penny.
>
> He always gave me just enough rope to hang myself— well, not quite enough. He kept me on the right track and kept pumping me to have ambitious expectations. When I had to

go call on a big customer he said, "I'm not going to be there. You have to be prepared to run with it. It's yours. But get in here if you have problems and can't come up with any potential solutions." He let me feel in control. He built up my status—I felt like I owned my own ten-million-dollar business. And he talked to me not just about what I did, but how I did it when I'd come back from the call. I learned to examine the business a lot closer. He gave me loads of feedback about how other people saw me. Sometimes I'd get mad—I didn't always want to hear what he had to say. But now I can use that information to help me know how to handle myself.

We had two-way conversations. We'd chit-chat about what was on my mind. He'd give me feedback and then ask me for feedback about how he was doing with me. They were frank discussions and he listened carefully.

This last manager also contrasted that former boss who had been his best teacher with another who had also given him freedom, but who had offered little guidance or feedback:

I got no support. He wasn't even around for me to ask him a question. I often didn't know where to find him. No development, no training, no encouragement. Just do the job and don't bring me lawsuits is what he said. He was too hands-off.

The bosses who had been good teachers also had allowed their subordinates the "sacred right to make a mistake." By so doing they had helped them learn to manage risk, both intellectually (weighing options and risks) and emotionally (coping with personal stresses). In short, by their actions these former bosses had led their subordinates to broaden their perspective beyond that of the producer and to think like businesspeople about both the technical and people aspects of doing business. And by role modeling they had demonstrated the value of and appropriate method for managing subordinates' career development. And finally, it seemed they had encouraged self-motivation and a "learning attitude" in their charges.

Good teachers are hard to come by in academic institutions, where one assumes they should be plentiful, and are even scarcer in corporate environments. Only about half the managers felt they had established mentor-like relationships with past bosses. Those who had been able to do so felt fortunate and turned to these bosses throughout their first year as managers for advice about dilemmas they faced on the job and for emotional support:

> I was facing a tough decision about whether to fire this broker or just reprimand him, for he had willingly and knowingly violated a company policy. I wrestled with it on my own for almost a week and had pretty much made up my mind about what I was going to do. But I gave him [his former boss] a call and talked it through with him. He was really sympathetic. He knew I was struggling. He just let me talk out my decision and asked me hard questions along the way. We looked at the problem from several perspectives: mine, my bosses', the brokers'. We talked about the business consequences and the personal consequences. We talked about compassion.
>
> He [a past boss] had experienced the same heartaches I was going through. He talked to me about how he got through them; he didn't try to hide them from me or play macho man. It's comforting to know that a manager as successful as he is had to go through this too. "We're just two decent people who don't claim to be infallible" was his attitude.

Current Bosses

The new managers who did not have such boss relationships to "lean on" were at a clear disadvantage, for few *initially* turned to their current bosses for support. One of the most consistent and troubling findings in this study was that the new managers did not perceive their current bosses to be resources for coping with their first-year challenges. Most saw the current boss as more of a threat then an ally:

> There can be no meaningful dialogue between us. He will never hear the truth as I see it. I feel he is always judging me. And so I don't dare even ask a question that could be perceived as naive or even stupid. Once I asked him a question and he made me feel like I was a kindergartner in the business.

It was as if he had said, "That was the dumbest thing I've ever seen. What the hell did you have in mind?"

I miss having someone I can talk to who won't be evaluating me. That would be a big plus if I had a person who really understood my job and I could just discuss things with, who wasn't testing me.

I know on one level that I should deal more with my branch manager because that is what he is there for. He's got the experience and I probably owe it to him to go to him and tell him what is up. He would probably have some good advice. But it's not safe to share with him. He's an unknown quantity and he is the last place I'd go for help. If you ask too many questions or for too much help, he may lose confidence in you and think things aren't going very well. He may see that you are a little bit out of control, and then you really have a tough job. Because he'll be down there lickety split asking lots of questions about what you are doing, and before you know it he'll be involved right in the middle of it. That's a really uncomfortable situation.

A few did turn to their superiors for assistance early in the year; their bosses had reputations in the company for being people developers. This repute seemed to give the new managers the confidence to approach their bosses as resources. As expected, these superiors exhibited the same characteristics as the bosses who had offered mentoring:

He has a reputation for being a fine businessperson, a fine developer of people, a hard person to work for. I mean, he is not an easy, I'm-going-to-make-the-world-for-you kind of person. If you work hard for him he will assist in your development and your career. He is demanding, but he enjoys a reputation for growing people and helping them, not throwing them to the wolves and saying, "If you swim I will support you." He truly represents an awful lot from a developmental standpoint. I wasn't sure after the first sixty days, though. Everything was so hard and I was so frustrated, but he didn't offer to help. It was driving me nuts—when I asked him a question, he asked me a question. I got no answers. Then I saw what he wanted. I had to come in with some ideas about how I would handle the situation, and then he would talk about them with me. He would spend all the time in the world with me.

People said, "You've got the gem right now." That was the opening everyone wanted. He spends a lot of time developing his people. He lets you exercise your own style. He doesn't tell you how to manage your folks at all. I've got a couple of situations I feel a little uncomfortable about right now and I've bounced some ideas off him. He is always very receptive and is willing to share with you, to play out various scenarios. And he certainly does not come down and tell you what you should do. He encourages you to develop your own style. He allows managers to learn by doing and making mistakes. He won't tell you you've made a mistake. He has it set up that your peers will. They'll pull you aside one by one, "Why did you make that decision?"

It was difficult to ascertain why most of the managers did not rely upon their current bosses as resources. Some inherent dilemmas in boss-subordinate relationships can undermine their capacity to foster development. Louis writes that newcomers to jobs are unlikely to see supervisors as available for impromptu help; they do not feel comfortable "interrupting them."[10] Moreover, the conflict between the boss's role as evaluator and as developer is an age-old dilemma that almost inevitably crops up. Consequently, both parties may be reluctant to take the risks to build a developmental relationship. For example, the subordinates may not be willing to disclose mistakes, or the superior will offer the official view, not the real story about what is going on in the company.

In both organizations, senior management acknowledged that many, perhaps most of the executives were not "good developers of management talent." In one report the human resource department concluded that only 10 percent of the executives could be considered good at coaching and development. Anecdotal evidence indicated that the cultures in both organizations embodied a sink-or-swim mentality.[11] They appeared to have clear norms against asking for help. One manager commented that this is a "very macho Wild West kind of place." Another described the predominant managerial style as "autocratic and not having much tolerance for mistakes." Senior managers in both organizations were actively engaged in trying to

223

change these aspects of their culture. (In fact, they had agreed to participate in this study as part of that effort.) A survey of medical interns and residents in their first year of practice found that almost half failed to inform supervising physicians of their mistakes. Reviewing these results, one physician concluded, "Any senior physician who teaches needs to reassess how he or she enables residents to ask about mistakes."[12]

On the other hand, the managers were in "no position to ask for help." As described earlier, they were still struggling with the idea that as boss they were to be the expert, the person in control. Psychologically, many were not willing to admit (especially in the early part of the year) that they needed assistance:

> It's difficult even to go back to an old friend and express a lot of frustration. You're afraid, "Oops, I might let something out." As if you have secrets. I'm still tentative about that. It's like leaving home. The first six months you want to be at college. You don't want to talk to mom and dad. Even if they keep asking you, "Do you need help?" You're not going to say yes and start pouring your heart out. You're a grown-up now, out on your own.

> If I had a major concern or question, I'd call a friend in the region and ask them to dig up the answer. I'd never call my boss even though I knew that would be the fastest way to find out. He might start worrying that I was in over my head if he really knew what I didn't know.

As the managers felt more confident in their new positions, they were more willing to call upon their current superiors for advice:

> It's a real plus in helping you grow if you can treat them like consultants, someone you can call and say, "Look, I have this situation. This is what has happened." Or "I need help here," or, "Here are my options, what do you think?" I found he was very helpful.

> Right now, [after seven months on the job] what I am beginning to sense is that I've been on the job a little bit longer, now I need a little more communication and interaction. I've been initiating some of that and he [his boss] has been very receptive. And so I think I need to start relating to my manager in the same way as I want my folks to relate to me. I've got

more people opening up to me now and so I think I am ready to do the same with him.

Eventually, about half the managers, often because of a looming crisis, turned to their bosses for assistance. They were relieved to find the superiors were more tolerant of their questions and mistakes than anticipated. One manager said, "He [the boss] recognized that I was still in the learning mode and was more than willing to help in any way he could." Managers who did encounter hostile, judgmental, or disinterested reactions from their bosses rarely initiated such interactions again. Their conversations with their bosses were generally very task-oriented and usually focused on a specific problem. These fledglings were reluctant to turn to their bosses for general advice or emotional support. Even at the end of the year the managers approached their bosses with trepidation, all too aware of the risks associated with revealing any weakness:

> I was always very professional in my conversations with him. I never brought up anything personal or even career-related issues. The guy is not my friend, and I don't think he would be sympathetic to hearing my real worries. I prepared before I called him so that I would look more in control than I really was. I'd lay out the options and the advantages and disadvantages of each. It's a real bind: you need some help and you know he is the guy who can help you, but each time you go for help you invite him to step into your operation.

The managers generally failed to take advantage of a potentially valuable resource, their immediate superiors. Consequently, the superior had little influence in the managers' earliest conceptions of their new position and the way they approached it. They presumably deprived themselves also of the organizational assets (such as resources that involved substantial financial outlays or critical information about senior management's interests) that superiors could best provide. Finally, one cannot help but wonder how the managers' attitudes toward their bosses influenced their treatment of their own subordinates. It took them some time to acknowledge their responsibilities for developing subordinates.

Previous and Current Peers

The individuals to whom the managers most often turned were former peers (who had been producers with them at one time but currently held a managerial position) and current peers (individuals in the same positions as the new managers or in managerial positions in other functional areas, with whom the new managers became acquainted during the year). Managers who had a more extensive and varied network, and who were willing to ask for help, found it easier to cope with the many first-year challenges:

> At first I didn't know how to utilize different people I'd meet. I'd call and talk pleasure when I should have been talking business and wait and see if they'd give me an in to ask a question or two. As I saw what an opportunity for learning it was to talk to as wide a range of people as I could, I got better at calling up managers around the country and getting to the point. I'd admit I was just looking for new ideas. "Here is a situation. What would you do in this situation?" Then, you just sit back and absorb all that wisdom.

> I don't think you need just one mentor. You need to have lots of people you can turn to for advice. You need to have friends who are experts about different things.

They depended on peers throughout the organization, both inside and outside their functional areas or regions. In fact, some preferred to call upon those in other parts of the organization because they feared they might reveal shortcomings to people who could use the information against them:

> This is all a competition, and we can't all move up. You'd just be giving them ammunition. I draw on people from other regions in the company whose career paths I am not likely to cross any time soon.

For this reason a few even chose to rely upon peers in other corporations they had met outside of work. There appeared to be real individual differences in the managers' willingness to admit mistakes and ask for help.

Most of the managers began the year relying upon peers

with whom they had relationships in the past. But as they grew to respect and trust some of their current peer managers, especially those with more experience, they established fruitful developmental relationships with them. At first a new sales manager was very wary of his branch manager's notion of "peer management"—that all sales managers in the branch should assist and coach one another. By his third month on the job, though he still expressed ambivalence about his peers, he clearly recognized the benefits:

> We're all good analysts. We can all sit down and analyze. The personnel side is much subtler, and what we have tried to create here is an interesting peer structure. The trappings of management elude us at first. I'm much more collegial even with the people I work with than I probably should be. I should be a little more aloof, but I really think the secret is to make sure you have a peer management support setup. It's much more effective to be critically analyzed by your peers than by your boss, because your boss has career or performance implications. From a peer it's almost penalty-free, and the way we do it here is active, not passive. We don't wait for them to come to us. If we really think they've done something wrong we go to them.

Managers in the computer company found it somewhat easier to establish supportive peer relationships than those in the securities firm. The former were located in branches with other peer managers; hence, they had a natural cohort to whom they could turn:

> I will tell you what I did have. One of the best things that happened to me is a very, very good peer manager, a sales manager in the office, had been a manager for a long time. He probably helped me out more than anyone in feedback, critique, good style: "Well, you may want to do it that way," or "You may want to think about doing it this way." He knew the plumbing of the job very well. He knew the systems that you had to work with to get things done. Any time I had a problem, I had someone I could bounce things off back and forth as a peer.
> When I first got here I was confused about the regional

office. I understood the corporate headquarters standpoint because I had worked with people there. I didn't know how to use the region. My peer managers taught me the region point of view, and now I'm using them a heck of a lot more than when I first got here.

I rely on the systems engineering manager a lot. She has been with the company seventeen years. We spend an awful lot of time together bouncing ideas, talking about the right thing to do. We don't step on each other and that is real rewarding. We can just try out ideas, even crazy ones, and not worry about the consequences. No question or idea is too stupid or naive. Without her, this year would have been much more difficult.

Unlike the interactions the managers had with past or current bosses, those with peers were generally very informal, supportive discussions in which the managers felt free simply to explore ideas and disclose their real problems. Many of the managers had peers they chatted with weekly or more often:

We just shared a lot of stories. He had a couple of years' experience on me [they had been sales representatives together in the same branch]. We'd shoot the breeze and swap ideas. I just liked to hear what he was doing. He was willing to share with me the way he looked at things. Beyond that, I'd learn a lot about different aspects of the firm from him.

It was the "people side" of management that dominated the new managers' discussions with peers. They needed peers as confidants and sounding boards for their ideas, for feedback, and for emotional support about handling the dilemmas that arose in managing people. They sought advice not only about what to do, but also how to do it. The new managers were especially anxious about the latter. They often felt that they could figure out for themselves the right thing to do, but did not trust their judgment about how to implement their decisions: "The decision was really cut and dry. I wanted to hear what his thoughts were about how to carry it out. Who would resist? What could I do about it?"

Typically, the managers described in detail how they would handle or had actually handled a circumstance. In a discussion they would often move back and forth from the specific to the general:

> Let me tell you what happened [about a meeting with a problem subordinate]. I did this. She did that. I said this. She said that. Then I'd swallow hard and listen. After that conversation I knew I had to go back the next day and make amends with her. [His peer] helped me see, without saying it outright, that I hadn't considered all the facts. I had made a pretty big mistake in how I handled it. I felt loads better after the talk even though I had to face the fact that I had been wrong. You need a sanity check every now and then.
>
> The guy I call a lot is very opinionated. He's fun to be around. I'd get home at seven or eight at night and pick up the phone, "[The peer's name] I did the dumbest thing today. Let me tell you what I did. Or is this unique? Have you ever heard of this happening with a rep before?" We'd talk and we'd cuss and swear. By the time it was over, the frustration would have ended and I'd feel a little bit better and would have learned a few things about myself and maybe some pointers about how to do things differently the next time. These talks have pulled me through a lot of times.

From the peers' comments and questions, the managers would gain feedback on their ideas and performance. Informal as it was, this feedback greatly enhanced the managers' ability to learn from experience. Such learning is not automatic.[13] Succeeding or failing to handle a situation did not tell the new managers much. They often had difficulty ascertaining if their actions really mattered and deciding how much responsibility they should take for various outcomes in the organization:

> Good sales results can mask the truth. They can hide deficiencies on my part. Maybe I didn't put the best person on the account, or maybe I used more of the company resources than I needed to. I don't necessarily know if it worked because of me or in spite of me. I could be pushing people too hard and they could be planning to walk out the door. You never know. You can't get comfortable just because the dollars are rolling in the door today.[14]

229

The managers used feedback from others to help them interpret their experiences and establish cause-and-effect linkages between their decisions and actions and outcomes. As they talked through a situation with a peer, the cause-and-effect relations would become clearer, they would begin to appreciate the consequences of their actions and their contribution in creating or resolving a problem. These conversations were collaborative efforts at making sense.[15] The managers were eager to ascertain not the right answer but rather how their peers framed or thought about a problem or situation. The sales manager in the branch with the peer-management system mentioned above provided this example:

> At first when you meet in these review sessions [with peer managers] you are lobbying or positioning yourself. Then an interesting phenomenon takes place: they become a safety valve.
>
> Some of the things that get said are outrageous. "You're going to give that jerk an award like that? What the hell for? He didn't do anything." But it's all really positive in terms of motivation. It's really oriented toward making the person think reflectively about why they want to take an action; not that we're making the decision for them, but we're trying to stretch out the dimensions of the decisions that they're making. One of the managers runs the meeting each time. It's amazing what you can do. You get very sophisticated very quickly in your thinking about what you want to do and why you want to do it. What is an award going to say to that person? What is it going to say to the other people? Should we do it now? What if what we are giving him an award for doesn't pan out in the long term?

Because many of the discussions were focused on *how* to get the job done and the logic in making "people decisions," the managers gleaned valuable insights into managerial thinking and appropriate criteria for performance evaluation. These discussions helped them appreciate the varied expectations about the managerial role. One manager reported that he often learned of "missed opportunities or mistakes of omission [not commission]" from these conversations, things he just hadn't thought of. Another manager said that reviewing a situation with a peer often "broadened [his] horizons and made him conscious of a whole set of assumptions he had made about management without knowing it." Once the managers became aware of their assumptions, they realized that some were invalid and others unrealistic.

The managers also relied on peers for feedback on how they were perceived and on their performance. They seemed especially receptive to peer evaluations. As many have found, although you may be able to appreciate intellectually the need for change, emotionally you may not be able to. When negative feedback came from a peer whom the new manager perceived to be in the same boat, the feedback was generally taken as objective and constructive, and the managers often modified their behavior accordingly. Positive feedback from peers also strongly influenced the managers' development. Many felt it was easier to recognize and learn from their mistakes than from their successes. They were much more aware of their shortcomings than their strengths as managers and so suspected that they did not fully capitalize on the latter. One manager said, "You are less likely to bother to do an autopsy on an apparent success than a failure."

Finally, the managers received critical emotional support from peers. They reported that their peers helped them cope with the anxiety of not knowing how they were doing; they craved performance feedback. Many contended that having no feedback was even more disconcerting than having negative feedback: "At least with negative feedback, you have an anchor to hold on to in figuring out what to do next."

Clearly, conversations with peers were cathartic. They allowed the new managers to release pent-up frustration and tension and freed them to focus on the substantive problem at hand:

> You know what we [new managers] need most, a suicide hotline and a newcomer club to draw on. If you're lucky, your peers serve the function for you.

Most new managers believed that access to a network of peers was a key to having a successful year. After they overcame the inhibitory effects of competitive pressures with peers, peer interactions provided a supportive forum in which they could explore how they thought and felt about the challenges they faced. And peers gave them the most candid and timely feedback. Relationships with peers, not superiors, seemed the developmental relationships that mattered.

FORMAL TRAINING

The managers all agreed that they learned how to be managers primarily from on-the-job experience. Nevertheless, most felt that formal training played an important although limited role in their development:[16]

> I learned how to do this job 60 percent from job experience, 25 percent from relationships, and 15 percent from training.
>
> How'd I learn this job? Mostly through o-j-t, trial and error, gut feel, and mistakes. I guess there was some influence from courses and seminars and what you pick up from others. "What would I do if I was in your position?" I also read a lot about management and sales.

In both companies, new manager training was mandatory. The managers received an average of a week to ten days of off-site training, most of which was designed specifically for new managers. These programs were designed to provide the new managers with a broad orientation, primarily addressing the company's administrative and personnel practices and procedures. The sessions were generally taught by in-house trainers. Some of the training, however, was strategy analysis or product training provided by the regional, not the corporate office. Three managers in the study did not attend the required training until well into their first year because of "work pressures." One commented that when he finally attended the course, he realized that he had wasted a great deal of time and effort "reinventing the wheel." Another said he had already formed some "bad habits that were difficult to break." Interestingly, almost all had a file or box of materials from new manager training that they kept close at hand:

> That [pointing to a box in the corner] is the material from new manager school. I thought I would have unpacked it by now, but I haven't. I guess what I know is already in my head. If it's not there or in my gut, it must not be that important. But I'm not throwing that box away. You never know when you'll want to look up something specific.

The managers reported that formal training fulfilled five critical functions: 1) it acquainted them with corporate policies, procedures, and resources; 2) it provided valuable insight into corporate culture; 3) it was a forum in which they could receive more systematic and objective feedback; 4) it facilitated developmental relationships with peers and sometimes superiors; and 5) it was a rite of passage.

The new managers described the new manager training as a formal orientation to their new positions and relevant corporate policies, practices, and resources:

> You get the nuts and bolts. A lot of it seems pretty mundane, but it's nice that they do it. They lay the ground work.

From the training they began to understand the reality of what they were getting into. They saw the training programs as especially useful in helping them master the administrative aspects of the new position. The training gave them a picture of the organization's structure and the corporate resources that were available:

> You understand who the folks are, what their responsibilities are, whom you should be calling, and what are appropriate expectations from them. Actually, you don't really learn the last thing until you're back on the job and you call the person you think should be able to help you and they let you know "that's not in my job description." But you get the general lay of the land from management training.

The new managers found the training valuable because at least it let them know the "official party line":

> And so it was valuable because it taught you where you could use your discretion and where you absolutely could not. It established the parameters for you. You're taught the tradi-

tion; it's sort of like teaching a child that you cannot walk in the street.

They were relieved to discover that the company, in fact, had policies about many matters. From formal training, the managers gained specific knowledge about how to do their jobs and much-needed confidence:

> You see you are not managing in a vacuum. Somebody out there has thought about of lot of the situations that can come up and about ways to handle them. That helps build your confidence.
>
> It's a course designed to keep you out of trouble, to make sure you stay in bounds. For example, you have an employee who is moonlighting. Can you go out and tell the employee to stop doing that? You have an employee who comes in to you and says, "Look, I'm broke. My creditors are coming and going." How do you react to that employee? You go through tons of options.

Perhaps more important, they gained insight into the corporate culture, often by "reading between the lines":

> You learn [the company] way. How they think you should handle a situation. They don't really spell it out for you, but you can figure out that there is a value system behind what they are telling you about which options are best.
>
> They're not just giving you the mechanics. They are imposing a value system on you, especially about how we deal with each other internally. The personnel policies are fundamentally about how we are to execute our jobs. The training inculcates the culture in you. Symbolically it is indispensable because it helps you understand what senior management thinks is most important.

Formal training conveyed to the managers vital corporate assumptions, norms, and values.[17] With this information they had a framework for thinking about how to handle common dilemmas. It helped one manager understand what "best company practice" was; therefore, the training lessons served as "calibration tools" with which she could evaluate her behavior and performance.

The managers found too that training enabled them to get even more direct feedback on their performance. As part of management training in the computer company, new managers were required to have their subordinates complete opinion surveys. The results were taken quite seriously and often profoundly influenced their behavior:

> As soon as [the managers] reflect on or just stop and think about a situation, it's quite clear to them that they should have done it this way or that way; they just did not stop and think about it. My reading about why they didn't stop and think about it usually is that so many other things are going on. One of the reasons the surveys are so effective is that they force you to deal with this feedback, and you have to reflect whether you want to or not. Even if the feedback isn't accurate, just having to think it through makes you sort of ask yourself and think about some things.

The feedback at first seemed devastating, even to managers who received positive overall evaluations. All were surprised to discover areas of "breakage":

> Once you grapple with that ego, you've had a real shock to the ego and you're just floored. How could they think that of me, that I'm cold and aloof? They're wrong. "I'll teach them," and then you can't do that. A professional counselor from human resources sits down and walks you through it. "Here's what they are saying. Why are they saying that? What do you think?"
>
> I was doing an okay job. But my biggest surprise was my biggest weakness. I wasn't listening to people. I didn't let people speak their minds; I had made up my mind before they started talking. My boss had been telling me this, but I didn't believe him until I heard it from my subordinates. When I saw it in black and white I had to face it. When I got back from training I told myself I would change my style. But the next day I went in and said to them, "I understand you think I don't listen. Well, you have to yell louder." I was still being defensive. I talked it over with [a peer manager] and knew I just had to try to be different. Just doing it after a few months, it began to feel easier. But it took months of talking it through

with [one of her peers] over and over again and just doing it before I began to feel natural.

Was it motivating? I'm competitive, and seeing where I came in as a manager was motivating. I wasn't number one and that got me going. I said I have to watch my p's and q's. Really, I didn't learn anything much that I didn't know. I would have rated myself the same way. But it reminded me that I needed to work on my sensitivity. Not be so crass or so straighforward as I used to be, to my people, my boss, or my wife. I've learned to temper what I want to say, to watch my tone of voice. You can't wipe them out or destroy them; sometimes you have to feed them milk. "I understand how you feel. If I were you, I'd probably feel the same way. However . . ." Then I explain what I want to get across in a more empathic way. Yes, I am behaving differently since the survey.

Another manager, who got feedback after five months on the job, remarked:

I didn't get religion right afterward. But there was a greater awareness that they [his subordinates] thought I should work for them. Now, I tell them more, explain things, and try to be a little looser. I don't just talk the business issue, I talk about what they want to [talk about] sometimes.

The feedback also taught the managers to adapt their style to the subordinate. They saw "in black and white" that an amount of delegation that seemed appropriate to one subordinate was described as controlling by another, and a lack of guidance by yet another.

The new managers in the securities firm did not get such feedback from subordinates. During selection, however, they were evaluated on a number of criteria by more experienced and senior managers. This information was summarized and communicated to them by the human resource department. The managers took any criticisms quite seriously:

[The feedback] was based on the opinions of so many people looking at you from so many angles that you had to take it seriously. It was a very valuable tool that let me see for the first time really how people saw me.

> At first I felt angry and misunderstood. I dismissed some of it consciously, but it was eating at me. And after I got some distance, I saw it as an interesting opportunity for self-analysis, and I was able to laugh at myself a little. They were entitled to their perception, and I'd damn well better understand why I was being misperceived, if that was all there was to it.

One manager listed "things to work on" based on this feedback, which he referred to as a reminder from time to time. In both companies the feedback was considered valuable because it was objective and also was often at the behavioral level; that is, about how the person actually performed or behaved in a specific situation.

Another function that the formal training served for the new managers was facilitating the establishment of developmental relationships, especially with peer managers:

> I got a sense that they cared. I lead a sheltered life out in the branch. The only time I see other managers is when we come together in training or seminars. I get to talk to all these people, get their ideas, and really learn from them. I would like to spend time with the guy in California because he seems like such a good manager. There's not time. I'm going to write him a letter and see if we can get together for an hour at the next meeting.

> It was wonderful. I got to pick the brains of managers with fifteen years of experience with such things as how to handle the trainee and the local lawyer who is handling a lawsuit for me. I came right back and implemented those ideas. [A more experienced manager] had explained his philosophy of how he handled [a lawsuit] and so I could apply what was appropriate to my situation.

> The biggest benefit that I received from the training was a chance to interact with my peers. Talk with them, see what they were doing right, what they were doing wrong. You know, swap ideas. There's lots of what if's when we get together. They've become my mastermind group.

> I was at one of these programs and [one of the most successful branch managers in the history of the securities firm] was on a panel. I walked up to him afterward and asked him for a moment of his time and said, "I've heard nothing

237

but good things about you. I've just been appointed resident manager of a very small office and would not mind listening to some of your thoughts." Four hours later I was driving to his house for dinner and we spent the evening just talking. He told me to call him up, or better yet come by and visit his office any time. I'm going to take him up on the invitation and go watch him as soon as I can.

Again, the managers felt that they learned more from the informal than the formal aspects of the training, from socializing with peers, and thereby being socialized into their new role:

> You probably learn more at night going to dinner than during the day. At night the lessons are very practical; people are candid and share failures. It's nice to know you aren't the only one screwing up and it's nice to have new ideas and friends.

Not only did the managers gain skills and knowledge from formal training, but they also augmented their networks of relationships. In fact, the relationships they formed during training came to be an important support group.[18] According to research on management training experiences, this group will be influential in the managers' development throughout their career. Trice and Morand found that training provides a camaraderie or "supervisors anonymous" feeling that persists for years after training.[19]

Finally, training served as a rite of passage, symbolizing the company's faith in the new managers' ability to master their new role successfully, and its willingness to invest in them. The opportunity to mingle with some of the most successful and seasoned executives in the company suggested that they had arrived and "entered a new order":

> At first, I didn't quite get it. [The training department] had me here rubbing elbows with these guys to let me know just how much they expected of me, to let me see what my responsibilities as manager really were.
>
> It helped me make the mental adjustment from the old job to the new job. They treat you with a great deal of respect—you're very valuable. They build you up. Senior

management becomes involved socially. They make you part of the team.

One of the new branch managers remarked that a closing dinner held at one of the finest restaurants in the area clearly communicated to the new managers that they were now valued members of the corporate management team. The ritualistic quality of the formal training programs was not lost on the new managers. They appreciated the company's efforts to help them fit into their new status.[20]

When asked to critique the formal training they had received, the new managers made a number of observations. They said their organizations in fact provided more training for new managers than did most competitors in their respective industries. One manager reported that most of their competitors spent more money in training the salespeople than the sales managers. He was grateful to be in a company that recognized the value of education and training for management. In general, though, the managers felt the training did not go far enough. The relation between what was taught in the program and what occurred on the job was by no means perfect.[21] Many complained that they gained little insight into the rationale for particular corporate policies and procedures—"why things are done in this way." Consequently, the managers felt they were ill-prepared to handle the many dilemmas they encountered when trying to apply a company system or utilize a corporate resource. If they had been generally acquainted with the principles underlying a practice or policy, they would have found it easier to apply the practice or policy. Application was by no means mechanical, but rather required "subtle adaptations to the complexities and realities" of the job. They contended too that the training should have provided them with more insight into the common difficulties they would encounter in trying to apply company policies and practices:

> When I got back on the job and tried to apply what I'd learned, I found it wasn't mechanical at all. I kept running into brick walls and making mistakes. Many of my buddies [other new managers] did the same thing. Is it really necessary that

we learn everything by trial by fire? They could have at least warned us about some of the resistance we'd find out there.

The managers also felt skill should have been emphasized more than development of knowledge. They said pedagogies which focused on real or very life-like problems, and which permitted them to apply new knowledge, were most useful. More than half explicitly mentioned the value of the case method, role playing, and simulations. These methods helped them see what it felt like to be a manager and how difficult a job it really was. One manager said he learned best by taking action. The simulation experiences especially provided him with a useful "surrogate for on-the-job experience." As this manager and others discussed, simulations forced them to problem solve amid uncertainty and ambiguity, helping them learn how to cope with the *emotions* associated with stress and taking risks. And any opportunity to practice their people management skills was especially appreciated.

The managers expressed the desire for more feedback on their behavior and performance, formally with videotaping and opinion surveys, or informally from colleagues. When they received explicit feedback on their performance, they found it much easier to learn from their experiences.

Researchers who have studied adult learning and specifically management development concur with the new managers' recommendations. Action learning seems to be especially helpful in acquiring interpersonal skills.[22] People find it easier to act themselves into a new way of thinking than to think themselves into a new way of acting. People learn skills best by practice plus systematic feedback. Mintzberg observes:

> Management schools will begin the serious training of managers when skill training takes a serious place next to cognitive learning. Cognitive learning is detached and informational, like reading a book or listening to a lecture. No doubt much important cognitive material must be assimilated by the manager-to-be. But cognitive learning no more makes a manager than it does a swimmer. The latter will drown the first time he jumps into the water if his coach never takes him out

of the lecture hall, gets him wet, and gives him feedback on his performance.[23]

This parallel between management training and swimming is strikingly similar to the bike-riding analogy in the opening of this chapter. The new managers knew that their key to success was learning how to learn from experience.

CONCLUDING REMARKS

We are reminded that management development is a long-term process based on exposure to diverse experiences. Crash courses are not available. Also, becoming a manager is both an intellectual and an emotional exercise. The managers were as desperate for help in managing the new position's emotions and stresses as for help in making correct decisions about specific business problems that came up. Since experience counts so heavily in acquiring managerial knowledge, skills, and identity we might ask what would improve the odds that the new managers might learn from experience. They found it easiest to learn from experience when they had strong developmental relationships with superiors and peers, and when they received candid and timely feedback on their performance. In particular we saw the important role that peer relationships played. We learned too how limited the managers' resources were for adjusting to their work. It seems good management teachers were hard to come by, feedback was all too rare, and training often failed to adequately address development of managerial skill.[24]

The new managers' organizations failed to take advantage of a unique opportunity to shape their pool of future executive talent, for transitions between roles are generally the times at which individuals are most receptive to development and socialization.[25] During such transitions individuals generally are strongly motivated and ready to change. This motivation is especially crucial in acquiring new interpersonal skills, unlike intellectual or technical knowledge and skill.[26] In fact, the managers were especially open to feedback and change. They approached their formal training like ethnographers, eagerly collecting, sifting through, and evaluating tangible and intangible data about the organization's culture and themselves. One manager said he was hungry for feedback, unlike some of their senior counterparts, who freely admitted that they were "somewhat immune" to feedback. They were surprisingly able to hear, both intellectually and emotionally, what their deficiencies were, and they had yet to establish bad habits. These findings are consistent with those of others who have found that time in the job is a good predictor of the impact of perceived feedback on job performance. Those with less time are more likely to value and seek feedback by direct inquiry or monitoring.[27]

It is no wonder that others have found that the first managerial assignment has a lasting influence on executive development. When McCall et al. asked executives to identify key events in their careers—that is, things that made a difference in the way they managed—the executives pointed to their first managerial role.[28] That is the time when executives are perhaps most open to experience and to learning the basics about how things work in organizations and how to deal with people. From this foundation they build the skills and judgments they rely upon later in their career.

Both the new managers and their organizations could have been more thoughtful and proactive in managing their first-year learning. Instead, except for initial new manager training, the learning was left mainly to chance. In Chapter 9, we consider how individuals and organizations can capitalize on the new manager experience.

NOTES

1. Burgoyne and Stuart (1976) report that "the greater part of learning of managerial skills comes from 'natural' experiential sources—work and other events and experiences not deliberately planned for learning purposes" (p. 29). They identify nine sources of learning for managerial skills in order of importance: doing the job, noncompany education, living, in-company training, self, doing other jobs, media, parents, and innate. The managers in this

study mentioned each of these, but the three discussed in this chapter were considered most critical.

2. Kotter (1982), p. 134.

3. McCall et al. (1988).

4. See Kram (1988) on the instrumental and developmental support managers derive from coworkers. McCall et al. (1988) conclude that experiences with bosses specifically affect managers' values (p. 73).

5. McCall et al. (1988).

6. Three of the women felt at a disadvantage, having no woman bosses; they felt they had no real role model.

7. These managers can be thought of as "heroes"—individuals who have no personal relationship with the people for whom they serve as role models.

8. See Hill and Kamprath (1991) or Kram (1986) for reviews on the literature on mentoring.

9. Hall (1986), p. 76.

10. Louis (1990), p. 99.

11. McCall et al. (1988) observe:

> It is nearly always the immediate boss who passes on the organization's attitude toward mistakes. But because bosses each have a uniquely personal response to mistakes, this is akin to handing out shotguns randomly laced with either buckshot or flowers. For every story of a boss helping a subordinate to learn from mistakes, there is one for a boss who cruelly metes out punishment and scorn (p. 110).

12. Shuchman (1991), p. B16.

13. See Bandura and Wood (1989) for some of the difficulties in learning rules from the results of actions alone (p. 812).

14. Falvey (1989) describes this phenomenon:

> Unfortunately, Pete's story has a happy ending. Not only was he promoted to the management ranks but he eventually became sales vice president! The missed opportunities and hidden costs for Zappo were enormous. Only a strong product line, a handful of star performers, and luck kept the sales effort afloat (p. 83).

15. See Louis (1980) for additional research (p. 247).

16. By formal training, I mean corporate training. No managers in this study had completed an MBA, but two were taking MBA courses.

17. Van Mannen (1977) suggests how little we appreciate and understand how much individuals need to learn the cultures of their organizations (p. 232).

18. Trice and Morand (1989) propose that such rites of passage or "rites of integration," can deeply influence an individual's socialization into an organization (p. 402).

19. Louis (1990), however, raises a number of reservations about newcomers relying too heavily upon other newcomers as sources of help in acculturation:

> Newcomers are not well equipped to interpret uncertainties and surprises in the new situation; they are likely to disseminate inaccurate information since they are not well informed about the local culture. Newcomers do, however, provide social support for one another

(Fisher, 1985); they are going through similar experiences, so can be "kindred spirits" to one another. Effects of social support on acculturation have not yet been identified. Social support may enhance the newcomer's sense of psychological safety or security, a condition necessary for personal change (Schein, 1979). However, in the absence of veterans who can provide reliable information about local cultures, the effects of newcomers on one another are likely to be mixed (pp. 97–98).

Louis also cites research suggesting that if other newcomers are available, a newcomer is less likely to build relationships with veterans who could provide them with more accurate information and advice about the organization.

20. The significance of these rites of passage is not known. Myerhoff (1982) writes thus about their potential importance:

There is, however, every reason to believe that rites of passage are as important now as they have always been for our social and psychological well-being. Indeed, given the fragmented, confusing, complex, and disorderly nature of modern experience, perhaps they are more important (p. 129).

21. For this reason a number of researchers advocated tailoring training to fit the job for which the training was undertaken. See Badawy (1982), Bigelow (1986), Carnevale et al. (1990), and Hill and Elias (1990).

22. See Bigelow (1986), Cross (1981), and Medcoff (1985) for discussions of the value of more interactive pedagogies. Medcoff (1985) writes:

Dramatization is a powerful device for creating the feel of managerial experiences, for acquainting students not just with the factual outlines of specific situations but with the sensations and stresses of the executive's life. . . . At its best, the teaching case should heighten students' awareness of managerial consciousness of self (p. 152).

23. Mintzberg (1973), p. 58.

24. Nicholson and West (1988) observe:

Most organizations are described as having a low concern for people, and indeed, as if to corroborate this, our managers themselves are more concerned with the cognitive tasks of job performance than the human tasks of developing their subordinates. It is, therefore, hardly surprising that they find themselves subjected to a similar neglect. Both are equally prisoners of the cultural norms of business. Structured and informal feedback are rarely received, and it seems that what little assistance and support organizations may attempt to give managers when they are settling into their new jobs is actually found to be of negligible practical value (p. 183).

25. See Nicholson and West (1988) for research corroborating this observation (p. 193).

26. See Louis (1990), p. 49.

27. See Ashford (1986).

28. McCall et al. (1988).

9

Easing the Transformation

With this study we have had a rare glimpse into the subjective experience of becoming a manager and proposed a framework for understanding that very complex transition. The new managers provided surprisingly consistent accounts of their first year as managers and from those we have extracted two themes:

1. Becoming a manager required a profound psychological adjustment—a *transformation*. Some transitions are changes that keep an individual on a fixed career track, like the pilot's minor adjustments in heading an airplane to maintain a steady course. Others—like the promotion to management—are turning points shifting the entire balance and direction of one's career, like the pilot's submitting a new flight plan when changing destinations. The new managers had to learn how to think, feel, and value as managers instead of as individual contributors. To

make the psychological adjustment, they had to address four tasks:

- Learning what it means to be a manager
- Developing interpersonal judgment
- Gaining self-knowledge
- Coping with stress and emotion

2. Becoming a manager was largely a process of *learning from experience*. New managers could only grasp their new role and identity through action, not contemplation. They learned by facing real problems and real consequences. Consequently, the transformation was iterative, slow, and difficult, both intellectually and emotionally.

Most future managers in this study succeeded. Their superiors said all but three made it through the first year. That is, they accomplished as much as their superiors expected from a manager with their experience. Although none of them felt he or she had mastered the new job after a year, they all had, in fact, learned a remarkable amount in a relatively short time. One said that although he was still not delivering all he wanted to, he felt he had made a large step in the right direction by the year's end. And another observed that her point of view about things had changed profoundly over the year. It was a year of coming of age, a move from naïveté to realism about managerial life and of unlearning the individual contributor's identity and moving toward that of the manager. By the end of the year most had begun to understand and even accept what it meant to be the formal authority for a unit and to get work done through others.

WHAT IS MANAGEMENT DEVELOPMENT?

The new managers' experiences remind us that managing is a complex, often inscrutable, and demanding task. Their experiences challenge us to adopt a more realistic and ambitious view of managerial development: 1) management development is not simply a matter of changing people's knowledge and skills, but involves changing their attitudes; and 2) management development is a difficult and stressful task that individuals must go through themselves, with no short cuts or quick fixes. Managers develop most effectively when given the opportunity to make and implement tough decisions.[1] McCall et al., in their study of executive development, made this unsettling but all too accurate observation:

> The essence of development is that diversity and adversity beat repetition every time. The more dramatic the change in skill demands, the more severe the personnel problems, the more the bottom line pressure, and the more sinuous and unexpected the turns in the road, the more opportunity there is for learning. Unappealing as that may seem, being shocked and pressured and having problems with other people teach the most. For future executives, comfortable circumstances are hardly the road to the top.[2]

Moreover, as described earlier, management development is a paradoxical proposition. Those responsible for it cannot tell new managers what they need to know, even if they know what to tell them. And the managers cannot understand what they have to say. For managers must *act* as managers before they really understand what their job is or what they are supposed to do.

Management development is best understood as an organization's conscious endeavor to provide managers (or potential managers) with the opportunities and resources to learn and develop from experience. From this perspective, development requires deliberate and careful career planning and not, as many have pointed out, the fragmentary, reactive, and intuitive approaches followed by numerous organizations.[3] On the one hand, many companies treat development as a sink-or-swim or survival-of-the-fittest proposition. On the other hand, some companies adopt a myopic view that limits development to formal education and training. Management development should, instead, be broadly conceived as experiences (both pre- and postmanagement promotion, and both formal and informal) meant to enhance an individual's current and future effectiveness. From this research, we can anticipate the dilemmas the new managers will face as well as some of the conditions most likely to facilitate the transition and thus management development.

Managing the transition from producer to manager is a joint responsibility of the individual and the organization. It is the new manager's responsibility to make every effort to ensure that the fit between him- or herself and the managerial role is a good one, to develop managerial knowledge, skills, and attitudes, and to seek the support needed for a successful transition.[4] The corporation is obliged to provide a supportive environment and resources to ease the demands of the transition. In this chapter we examine the conditions that support this more ambitious view of management development: What can the new manager (or managerial candidate) do to ease the transition? What can those responsible for new manager development—line managers and human resource managers—do to make the transition smooth and successful? And finally, what are the implications of this research for corporate training and MBA programs?

NEW MANAGER RESPONSIBILITIES: CHOOSING MANAGEMENT

Based on the above framework of analyzing managerial development, we suggest broad outlines to help new managers think about the challenges of the transition.

No one *has* to become a manager. As this research makes all too apparent, the decision to pursue a managerial career should not be taken lightly or abdicated to others. In accepting the promotion to manager, the new managers consented to more than new job responsibilities. They committed themselves to form a new professional and personal identity. A newcomer to any position will encounter some unmet expectations and some surprises, but too often the new managers were caught off guard by the sharp transition from individual contributor to manager. Potential managers should familiarize themselves as much as possible with the realities of managerial work and the challenges of making the transition from individual contributor to manager so that they can make intelligent career choices and prepare for their new assignment.[5] Managerial candidates should take the time to carefully observe their own managers at work: What does their typical day or week look like? Whom do they work with? They should speak to as many managers as they can about what the managerial role entails: What are your primary responsibilities? What do others expect of you? In their exploratory conversations, candidates should ask not just "what," but also, "how" and "why" questions: How do you go about fulfilling your primary responsibilities? Why do you do things as you do? Before becoming a manager they should ask for opportunities to do more manager-like tasks, so that they can enhance their conceptual and interpersonal skills: Are there opportunities to be a product coordinator or trainer, serve on a task force, fill in for a vacationing manager, or act as liaison with other functional areas or the corporate office?

Potential managers should also engage in constructive introspection. Research indicates that self-awareness is one of the fundamental requisites for managerial effectiveness.[6] The managerial candidates must be as brutally honest with themselves as possible. Am I being realistic about what, as far as I can discern, the managerial role entails? Do my career interests, aptitudes, knowledge, and skills fit the job's requirements? Is my technical background solid enough to build a managerial career on? Have I had the kinds of experiences that give conceptual and interpersonal skills? Do I have others upon whom I can rely for help in dealing with this new challenge?

Managerial candidates will need to call upon people who know them in different capacities to assist in their self-diagnosis. It is difficult to be objective about one's self; the mechanisms that keep individuals from evaluating themselves squarely are well documented. The more feedback they can obtain from varied sources, the more accurate their assessment will be. They should look for information not only about what they have accomplished, but also how they have done so. Also, they should decide what kind of work they find most interesting and fulfilling. Have they been team players? Do they enjoy collaborative work? Do they find it exciting to work on thorny, ambiguous problems? Do they have the managerial character? Do they cope well with stress?

If an individual finds his or her career history wanting, spend more time building the experience and relationships upon which a successful managerial career can be launched. It takes time to assemble the managerial building blocks; judgment and skill come gradually through experience. As others have pointed out, fast-tracking of high-potential managers can impede sound technical and managerial development.[7] Bonoma and Lawler observed that

> Juniors are often their own worst enemies, mistaking the first five years of a career for the career itself, and forgetting that rapidity at some stages may stall a career later on. Those who have paid their dues gaining functional expertise may find it difficult to respect those who have not. . . . A successful career in general management is analogous to climbing a ladder—skipped rungs almost always create a safety hazard for the whole crew.[8]

NEW MANAGER RESPONSIBILITIES: MAKING THE BEST OF IT

One primary objective of this study was to provide new managers with a map for making sense of the experience of becoming a manager—a reference point to hold on to as they went through the transition. This research suggests that new managers should see themselves as engaged in strenuous self-development. Their task is to learn how to capitalize on their on-the-job learning. This requires a commitment to continual learning, self-diagnosis, and self-management. The transition is daunting at best, and most organizations offer little support. New managers must therefore set reasonable expectations for themselves and be patient—accept, one new manager said, that they will take two steps back for every step forward.

Anticipating Common Pitfalls

Because becoming a manager requires learning by experience, the managerial candidate must recognize and avoid the pitfalls of real-time learning.[9] People are prone to put most of their energy into demands and problems they have seen before and to rely on proven skills and approaches, especially in fast-paced and pressured circumstances. The new managers, as we have seen, had to see that past experience and old ways of thinking were not much help in making sense of, and making decisions in, their new managerial positions. This limitation was especially difficult amid the stresses and emotions they were struggling with.

Managers must therefore be prepared to engage periodically in introspection—to collect feedback on, analyze, and alter their behavior when necessary.[10] They have to learn how to manage themselves and their emotions.[11] The new managers were ill-prepared for the inevitable trauma associated with the mental change of clothes. They had to let go of the old, comfortable doer role and identity and embrace the new, ambiguous managerial role and identity. As in most "divorces," the transition phase was often bewildering. Marginal and insecure feelings profoundly affected their daily functioning. In response, they all too willingly retreated to the doer's familiar attitudes and behaviors. This regression interfered with their ability to fulfill the requirements of the new position. Only when the managers understood why they were reverting to old habits were they able to combat this tendency. Many discovered that their eagerness to help subordinates manage client relationships reflected their own desire for approval and achievement; they knew how to manage client relationships and enjoyed doing it. As a new manager, an individual has to anticipate and consciously manage this regression.

The new managers' experiences revealed other typical misconceptions and mistakes. They should recognize that their frame of reference for understanding the new role is biased in predictable ways. They should begin the year by listing individu-

251

als on whom they will depend to get their job done, making sure to include subordinates, superiors, and associates both within and outside the company. They should seek these groups and query them about their expectations, no matter how threatening and overwhelming the responses: What do they expect from me? What do they need from me to get their job done? When reviewing corporate policies and practices, they should work to discover their rationale: Why does the company do things in this way? What does this choice tell me about the company's interests or priorities?

As the year proceeds, managers may want to record in a journal how they spend their time: Am I allocating my time appropriately among my responsibilities and relationships? They should repeatedly ask themselves how much time they spend on "doing" as opposed to managing. To monitor progress, they might keep and update a list of what they have learned, especially about managing subordinates' performance and relationships. These lessons were the core of the managers' curriculum. When coaching new managers, I frequently ask them to maintain such a developmental report. It helps them achieve some sense of closure and success, with a much-needed boost in self-confidence. These simple techniques will force new managers to confront—sooner—their misconceptions about managerial work and to direct their search through the messy and often overwhelming world of management. I make no pretense, however, that managers absorb, let alone act on, all the information they glean. But the manager can profit by adopting the detective's inquisitiveness and techniques, collecting and utilizing all clues to make sense of this new world. These tools are also meant to encourage managers to reflect on and consolidate lessons from their experience. Much research shows that reflection is a key part in learning by doing. Bennis writes:

> Reflecting on experience is a means of having a Socratic dialogue with yourself, asking the right questions at the right time, in order to discover the truth of yourself and your life. What really happened? Why did it happen? What did it do to me? What did it mean to me? In this way, one locates and appropriates the knowledge one needs or, more precisely, re-

covers what one knew but had forgotten, and becomes, in Goethe's phrase, the hammer rather than the anvil.[12]

Creating a Resource Base

Recognize that the challenges of becoming a manager cannot be handled alone, even with the tools mentioned here. New managers must be prepared to seek assistance. They will certainly want to take advantage of the formal resources and systems of support in the company; they must inquire about them. Some of the managers' superiors were not familiar with new manager training and other human resource programs. Moreover, it is worth the time to attend formal training. Managers who chose to postpone formal training courses because of pressures of the job regretted it. New managers must begin to think ahead, not only about their work but also about their personal development.

Perhaps more important than the organization's formal resources are the more informal ones that new managers must create for themselves. They cannot fail to devote time and energy to building and maintaining a network of relationships (superior and lateral, internal and perhaps external to the organization) from which they can derive support, feedback, and advice.[13] These relationships can be helpful only if the managers are willing to take some risk, disclose some of their problems, *and* open themselves to constructive criticism. They will have to fight the tendency to avoid their superiors. The superior holds the most accurate and thoroughly elaborated point of view about managerial work. It is beyond the purview of this book to provide specific advice on how to manage superior relationships, but it is the new manager's responsibility to do so.[14]

Is Management Really for Me?

Individuals cannot really know how they feel about management until they are in the job. Once an individual has elected to become a manager, he or she must work to abandon illusions about his or her motivations and abilities. How am I doing? Do I find managerial work satisfying? Am I seeking and willing to accept feedback and counsel from others? Am I prepared to make necessary changes in my attitudes and behavior? This self-development can be painful, and we know that people often fight it. Again, it seems that one of the most effective ways to undertake periodic self-assessments is by exploring freely with trusted confidants the sensitive issues that inevitably arise.

If in time you find greater rewards in excelling at the job's technical aspects, carefully reconsider your choice of a managerial career. Reversing your decisions is by no means easy: in most companies, even those with dual-career ladders, managers reap the lion's share of corporate rewards and power.[15] Admittedly, returning to the individual contributor's role means giving up access to valued opportunities for advancement and compensation. It also implies defeat. Each occupation needs its craftspeople, however. An individual whose career anchor turns out to be technical rather than managerial may be better suited to a life of functional specialization. Such specialists owe it to themselves and the organization to undo the mistake as soon as possible.[16]

RESPONSIBILITIES OF THE LINE MANAGER AND HUMAN RESOURCE MANAGER: SELECTING NEW MANAGERS

"I have this theory," says Andy Stone, seated in his office at Prudential-Bache Securities. "Wall Street makes its best producers into managers. The reward for being a good producer is to be made a manager. The best producers are cutthroat, competitive, and often neurotic and paranoid. You turn these people into managers, and they go after each other. They no longer have the outlet for their instincts that producing gave them. They usually aren't well suited to be managers. Half of them get thrown out because they are bad. Another quarter get muscled out because of politics. The guys left behind are just the most ruthless of the bunch. That's why there are cycles on Wall Street . . . because the ruthless people are bad for the business but can only be washed out by proven failure.[17]

Criteria for Selecting Managers

This inflammatory statement from *Liar's Poker* unfortunately reflects a growing concern in many industries that the wrong people are being selected for management. Ruthlessness aside, the common practice of rewarding technical success with a promotion to management has increasingly come to be regarded with skepticism. Technical experts may not have basic managerial competencies, much less the right temperament or motivation for management.[18] Certainly we saw that the new managers in this study pondered why and how they had become managers. They came to understand that technical prowess, no matter how great, was insufficient for the people-managing tasks that so filled their days.

What criteria should be used to identify potential managers? You will not find much in this study to add to the current wisdom; it simply confirms what others have been saying.[19] The results suggest that managerial candidates should have technical, human, conceptual, or analytic competence, find managerial work intrinsically rewarding, and exhibit the managerial character. They should display the attributes critical for getting the most from on-the-job learning: self-insight and a penchant for learning. Individuals vary in these two attributes, and effective leaders are highly proficient at learning from experience in an organizational context.[20] People who enjoy learning actively seek opportunities for personal growth and development. They tend to be more introspective, and show resilience under stress.

How to Select Managers

This study has more to say about how to select new managers than about the criteria for choosing them. The new managers described how they relied heavily upon the lessons of experience as resources for managing their new positions. In selecting managers, then, senior executives and human resource personnel should scrutinize managerial candidates' career histories. These career histories represent the experiential base from which managerial candidates could have developed (and tested) competencies, qualities, and developmental relationships critical for management and should be judiciously analyzed. What experiences have they had—what were their *specific* assignments or tasks? With whom have they worked? How well have they performed on the job? What competencies have they acquired from those experiences? What managerial qualities have they displayed? With whom have they established developmental relationships?

Has a potential manager had the opportunity to develop a solid technical foundation upon which to build managerial competence? (The candidate need not be a *star* individual contributor, but probably should demonstrate above-average proficiency at the technical task.) As we saw, the new managers relied upon their technical background in three ways: the expert knowledge they needed to make the technical judgments that arose; a source of self-confidence when faced with bouts of self-doubt; and a base upon which to build credibility and exercise influence among those they worked with. Katz, updating his classic article on managerial competence, concludes that technical competencies are becoming crucial for all managers, even very senior ones.[21] According to Katz, being a good general manager is not enough in today's business environment; executives must understand the basics of the business. Because technical judgment and skill are also acquired primarily through experience, potential managers should have been exposed to broad technical challenges. Formal training and education, such as an MBA, should be supplemented by firsthand experience and a proven record of meeting technical demands. But technical competence is only the first hurdle a managerial candidate should have to clear. Human and conceptual competencies must also be considered. Has the potential manager had any manager-like experiences, such as being a trainer, leading a task force, or being a product coordinator?

In evaluating candidates, senior executives and human resource managers should consider more than the outcomes or what candidates achieved in assignments. They should also examine "how" those candidates achieved those outcomes. How well did they work with others? Were they sensitive to others' concerns and needs? Did they exhibit a sense of the relevance of their assignment to broader corporate objectives? Did they stay well within company policies? In other words, did they display good interpersonal and conceptual judgment or instincts? These are raw materials a new manager should bring to the job.

Ask whether candidates have the managerial character. The new managers themselves indicated that this quality was vital for managing interpersonal relationships effectively and coping with the stress in their new role. When faced with pressure and ambiguity, how well does the candidate handle him- or herself? Does the candidate seem to have the motivation and ability to learn from experience?[22] Does the candidate seem aware of his or her strengths and weaknesses? Is he or she open to constructive criticism? Does he or she initiate or seek opportunities for development?

Care should also be taken in considering managerial candidates' motivation for management, for many companies have found that wrong motivation is the most common reason for managerial failure.[23] Have they ever sought or initiated tasks that were managerial? Do they seem to enjoy thinking about and working on people problems?

The managerial competence that potential managers have acquired can be further developed and refined once on the job. Many contend, however, that managerial character and the motivation and ability to learn from experience are inborn, or produced by prework socialization. Try to choose candidates who seem to have these qualities.[24] Only a caterpillar has the potential to turn into a butterfly![25]

When analyzing the career histories of potential managers,

carefully consider those with whom they have worked. Have they had assignments exposing them to many points of view? Have they worked with positive managerial role models? Have they developed mentor-like relationships with superiors or human resource personnel upon which they can rely? What are their relationships with peers?

Proper diagnosis of a managerial candidate's career history requires much time and effort, and the right information about behavior and attitudes. The firm's middle and senior managers must be given guidance on how to conduct periodic performance appraisals from which such information can be discerned. Many companies have also found it valuable to institute assessment centers for evaluating promising managerial candidates. Such centers are expensive, but they give the company insight into how a managerial candidate thinks about or approaches issues and behaves under stress.[26] For the candidate who is selected, feedback from this examination gives the candidate a head start in understanding how he or she is perceived and in identifying strengths and weaknesses. The candidate also gets to see how the company looks at management and what it considers critical for managerial effectiveness.

Previewing Managerial Work

Senior executives and human resource personnel must make every effort to provide potential managers with an accurate picture of the managerial position *and* of the challenges in making the transition from individual contributor to manager. They should be encouraged to observe and talk to seasoned managers. One new manager remarked on how useful it had been for him to visit branch offices as part of a corporate assignment and see the varied approaches managers took to the job.

The best preview can be done by providing managers with management internships. In fact, during my research, one of the firms in this study decided to implement such a program. Potential managers were asked to assume some managerial responsibilities for at least a year before being promoted to the first-line management position; specifically, they were given responsibility for younger people in the branch or asked to spend time in a staff job at the corporate office. The benefits in this approach are obvious. Each side can observe the other, the candidate experiences management in action, and executives can assess whether the candidate has what it takes. Potential managers can begin to form a managerial perspective (broader and more forward looking) and managerial knowledge and skills (conceptual and interpersonal). Moreover, they can see if managerial work is intrinsically satisfying to them. When they do become managers, they should be better prepared to hit the ground running. And of course the company has more reliable evidence of their proclivity for management than could be ascertained from even the best-designed and implemented assessment center.

Such a program requires close attention to placing the candidate in a supportive, fostering relationship. We have seen that the new managers in the study considered their relationships with their former bosses and other associates crucial—for reality checks, feedback, concrete advice, and emotional support. An ideal management internship would encourage establishing developmental relationships. At least candidates would be matched with positive role models. This arrangement may sound obvious, but an unfortunate tendency in many of these programs is to pair a candidate with a weak manager to prop up or improve the latter's performance; short-term practical needs often outweigh more distant developmental goals.[27] Such a practice jeopardizes the potential manager's development in two ways. It increases the probability that the candidate will receive an impoverished portrait of the managerial role and be exposed to—and thereby develop—bad habits. Further, it reduces the likelihood that the candidate will receive the attention and coaching the program should provide in the first place. The weak manager is too busy fighting fires to take care of the candidate's developmental needs.[28]

RESPONSIBILITIES OF LINE EXECUTIVES AND HUMAN RESOURCE MANAGERS: SUPPORTING THE NEW MANAGER

> Nobody really tells you what you are supposed to do or what is this thing called management. They assume you know that and just get on with how to be a manager.

This *cri de coeur* from one of the study's new managers reflects the feeling they all had when newly promoted. Managers who had participated in manager-like assignments or had a network of relationships upon which they could rely had more insight into the managerial role than those who had not. But even the best prepared new manager had much to learn. What resources will ensure that new managers will in fact learn and develop as much as they can? The challenge in management development is to help new managers capitalize fully upon on-the-job experience—to provide the resources, attitudes, and skills so that they can effectively learn from experience.

As we have seen, the new managers were ready and eager to learn. In fact, for reasons outlined in Chapter 8, during career transitions we are most strongly motivated to learn and become socialized. As many have found, however, career transitions in general and the first managerial assignment in particular are opportunities that many organizations neglect.[29] Instead, line executives and human resource managers should capitalize on these unique opportunities and manage the new manager experience in a deliberate way. Nicholson and West, in one of the most comprehensive studies of managerial career transitions, vigorously criticize corporate efforts in management development:

> If job change has the power to effect changes in identity as well as in organizational performance then how the transition process is managed has a vital bearing on the well-being and effectiveness of organizations. Human resource management seems to end at the point where it could most profitably begin, i.e., when the human resource has been secured. The new manager is a capital asset yet to be converted into a func-

tional resource. This does not mean a lot of handholding and cosseting of newcomers is needed; quite the opposite, for most job-changing managers thrive on freedom and expanded horizons. But a good deal of attentiveness to the process of adjustment is required, to ensure that newcomers have access to the people and relationships they need to help them embed and amplify their personal effectiveness.[30]

Developing the New Managers' Superiors

One of the more provocative findings in this study was that the new managers were reluctant to discuss their concerns with their direct superiors. Efforts should be made to avoid such common pitfalls. The conflict between evaluation and development goals is an age-old dilemma. I do not advocate that new managers turn to the boss first when they have a problem, or that they even bring most problems to the boss. It seems unfortunate, though, that their bosses had so little effect on the managers' earliest notions of managerial work. More than any others with whom they interacted, their bosses appreciated what the job entailed. Besides, the bosses too had gone through the transition from producer to manager, putting them in a unique position to understand and help the managers.

Many of the senior executives with whom I spoke sought my advice on how to handle their charges. They recognized that they could achieve much, but did not believe they were effective developers. They lamented that they rarely received feedback, much less training, on how to manage effectively and develop subordinates.

If an organization could make only one intervention that would improve development of new management, I believe it should be to provide senior executives with training on how to be better *coaches*. Senior managers can be educated—more accurately, reminded—about the challenges of the transition from individual contributor to manager, its critical lessons, and the resources new managers find most helpful in making the transition. Specifically, they should be given training in setting appropriate expectations for new managers, providing feedback effectively, and responding appropriately to the inevitable mistakes that new managers will make. One senior executive declared how he wished he could find some graceful way to sit in on the new manager training on how to do performance appraisals. When he became a manager some twenty years earlier, the company provided no formal training. He recognized that he had always been ineffectual in providing developmental feedback to subordinates.

Finally, if a corporation is serious about developing new managers, it must evaluate and reward senior executives in part for their subordinates' development. Such practices are scarce in organizations. The executives in this study complained about unrelenting pressure from their superiors to meet short-term profit objectives, at the expense of developing their people. Many of the company legends I spoke of in Chapter 8 said that when they instituted practices that would encourage subordinate development they took considerable risk in letting subordinates take on significant responsibilities and "eating" the inevitable missteps. One said he went well beyond the call of duty and it was a long while before the company began to reward him financially for his labors.

Another challenge that corporations must address in preparing senior executives for their developmental function is updating or upgrading the senior managers' conceptions of management. As stated earlier, senior managers rarely received training. They too were often at a loss in dealing with realities in the new business environment. Organizations are becoming leaner, less bureaucratic, and more entrepreneurial.[31] Consequently, leadership and the skill of exercising influence without authority to build partnerships both within and across units are ever more important. Managing today's diverse work force (with new balances in gender, ethnicity, race, and nationality) is no mean feat. Employees are less loyal to the organization and also expect a more participative management approach. Today's competitive and global business environment places a premium on managers' interpersonal skills and it also taxes their conceptual ability. Organizations are discovering that they need managers at all levels constantly on the lookout for opportunities and threats in the environment, if strategic initiatives are to be realized.

Encouraging Developmental Relationships

Once again we can profit by going to the new managers for advice on what senior executives and human resource personnel can do to help them move from individual contributor to manager. As we saw in Chapter 8, the managers found people with whom they could air their experiences. All spoke about relationships, from premanagerial days or newly established, upon which they relied. Having varied relationships seemed most useful. Such relationships should be encouraged between new and veteran managers; both formal and informal channels can be used to expose new managers to competent peers and superior managers. When feasible, new managers can be placed on task forces in which they will have a chance to meet people from other parts of the organization. Formal working sessions such as regional meetings and training sessions should be scheduled so that time remains for informal or social activities. On the surface such activities may seem trivial, but as we saw, they were company-sanctioned events at which new managers could interact with senior executives with whom they would rarely come in contact, and to establish camaraderie and trust with their cohort of new managers. At these times the managers could have rich discussions about what they should be doing, and how they should be doing it.

Such simple tactics have a second benefit. New managers more clearly see themselves as part of the larger organization. In working on issues face-to-face with individuals from different parts of the organization, they experience the perspectives of the constituencies with whom they must interact. Recall that in Chapter 1 many of the new managers complained about their administrative responsibilities, for they did not understand their significance. Also, when newly promoted they were frustrated by the politics of their new positions and the need to network. Getting to know those who request administrative tasks and those on whom they depend ameliorates the new managers' frustration. Corporate policies become associated with specific individuals and "politics" is no longer a dirty word—it now means working effectively with specific people. Procedures, functions, titles, and the like become personal matters.

Some corporations, mainly professional service firms, are experimenting with mentor programs, matching senior with junior people. In some programs, the senior person is instructed to assist a junior colleague with career development. In others, the junior person is encouraged to select a senior person from whom to get performance feedback—someone who is not a direct superior with whom he or she feels comfortable. Such programs have had mixed results; they seem to work much better in theory than in practice. Some reasons cited for their failure are: the senior people are poor at providing feedback and developing subordinates and are given little incentive to spend time on these activities; the juniors do not trust their mentors and are unwilling to admit their shortcomings and problems. I would add that both parties often have unrealistic expectations of what can be accomplished in such relationships.

The popular press has exalted mentoring as a key to career success and satisfaction. Individuals are advised on how to search for a mentor who will guide and support them all through their career. These accounts imply that somewhere stands the perfect mentor—benevolent, experienced, willing, and able to help a younger colleague navigate through the world of work. (In Homer's *Odyssey*, the goddess Athena, in the shape of the nobleman Mentor, was trusted counselor to the young Telemachus.) If only each of us had a goddess to accompany us on our journey through our work lives. Although perfect mentors can be found in literature, they rarely exist in reality. The fact is that mentor-protégé relationships are difficult to establish and maintain; they cannot be created by fiat or force. And mentors are neither omnipresent nor omnipotent. Both parties take on heavy investment and risk. Only two of the new managers in this study had true mentors. But, as we have learned from the new managers, alternatives to full mentor relationships can provide mentor-like functions, including both superior and peer relationships. Those responsible for developing managers should help them understand how useful having a range of developmental relationships can be and provide opportunities to facilitate them.

CORPORATE TRAINING

Corporations make substantial financial outlays for management training programs. The managers described how they utilized formal training and delineated some shortcomings, reminding us of the broader and more intangible results of corporate training. That training provided the new managers with a framework for thinking about appropriate ways of handling common dilemmas, corporate resources to help tackle those dilemmas, much-needed feedback, and a network of relationships. In other words, formal training plays a limited but necessary role. It should be designed to support the new managers' on-the-job training, helping them learn how to learn by experience. Johnston and his associates define the skills required for learning as "the capacity to critically conceptualize and communicate, obtain and integrate information and act with initiative and self-confidence."[32]

From the new managers' observations, it seems current emphasis on the acquisition of managerial competencies (especially managerial knowledge as distinguished from skill) and on classroom learning, may be misplaced.[33]

Content of New Manager Training

This research alerted us to some of the critical lessons new managers have to learn and some of the mistakes they will make. Management training should focus on these issues. Training should be designed to provide managers with the concepts and distinctions they need to adapt to their new world. They need to know what they should be doing, and also how and why. Only if they understand the latter will they be able to apply the classroom lessons on the job. But training objectives should include not just knowledge, but also skills and attitudes. When we considered how the managers learned the managerial role and interpersonal judgment, we saw that they went through a continual heuristic reframing. They observed a relatively unstructured or ambiguous situation, gathered and synthesized information to make problem solving and decision making possible, and experimented with possible solutions to address the situation. New managers should be taught induction—how to seek information and solve problems in semistructured situations. They should be taught how to observe and diagnose interpersonal problems.[34]

New managers should be exposed to both the intellectual and emotional challenges that lie ahead. Management training should focus on what it means to be and what it feels like to be a manager. They must recognize that both task and personal learning are required to be a manager. In task learning they acquire competencies and build relationships they need to perform the job effectively. Although aware of this kind of learning, the new managers underestimated its demands, especially in acquiring interpersonal judgment.

Personal learning was mostly an obscure subject for the managers. The need to constantly examine and change one's attitudes and identity was a major revelation. Like the new managers, corporations too often neglect or underestimate the demands of personal learning.[35] Corporate training programs should recognize and address the emotional strain and soul-searching imposed by the transition from individual contributor to manager for even the most talented individual. Managers need help realizing they are not alone in their anxiety and need help coping with the emotions and undesirable effects of the transition. They should be forewarned of the link between these feelings and regressive behavior—that they will be both unlearning an old role and identity and learning new ones. Handling of stress and emotion tailored to the challenges managers face must be considered.

New managers need an accurate portrait of managerial work and its tensions and stresses. Sayles and other leading managerial researchers point out the gap—really the gulf—between the rhetoric in most management texts and seminars and the exigencies of managerial life.[36] New managers need to see the differences between individual contributor and manager and their new agenda-setting and network-building responsibilities. Now that they are managers they need instruction in dealing with clients differently than they did as individual contributors. In so doing, the new managers can gain some insight into the differences between being primarily responsible for people as opposed to task. Such basic orientation is too often ignored.

With regard to agenda setting, the managers need guidance on how the corporation expects them to balance the trade-offs faced in making managerial decisions such as long- versus short-term interests or one functional area's interests versus those of another. One manager commented: "I am bombarded with variables that will occupy my mind rent-free and cost me a fortune. It takes tremendous discipline to fend off the things that are irrelevant."

The new managers need practical advice on how to prioritize and allocate their time. Dorney, an expert in time management, writes that his subject is more about management than time. Managers, he says, need to learn how to apply Vilfredo Pareto's 80–20 taxation principle:

> Only instead of applying it to taxation of the "vital few" who pay 80 percent of the taxes, I apply it to the significant functions that produce 80 percent or more of the return while still giving the "trivial many" the time they are worth.[37]

The managers also need to have corporate policies and practices delineated. They must understand the corporate perspectives and anticipate problems they may encounter when they attempt to implement the policies.

Curricula for managers in the lower ranks rarely include much on conceptual skills and on the corporation's strategy. Introducing new managers to the strategic issues early and broadening their view about the relation between business and environment has clear advantages.[38] For, as we saw, if left to their own devices, new managers give little attention to these matters, until rather late in the year. Training should stretch the new managers' notion of the managerial role.

Of course, training should also address managers' responsibilities for building networks. Training should emphasize the managers' most pressing needs: the challenge of making interpersonal judgments. As we have seen, they approached their jobs from the "right-to-manage" viewpoint.[39] The curriculum should therefore address how to exercise power and influence without relying heavily on formal authority. Training should also cover such subjects as tailoring management style and approach to the individual; effective delegation; and leadership in managing the group. Managers should be encouraged to deal with these subjects in all their complexity, to recognize the balancing act in which they will be engaged—for instance, between maintaining control, yet providing subordinate autonomy. Too often, managers are simply given prescriptive how-to lists of preferred practices, ignoring the complexities in managing relationships. When they try to apply these practices, they run into difficulty.

It is imperative to place the new managers' responsibilities for managing subordinates in context—to help them understand that they must manage relationships not only with subordinates but also with others outside their unit. They need to understand the perspectives of those on whom they depend to get their job done. More companies are finding it useful to expose managers to the fundamentals of other functional specialties, so that they can take into account the corporate picture.[40] The new managers were understandably preoccupied by their relationships with subordinates. Management training has too often focused on subordinate relationships, neglecting critical lateral and superior relationships.

Pedagogy of New Manager Training

The pedagogies that should be relied on are those which best capture the realities of managerial work and encourage learning from experience.[41] Management training should be based on a practicum approach (more experience than theory), combining conceptual and skill learning and practice.[42] This approach is most appropriate because it requires the person to act and encourages new attitudes. As we have seen, changes in attitude are required for changes in behavior. The managers could not become effective delegators until they knew the difference between responsibility for people and for the task. Receptive methods such as reading and lecturing are not very effective in improving interpersonal performance or changing attitudes and identity. But Hall and many others point out that "in many contemporary organizations, executive development is synonymous with formal receptive classroom teaching methods."[43]

Instead, the case method, role playing, and simulation exercises should be incorporated into training as much as possible. Corporations are beginning to realize that training programs including exercises on business simulation or better yet, projects with real corporate problems, are beneficial. Companies such as General Electric and IBM, well known for investing in management development, are creating practice fields in which managers can experiment and learn in environments that force them to confront managerial stresses and emotions. To reinforce this kind of learning the new managers must have feedback, not simply about what they have accomplished but also about how they did it. How well did they work with others participating in the exercise? Did they act as leaders? The managers, as we have seen, craved feedback on performance. They had to learn their strengths and weaknesses. Ideally, training should include self-assessment exercises as well as feedback to help the managers outline a personal agenda for development. Time should also be built in to allow managers to reflect on and consolidate their lessons.

One other general recommendation, as outlined in Chapter 8, time should be set aside to allow the managers to build strong developmental relationships. As we know from much research, acquiring and applying knowledge and skills are fundamentally social acts. Garvin presents this point of view:

> Children acquire language, for example, through complex social interactions with adults and [with] other children.

Carpenters, bookmakers, chefs, surgeons, experimental scientists, and practitioners of other occupations requiring complex strategies of estimation and decision making acquire a large portion of their practical knowledge from observing and interacting with other skilled practitioners. . . . Although the social dimension of learning is critical to the practical application of knowledge, we construct formal learning . . . in ways that discourage social interaction. We emphasize individual cognition over social interaction, abstract manipulation of symbols over concrete application in practical settings, and generalized learning over applications in specific social contexts.[44]

New manager training cohorts can help new managers survive the first year. Such cohorts might be encouraged to meet periodically to discuss common problems and share ideas. Companies have begun to include new manager forums and buddy systems to facilitate this interchange.[45] When possible, the managers should also be exposed to, or encouraged to work on issues with, seasoned and effective managers. After completing a project in a training program, they might be required to present their work to a senior management committee.[46]

A Prototypical New Manager Program

Considering how the new managers learned their roles and identities and the resources upon which they relied, the ideal management development program should be designed as an apprenticeship. Apprenticeships work best when individualized. Novices come to their craft with unique strengths and weaknesses or gaps in development. Like other artisans, new managers acquire their craft principally with actual and vicarious experiences and coaching by other craftspeople. In a perfect world, development plans would be delineated to suit the person's specific needs. The individual's talents would be matched with the demands of the first assignment in an effort to provide the manager with experiences fitted to his or her unique strengths and help close gaps in development. Each new manager would be matched with an ''old'' managerial hand who would listen and sagely offer advice. Similarly, each would be paired with new managerial hands, with whom they could commiserate and obtain socioemotional support.

But the world is not perfect and more practical ways must be found. What should a new management development program look like? Instead of assigning a new manager to a mentor, he or she should be assigned a coach, who will assist throughout the year. This coach should be trained in the experience of moving from individual contributor to manager and how best to develop new managers. At first the coach should be very proactive in making him- or herself available, initiating interactions to establish rapport with the new manager. Later, the coach should allow the new manager to be the primary instigator of their conversations.

We must consider how the study itself affected the new managers.[47] Over and over, they stressed how valuable it was to talk with me. In fact, they were usually talking to themselves; most of the time I served as confidante and sounding board. They were forced to reflect upon and therefore consolidate lessons from their experience. They had a forum in which to explain to themselves what they were undergoing. As I have said, I came to the project with no hypotheses. I was intentionally the listener and strove to be nonjudgmental in interacting with the new managers. They were therefore willing to explore the anxieties and frustrations that naturally accompany the transformation, thereby combating some of the pressure to regress to their former role.

Conceivably, corporations could formally establish the coaching I inadvertently supplied. One new manager suggested a name for this role: "field training officer." Such an officer could work one-on-one with a new manager. Indeed, that might be one of the more expedient ways in which a company could improve new manager development. Whether the coach's developmental function is best filled by someone inside the organization (such as a human resource manager or line manager to whom the new manager does not report) or an outside consultant, is debatable. Insiders would be in a better position to provide organizationally specific feedback and advice. They could transmit the "party line" on how to handle the real subtleties of the organization's culture. They might also have more credibility with the new managers. On the other hand, recalling the managers' reluctance to admit shortcomings, especially emotional reactions to the transformation, to those in their organization, an outsider would be less threatening. The managers might actually make more use of an external coach.

In the classroom the managers should be introduced (with interactive methods such as case study discussions) to managerial concepts and techniques. As more basic ones are mastered and experienced in action on the job, the managers should be introduced to ever more complex and refined frameworks with which to understand their new position. They should not be overloaded with new information; they are already overwhelmed by their workload and need guidance in choosing their priorities.

Classroom training should be supplemented with a practicum such as working as a group on a specific problem that one of the new managers has encountered, or on a strategic issue that a senior manager deems important. The instructors in the program would be available during these exercises to answer questions and facilitate proceedings when necessary. But the new managers would pretty much be allowed to go it alone. Such experiences would give them a chance to test the concepts and skills they had acquired in the classroom and identify difficulties they might have applying them on the job. They should also be assigned to a new manager support group, ideally the one with which the manager goes through formal training. And time should be set aside to allow them to interact in their support group informally and to meet with others from various parts of the corporation.

It seems new manager training would work best if it took place periodically, perhaps in four three- to four-day sessions, throughout the new managers' first year. Topics should be introduced when the managers are ready to hear them; that is, after they have encountered them on the job. Shortly before beginning the new job, they should undergo self-assessment. They should be told what management thought their strengths and weaknesses were. They should also receive orientation to the content and responsibilities of management and to corporate policies and practices. At this session, formal training as a rite of passage should be addressed. Senior executives should be included in the program to officially welcome their new colleagues and help them assume their new status in the organization. And once again, formal and informal time should be set aside for the new managers to meet and establish some rapport.

During the first three months, after some firsthand experience with managerial challenges, the managers should receive additional training exposing them to a more elaborate conception of management and to interpersonal skills, especially those critical in managing subordinates. Special emphasis should be given matters on which new managers are prone to make mistakes, as in managing the more experienced subordinate. At this session and the others, individuals representing various parts and levels of the organization should be invited to take part formally or informally. Perhaps a panel of individual contributors with different levels of experience could speak. This panel should include relatively new managers as well as those with more experience. The former would be in a position to talk about the vulnerabilities and stresses new managers often feel, and the latter could answer questions about how to get the job done.

At some time during the second half of the year, the new managers should return for additional training. The curriculum should focus on managing superior and lateral relationships and devote some attention to developing their conceptual skills. Emphasis should be given to interdependence in managerial work and the manager's function as integrator, to help them understand how best to represent their groups' interests and appreciate the needs of other groups depending on them to get their work done. This session should consider the skills needed for effective group and intergroup relationships, diagnosing and resolving problems within and among work groups, and negotiating with peers. During this session they should perhaps undergo another self-assessment. They should be given systematic feedback as with employee surveys. The feedback should be collected from subordinates and also from peers. Only the new manager should receive this confidential information for this process is development and not evaluation. The new managers should be encouraged to review their results with a session facilitator to help interpret them.

As the second year begins, the new managers should be brought back for leadership training exposing them to the principles of managing group performance. They should now be ready for such a discussion and should have some firsthand feel for the issues. They need to know how to evaluate and monitor group-level performance, how to encourage and reward cooperative behavior, how to build effective group cultures and teams and how to lead.

Admittedly, many of these recommendations are expensive and assume that corporate priorities have been reordered. But they are not at all magical—they are surprisingly straightforward. And if one compares the cost of such endeavors, with the financial and human cost of managerial failure and turnover, they may even seem most reasonable. The business press suggests that more and more companies are beginning to consider such programs and policies. Practices once considered unfeasible are being redefined as investments in the corporation's future vitality, as companies move toward a "learning culture."

MBA EDUCATION

Let us evaluate how business schools are doing in management development, especially with the impressive numbers pursuing the Master of Business Administration degree (MBA). If the population studied here had more MBAs, perhaps I would have gained more insight into the unique managerial preparation provided in universities. But the new managers' observations about corporate training presumably are generalizable to managerial education offered by universities. Indeed, a study of graduate business education quoted almost two-thirds of the graduates surveyed as reporting that they used their MBA skills marginally or not at all in their first management assignments.[48] The business press tells us that corporations are increasingly disillusioned with the MBAs they hire at great expense. When corporate recruiters were asked in a *Fortune* survey, "What one improvement would you suggest to deans concerning their MBA programs?" they recommended teaching the so-called soft skills (especially interpersonal skills, as well as conceptual ones) and instilling more realistic expectations for the first job.[49]

My study shows that these findings were predictable. In content and pedagogy, the education many business schools provide does little to prepare managers for their day-to-day realities. With few exceptions, the schools emphasize functional expertise and spend little time developing interpersonal judgment and skill. Usually students must themselves connect theory and practice. And classroom learning is rarely supplemented with experiential exercises. Many point out that these shortcomings are not new or unknown. From their inception, debate has raged over the business schools' mission and curriculum. Today, the schools are taking such criticism to heart, but administrators and faculties are only beginning to address them. Among other things, to do so requires reconsidering of the schools' mission and of the promotion requirements for faculty. Until the schools reconceptualize their traditional role of discovering and imparting cutting-edge knowledge to include that of helping future managers learn how to learn from experience, it is difficult to imagine how much progress they can make.

Interesting initiatives are under way, nonetheless. Many business schools are overhauling their curriculum. At the Wharton School, student teams work on four-day integrative case studies, for which they produce videotaped presentations of business plans.[50] They also expect their students to travel abroad and conduct field studies of European or Japanese business operations. The University of Chicago requires a leadership course, with an intensive weekend retreat engaging students in team projects. This course has been very positively received by students and the corporations who hire them. My institution, the Harvard Business School, is reexamining not only its curriculum but also the organization of the faculty. New "interest groups" bring together those in organizational behavior and human resource management, management of information systems, and strategy. The assumption is that to conduct useful research and construct relevant courses, we must have an inter-disciplinary organization reflecting the nature and complexity of pressing business demands. Moreover, the school is reaffirming its commitment to high-quality teaching. The book *Education for Judgment* is an outgrowth of the school's endeavor to help the faculty understand and fulfill their teaching responsibilities. And an informal seminar discusses how to effectively coach the neophyte faculty member.

These are just a sampling from the programs that business schools have set in motion in striving to equip the managers of the future. Clearly, much more work has to be done, but the dialogue has begun.

CONCLUDING REMARKS

Most estimates of the annual United States investment in management development reach tens of billions of dollars.[51] Companies faced with the business realities of the 1990s and the demand for superlative managerial talent are asking if these funds are being put to good use. Most management development programs are designed to help managers gain competencies (especially knowledge, not skills) and focus on classroom training. These emphases follow from the conceptual foundation upon which most are built. Of the countless articles and books on developing managerial talent, few are based on empirical research, and even fewer look at the phenomenon from the new managers' perspective. When one does consider that point of view, it becomes clear that corporations need to rethink and redirect their efforts in management development.

Of the manager's many career transitions, the first managerial assignment is one of the most pivotal, and many would argue, most demanding. Because it involves a transformation—a fundamental change in identity and point of view—it deserves to be better understood and managed. Our ambition in this book was to describe the transition's challenges from the new manager's perspective. The managers in this study have very obligingly taken us on a personal, often stressful, but exhilarating journey. They remind us how intellectually and emotionally demanding the manager's job can be and how much one has to learn to do it effectively.

In this chapter I have examined the conditions most likely to facilitate the transition and thus management development. These recommendations, like the findings in this project, are meant to provide a point of departure and to reframe our understanding. I hope both new managers and those responsible for their development will here gain insight on developing managerial talent more effectively—in short, helping new managers learn how to learn from experience and master a new identity.

NOTES

1. Davies and Easterby-Smith (1984) write:

> Development of greater awareness and perception is not enough; it is necessary for managers to learn from taking *action*. Our interviews with managers in this sample indicated that it was the fact of being given responsibility for a discrete area of the business or organization that was critical to their development: the need to take decisions under conditions of risk and uncertainty and to implement the resulting plans was, in some cases, exhilarating. Success under such circumstances led to increased confidence and thus, the willingness to launch out into the unknown again (p. 176).

2. McCall et al. (1988), p. 58.
3. See Hill (1985) for further discussion.
4. Others have mentioned that self-awareness is critical to managerial success. An individual's self-concept determines his or her perceptions and interpretations of the world. Only if people have accurate images of themselves can they make career choices appropriate to their interests and talents. Only if they are aware of their competencies will they try to improve themselves or acquire new capacities. Brouwer (1964) writes:

> The function of self-examination is to lay the groundwork for insight, without which no growth can occur. Insight is the "Oh, I see now" feeling which must consciously or unconsciously precede change in behavior. Insights—real, genuine glimpses of ourselves as we really are—are reached only with difficulty and sometimes with real psychic pain. But they are the building blocks of growth. Thus, self-examination is a preparation for insight, a groundbreaking for the seeds of self-understanding which gradually bloom into changed behavior (p. 156).

5. Considerable evidence shows the negative consequences of unrealistic job previews. For example, individuals with unrealistic expectations about new jobs are more likely to be hired for jobs for which they are not well suited, fail to receive necessary training, and subsequently perform poorly. See Feldman and Brett (1983), p. 259.

6. See Bennis (1989) or Kaplan (1989; 1990).

7. Gabarro (1987), pointing out that taking charge requires time and effort, therefore argues against brief, fast-track development assignments (p. 127).

8. Bonoma and Lawles (1989), p. 30.

9. Hannaway (1989) found in her research that explanations formed by managers who try to learn in a dynamic environment are overly influenced by interpretations of what happened in the past (p. 71).

10. For instance, Hall (1986) contends:

> Of all the qualities necessary for executive success, the capacity for self-learning is probably the most important. Personal learning is a "meta-skill." If the executive has learned how he or she learns . . . then he or she has acquired the capacity to master more specific tasks. And in fact, in their study of executive leaders, Bennis and Nanus (1985) found what we are calling personal learning to be their most prized personal quality (p. 256).

11. For example, London (1985) writes:

> Bennis (1984b) says that being a leader is like "learning to play the violin in public." Leaders need outside observers who can help them understand their own behaviors; Bennis feels that we give insufficient attention to the role of personality and self-understanding in leadership. Quoting Karl Marx's statement that "man's consciousness of self is the highest divinity," Bennis recommends that leaders learn how to manage themselves. Bennis calls this "the creative deployment of their characters," and he calls for a "restoration of self" in leadership theory (p. 200).

12. Bennis (1989) p. 61.

13. Gabarro (1987) found in his research on taking charge that managers who were most successful had enlisted the help of subordinates and superiors in assessing and diagnosing organizational problems far more than those who were unsuccessful. Consequently, they were able to establish trust, influence, and mutual expectations, and to implement decisions effectively.

14. See Gabarro and Kotter (1980) or Cohen and Bradford (1990).

15. For instance, Drucker (1988) concluded that most companies have been unable to implement an effective dual-career system. Most are structured in such a way that professional specialists reject them (p. 51).

16. Through the years some managers, even senior executives, have, very publicly, elected to return to being individual contributors. Waldholz (1991) in *The Wall Street Journal* reports that the head of Bristol-Myers's research and development division had decided to give up his post. He wished to be more actively engaged with hands-on scientific research (p. 10).

17. Lewis (1989), p. 141.

18. This limitation is especially troubling in the management of research and

278

development and sales and marketing. Webster (1983) concludes:

> A central conclusion of a classic study by Robert Davis involving field sales managers in 54 countries [was that] they excel at personal selling, at trouble shooting (which is usually customer-oriented) and at the mechanics of running the field office; they are weakest at developing and supervising salesmen and at analyzing and planning their operations. . . . Managers had received little or no management training and consequently . . . continued to do what they knew (p. 56).

This problem is also acute in professional service firms (consulting, medical, law), in which people are attracted by financial or status rewards that management offers, but may have neither the will nor the ability to manage. Organizations have failed to create career systems that enable such people to move out of managerial roles if they are not suited to them.

19. See Boyatzis (1982), Katz (1974), Bray et al. (1974), Robertson and Iles (1988), and Schein (1987). Katz (1974), in a classic article on the critical skills of management, identifies three basic skills:

> Technical skill involves specialized knowledge, analytical ability within that specialty, and facility in the use of tools and techniques of the specific discipline (p. 91).

> Human skill is the executive's ability to work effectively as a group member and to build cooperative effort within the team he leads. As technical skill is primarily concerned with working with "things" (processes or physical objects), so human skill is primarily concerned with working with people. This skill is demonstrated in the way the individual perceives (and recognizes the perceptions of) his superiors, equals, and subordinates, and in the way he behaves subsequently (p. 91).

> Conceptual skill involves the ability to see the enterprise as a whole; it includes recognizing how the various functions of the organization depend on one another, and how changes in any one part affect all the others; and it extends to visualizing the relationship of the individual business to the industry, the community, and the political, social, and economic forces of the nation as a whole (p. 93).

20. See Bennis (1989).

21. Katz (1974), updating his classic article, concludes that technical competencies are crucial for even the most senior manager. An executive must understand the basics of his or her business. Being a good general manager is not enough in today's business environment.

22. For example, London (1985) describes two domains of career motivation that are relevant to this discussion:

> Career resilience shows the extent to which we keep our spirits up when the going gets tough, how resistant we are to career barriers or disruptions affecting our work. People who are high in career resilience see themselves as competent individuals able to control what happens to them. They get a sense of accomplishment from what they

do. They are able to take risks. They also know when and how to cooperate with others and act independently.

Career insight demonstrates the extent of our realism about ourselves and our careers and how accurately we relate these perceptions to our career goals. People who are high in career insight try to understand themselves and their environments. They look for feedback about how well they are doing, and they set specific career goals and formulate plans to achieve them (p. 42).

23. See Badawy (1982), p. 59.
24. See Kaplan (1990), Levinson (1968), and Zaleznik (1990).
25. Many contend that managerial character cannot be taught by a corporation. More and more evidence suggests, however, that organizational culture profoundly affects motivation and ability to learn from experience and receptivity to change. See Hill and Elias (1990) and Kanter (1991). Nicholson and West (1988) summarize some of the literature on organizational culture and its influence on role transitions (p. 192).
26. See Bray et al. (1974) and Thornton and Byham (1982).
27. Bonoma and Lawles (1989) observed that

> Guiding managers and potential leaders on a career path often resembles the child's games of "Chutes and Ladders"; they are moved up, down, and around on the basis of organizational need or political convenience—not on the basis of their own developmental needs (p. 27).

Many have commented that heavy emphasis on short-term results is one of the major hindrances to building competence and personal development. See Hall (1989) or Zemke (1985).
28. Schein (1961) talked about the differing influences of role modeling and job rotation on management development:

> Apprenticeships, special jobs in the role of "assistant to" somebody, job rotation, junior management boards, and so on stand in sharp contrast to the above methods in the degree with which they facilitate, indeed almost demand, that the young manager learn by watching those who are senior or more competent. . . . It makes little difference whether the teacher, coach, or supervisor intends to influence the attitudes of the trainee or not. If a good emotional relationship develops between them, it will facilitate the learning of knowledge and skills, and will, at the same time, result in some degree of attitude change. . . . Job rotation, on the other hand, can facilitate growth and innovation provided it is managed in such a way as to insure the exposure of the trainee to a broad range of points of view as he moves from assignment to assignment (p. 77).

29. See Nicholson and West (1988), p. 193, or London (1985), p. 24.
30. This quotation is from Nicholson and West (1988), p. 213.
31. See Drucker (1988) or Kanter (1989) for descriptions of the new organization and its influence on managerial work. They argue that eventually business organizations will be more like a hospital or a symphony orchestra than a typical manufacturing company.

32. Johnston et al. (1986), p. 84.
33. It is instructive to consider subjects that the American Society for Training and Development (1989) found were commonly covered in management training. They reported that new managers are most often trained in employee selection, decision making, team building, strategic planning, and budgeting. Experienced managers receive developmental training in subjects that will make them more effective in groups and the external community. Their training includes subjects such as interpersonal skills, negotiation, teamwork, organizational development, and leadership. They also receive some training on relevant social and political issues (p. 26).
34. Weick (1974) comes to a similar conclusion:

> To the teacher the advice reads: get away from cognitive learning and train your students instead in eight basic managerial skills (for example, peer skills, resource-allocation skills, skills of introspection). Scientists are advised to provide managers with better descriptions of their jobs, treat induction as a topic rather than resource or research, and relax your aversion to quick and dirty analytic techniques (p. 112).

35. Schein (1961) writes:

> Yet we have given far more attention to the psychology which underlies change in the area of knowledge and abilities than we have to the psychology which underlies changes in attitudes. . . . But professionalization is not only a matter of teaching candidates increasing amounts about a set of relevant subjects and disciplines; it is equally a problem of preparing candidates for a role which requires a certain set of attitudes (p. 60).

Flamholtz and Randall (1987) in their research on the transition to management conclude:

> Changes at the behavioral and attitudinal levels of management are prerequisites for changes at the skill level. The managerial skills that are most directly affected by the underlying attitudes and behaviors are:
>
> Decision making
> Recruiting
> Day-to-day leadership and supervision
> Personnel development
> Time management
> Delegation
> Planning
>
> All these skills must be taught from an Inner Game perspective rather than merely as technical skills to be mastered (p. 203).

36. Sayles (1989).
37. Dorney (1988), p. 39.
38. Kraut et al. (1989) discussed the importance of teaching managers at all levels about the organization's competitive strategy (p. 291).

39. Others have mentioned this tendency in new managers. Cox and Cooper (1988) observed that new managers seem to work under the assumption that management is "mainly a matter of shouting orders to a waiting band of willing but not very bright workers, who would then scurry off to do the master's bidding" (p. 106).

40. Bernhard and Ingols (1988), p. 42.

41. Johnston et al. (1986) propose that companies place a premium on the capacity to learn effectively and quickly, to become a "fast study" (p. 89).

42. See Bigelow (1991) or Mumford (1987) for further discussion of this subject.

43. Hall (1976), p. 254.

44. Christensen et al. (1991), p. xiv.

45. In conversations with human resource managers about trends in the management development field, a number mentioned that they were instituting such programs. Reviewing programs from the annual conferences for human resource management professionals (such as the Human Resource Planning Society and the American Society of Training and Development) provided further confirmation.

46. Medcof (1985) extolled the benefits of a program for new R&D managers in which they met once a week for a number of months to discuss thier problems with fellow managers. Their sophistication as well as their awareness of themselves as managers gradually improved.

47. Clearly, my influence on the new managers' experiences must be taken into account in interpreting the results of this study. Presumably, the managers would not have been as conscious of the process they were going through if I had not been studying them. In addition, although I rarely gave "advice" to the managers, my questions and probes probably alerted them to issues they otherwise would not have considered. These issues, among others, are discussed in some detail in the Appendix.

48. Porter and McKibbin (1988).

49. Deutschman (1991), p. 76.

50. See Bryne (1990; 1991), Deutschman (1991), and Narisetti (1991).

51. See Galagan (1989) or Sonnenfeld (1985).

Selected Bibliography

Adams, J. (1977). *Transition: Understanding and Managing Personal Change*. Lanham, MD: Rowman and Littlefield.

Akin, G. (1987). "Varieties of Managerial Learning." *Organizational Dynamics, 16*(2), 36–48.

Allen, T. (1986, March). "Portrait of the Branch Manager." *Institutional Investor,* 209–218.

Allen, V.L., and E. Van de Vliert. (1984). *Role Transitions: Explorations and Explanations*. London: Plenum.

Argyris, C. (1982). "The Executive Mind and Double-Loop Learning." *Organizational Dynamics, 11*(2), 5–22a.

———. (1991, May–June). "Teaching Smart People How to Learn." *Harvard Business Review,* 99–109.

Arthur, M.B., D.T. Hall, and B.S. Lawrence, eds. (1989). *Handbook of Career Theory*. Cambridge, England: Cambridge University Press.

Ashford, S.J. (1986). "Feedback-Seeking in Individual Adaptation: A

Resource Perspective." *Academy of Management Journal, 29,* 465–487.

Badawy, M.K. (1982). *Developing Managerial Skills in Engineers and Scientists: Succeeding as a Technical Manager.* New York: Van Nostrand Reinhold.

Badiru, A.B. (1987). "Training the EE for a Management Role." *IE Career Strategies,* 18–23.

Baehler, J.R. (1980). *The Manager's Guide to Success.* New York: Praeger.

Bailyn, L. (1982). "Resolving Contradictions in Technical Careers, or What If I Like Being an Engineer?" *Technology Review, 85,* 40–47.

———. (1989). "Understanding Individual Experience at Work: Comments on the Theory and Practice of Careers." In M. Arthur, D. Hall, and B. Lawrence, eds., *Handbook of Career Theory* (475–476). Cambridge, England: Cambridge University Press.

Bailyn, L., and J.T. Lynch. (1983). "Engineering as a Life-Long Career: Its Meaning, Its Satisfaction, Its Difficulties." *Journal of Occupational Behavior, 4,* 263–283.

Bandura, A. (1986). *Social Foundations of Thought and Action: A Social Cognitive Theory.* Englewood Cliffs, NJ: Prentice-Hall.

———. (1989). "Human Agency in Social Cognitive Theory." *American Psychologist, 44,* 1175–1184.

Bandura, A., and R. Wood. (1989). "Effect of Perceived Controllability and Performance Standards on Self-Regulation of Complex Decision-Making." *Journal of Personality and Social Psychology, 56,* 805–814.

Barley, S. (1989). "Careers, Identities and Institutions: The Legacy of the Chicago School of Sociology." In M. Arthur, D. Hall, and B. Lawrence, eds., *Handbook of Career Theory* (41–65). Cambridge, England: Cambridge University Press.

Barnard, C.I. (1938). *The Functions of the Executive.* Cambridge, MA: Harvard University Press.

Barnes, L.B. (1981, March–April). "Managing the Paradox of Organizational Trust." *Harvard Business Review,* 107–116.

Bartolomé, F., and A. Laurent. (1988, October). "Managers: Torn Between Two Roles." *Personnel Journal,* 73–83.

Bayton, J.A., and R.L. Chapman. (1973, November). "Making Managers of Scientists and Engineers." *Research Management,* 33–36.

Becker, H.S., et al., eds. (1968). *Institutions and the Person*. Chicago: Aldine.

Belker, L.B. (1986). *The First-Time Manager: A Practical Guide to the Management of People*, 2d ed. New York: Amacom.

Bellenger, D.N., R.L. Berl, and M.D. Traylor. (1981). *Sales Management: A Review of the Current Literature*. (Research Monograph No. 89.) Atlanta, GA: College of Business Administration, Georgia State University.

Benbasat, I., D. Goldstein, and M. Mead. (1987). "The Case Research Strategy in Studies of Information Systems." *MIS Quarterly*, 369–386.

Benedict, R. (1989). *Patterns of Culture*. Boston: Houghton Mifflin.

Bennis, W. (1989). *On Becoming a Leader*. Reading, MA: Addison-Wesley.

Bennis, W.G., and B. Nanus. (1985). *Leaders: The Strategies for Taking Charge*. New York: Harper and Row.

Bernhard, H.B., and C.A. Ingols. (1988, September–October). "Six Lessons for the Corporate Classroom." *Harvard Business Review*, 40–46.

Bhaghat, R., and T. Beehr. (1985). "Conclusion." In R. Bhaghat and R. Beehr, eds., *Stress and Cognition in Organizations: An Integrated Perspective* (399–413). New York: John Wiley.

Biddle, B.J. (1979). *Role Theory: Expectations, Identities, and Behaviors*. New York: Academic Press.

Bigelow, J.D., ed. (1991). *Managerial Skills: Explorations in Practical Knowledge*. Newbury Park, CA: Sage Publications.

Bluehorn, A.C. (1984). *Management Development: Advances in Theory and Practice*. Chichester, England: John Wiley.

Bolt, J.F. (1985, November–December). "Tailor Executive Development to Strategy." *Harvard Business Review*, 168–176.

Bonoma, T., and J. Lawler. (1989, Spring). "Chutes and Ladders: Growing a General Manager." *Sloan Management Review, 30*(3), 27–37.

Boyatzis, R. (1982). *The Competent Manager: A Model for Effective Performance*. New York: John Wiley.

Boyd, H.W., Jr., and R.T. Davis. (1970). *Readings in Sales Management*. Homewood, IL: Richard D. Irwin.

Bray, D.W., R.J. Campbell, and D.L. Grant. (1974). *Formative Years in Business: A Long-Term AT&T Study of Managerial Lives*. New York: John Wiley.

Brewin, C. (1980). "Work Role Transitions and Stress in Managers: Illustrations from the Clinic." *Personnel Review, 9*(5), 27–30.

Broussine, M., and Y. Guerrier. (1982). *Surviving as a Middle Manager*. London: Croom Helm.

Brouwer, P.J. (1989). "The Power to See Ourselves." In H. Levinson, ed., *Designing and Managing Your Career* (11–21). Boston: Harvard Business School Press.

Brown, D., and L. Brooks, eds. (1984). *Career Choice and Development*. San Francisco, CA: Jossey-Bass.

Brown, R. (1968). *From Selling to Managing*. New York: Amacom.

Burgoyne, G., and V.E. Hodgson. (1983). "Natural Learning and Managerial Action: A Phenomenological Study in the Field Setting." *Journal of Management Studies* (U.K.), *20*(3), 387–399.

Burgoyne, J.G., and V.E. Hodgson. (1984). "An Experiential Approach to Understanding Managerial Action." In J. Hunt et al., eds., *Leaders and Managers: International Perspectives on Managerial Behavior and Leadership* (163–178). New York: Pergamon Press.

Burgoyne, G., and R. Stuart. (1976, Autumn). "The Nature, Use, and Acquisition of Managerial Skills and Other Attributes." *Personnel Review, 5*(4), 19–29.

Burke, R.J., and R. Weir. (1980). "Coping with the Stress of Managerial Occupations." In C. Cooper and R. Payne, eds., *Current Concerns in Occupational Stress* (299–336). New York: John Wiley.

Byrne, J. (1990, October 29). "The Best B Schools." *Business Week*, 52–66.

———. (1991, May 13). "Wharton Rewrites the Book on B Schools." *Business Week*, 43.

Campbell, J.P., et al. (1970). *Managerial Behavior, Performance, and Effectiveness*. New York: McGraw-Hill.

Carew, J. (1989, March). "When Salespeople Evaluate Their Managers." *Sales and Marketing Management*, 24–27.

Carlson, S. (1951). *Executive Behavior: A Study of the Work Load and Working Methods of Managing Directors*. Stockholm: Stromberg.

Carnevale, A.P., and L.J. Gainer. (1989, February). *The Learning Enterprise*. Washington, DC: U.S. Department of Labor, Employment and Training Administration.

Carnevale, A.P., L.J. Gainer, and J. Villet. (1990). *Training in America: The Organization and Strategic Role of Training*. San Francisco, CA: Jossey-Bass.

Carroll, S.J., and D.J. Gillen. (1987). "Are the Classical Management Functions Useful in Describing Managerial Work?" *Academy of Management Review, 12*, 38–51.

Chonko, L.B., and B.M. Enis. (1980). *Selling and Sales Management: A Bibliography* (Series No. 36). Chicago: American Marketing Association.

Christensen, C.R., D.A. Garvin, and A. Sweet, eds. (1991). *Education for Judgment: The Artistry of Discussion Leadership*. Boston: Harvard Business School Press.

Chubin, D.E. (1983). "Career Patterns of Scientists and Engineers." In T. Connolly, ed., *Scientists, Engineers, and Organizations* (310). Belmont, MA: Wadsworth.

Ciabattari, J. (1987, March). "When It's Your Turn to Be the Boss." *Working Woman*, 109–139.

Cohen, A.R., and D.L. Bradford. (1990). *Influence Without Authority*. New York: John Wiley.

Comer, J.M., and A.J. Dubinski. (1985). *Managing the Successful Sales Force*. Lexington, MA: Lexington Books.

Cooper, C.L., and J. Marshall. (1978). *Understanding Executive Stress*. London: Macmillan.

Cornelius, E.T., III, and F.B. Lane. (1984). "The Power Motive and Managerial Success in a Professionally Oriented Service Industry Organization." *Journal of Applied Psychology, 69*(1), 32–39.

Cox, C.J., and C.L. Cooper. (1988). *High Flyers: An Anatomy of Managerial Success*. New York: Basil Blackwell.

Crissy, W.J.E., G.A. Marple, and E. Conant. (1963, Winter). "Field Assignments for Individual Managerial Development." *Business Topics* 11, *1*, 49–63.

Cron, W.L., and J.W. Slocum. (1986, May). "The Influence of Career Stages on Salespeople's Job Attitudes, Work Perceptions, and Performance. *Journal of Marketing Research, XXIII*, 119–129.

Cross, P.K. (1981). *Adults as Learners*. San Francisco, CA: Jossey-Bass.

Dalton, G.W. (1989). "Developmental Views of Careers in Organizations." In M. Arthur, D. Hall, and B. Lawrence, eds., *Handbook of Career Theory* (89–109). Cambridge, England: Cambridge University Press.

Dalton, G.W., and P.H. Thompson. (1986). *Novations: Strategies for Career Management*. Glenview, IL: Scott, Foresman.

Dalton, G.W., P.H. Thompson, and R.L. Price. (1977, Summer). "The Four Stages of Professional Careers—A New Look at Performance by Professionals." *Organizational Dynamics*, 19–42.

Davies, J., and M. Easterby-Smith. (1984). "Learning and Developing from Managerial Work Experiences." *Journal of Management Studies, 21,* 169–183.

Davis, R.T. (1957). *Performance and Development of Field Sales Managers*. Boston: Division of Research, Harvard Business School.

———. (1958, January–February). "Sales Management in the Field." *Harvard Business Review*, 91–98.

———. (1970). "A Sales Manager in Action." In H.W. Boyd, Jr., and R.T. Davis, eds. *Readings in Sales Management* (259–268). Homewood, IL: Richard D. Irwin.

Dawis, R.V., and L.H. Lofquist. (1976). "Personality Style and the Process of Work Adjustment." *Journal of Counseling Psychology, 1,* 55–59.

———. (1984). *A Psychological Theory of Work Adjustment*. Minneapolis: University of Minnesota Press.

Deci, E.L., and R.M. Ryan. (1987). "The Support of Autonomy and the Control of Behavior." *Journal of Personality and Social Psychology, 53*(6), 1024–1037.

DeLong, T.J. (1982, May–June). "Re-Examining the Career Anchor Model." *Personnel*, 50–61.

Derr, C.B., C. Jones, and E.L. Toomey. (1988, Fall). "Managing High-Potential Employees: Current Practices in Thirty-Three U.S. Corporations." *Human Resource Management, 27*(3), 273–290.

Deutschman, A. (1991, July 29). "The Trouble with MBAs." *Fortune*, 67–78.

Dewhirst, H.D., V. Metts, and R. Ladd. (1987). "Exploring the Delegation Decision: Managerial Responses to Multiple Contingencies." *Academy of Management*, 35.

Dill, W.R., W.B.S. Crowston, and E.J. Elton. (1965, November–December). "Strategies for Self-Education." *Harvard Business Review*, 119–130.

Dorney, R.C. (1988, January–February). "Making Time to Manage." *Harvard Business Review*, 38–40.

Dougherty, D.E. (1984). *From Technical Professional to Corporate Manager: A Guide to Career Transition*. New York: John Wiley.

Driver, M.J. (1988). "Careers: A Review of Personal and Organizational Research." In C.L. Cooper and I. Robertson, eds. *International Review of Industrial and Organizational Psychology* (245–277). New York: John Wiley.

Drucker, P.F. (1988, January–February). "The Coming of the New Organization." *Harvard Business Review*, 45–53.

Eisenhardt, K.M. (1989, October). "Building Theories from Case Study Research." *Academy of Management Review, 14*, 532–551.

Everett, M. (1987). "Who Needs District Sales Managers?" *Sales and Marketing Management*, 54–56.

Falvey, J. (1989, March). "The Making of a Manager." *Sales and Marketing Management*, 42–83.

Feldman, D.C. (1976). "A Contingency Theory of Socialization." *Administrative Science Quarterly, 21*, 433–452.

Feldman, D.C., and J.M. Brett. (1983). "Coping with New Jobs: A Comparative Study of New Hires and Job Changers." *Academy of Management Journal, 26*(2), 258–272.

Ferguson, L.L. (1966, March–April). "Better Management of Managers' Careers." *Harvard Business Review*, 139–152.

Feurer, D. (1988, December). "Making the Leap: From Supervision to Management." *Training, 25*(12), 63–68.

Fielding, N.G., and J.L. Fielding. (1986). *Linking Data. Qualitative Research Methods, Series 4*. Beverly Hills, CA: Sage Publications.

Flamholtz, E. (1986). *How to Make the Transition from an Entrepreneurship to a Professionally Managed Firm*. San Francisco, CA: Jossey-Bass.

Flamholtz, E.G., and Y. Randle. (1987). *The Inner Game of Management: How to Make the Transition to a Managerial Role*. New York: Amacom.

Freedman, A. (1972, September). "The Medical Administrator's Life—Administration Here Today and Here Tomorrow." *Archives of General Psychiatry, 27*, 418–422.

Freese, M. (1982). "Occupational Socialization and Psychological Development: An Under-Emphasized Research Perspective in Industrial Psychology." *Journal of Occupational Psychology, 55,* 209–224.

Fury, K. (1988, August). "Are You Sure You Want to Be the Boss?" *Working Woman,* 96.

Gabarro, J.J. (1979, Winter). "Socialization at the Top—How CEOs and Subordinates Evolve Interpersonal Contracts." *Organizational Dynamics,* 3–23.

———. (1987). *The Dynamics of Taking Charge.* Boston: Harvard Business School Press.

Gabarro, J.J., and J.P. Kotter. (1980, January–February). "Managing Your Boss." *Harvard Business Review,* 92–100.

Galagan, P.A. (1989, January). "IBM Gets Its Arms around Education." *Training and Development Journal,* 35–41.

Given, W.B., Jr. (1955, January–February). "The Engineer Goes into Management." *Harvard Business Review,* 43–52.

Goffman, E. (1974). *Frame Analysis.* New York: Harper and Row.

Hackman, J.R., ed. (1990). *Groups That Work (and Those That Don't).* San Francisco, CA: Jossey-Bass.

Hales, C.P. (1986). "What Do Managers Do? A Critical Review of the Evidence." *Journal of Management Studies, 23*(1), 88–115.

Hall, D.T. (1968). "Identity Changes During the Transition from Student to Professor." *School Review, 76,* 445–469.

———. (1976). *Careers in Organizations.* Glenview, IL: Scott, Foresman.

———. (1986). "Dilemmas in Linking Succession Planning to Individual Executive Learning." *Human Resource Management, 25,* 235–265.

———. (1989, Spring). "How Top Management and the Organization Itself Can Block Effective Executive Succession." *Human Resource Management, 1,* 5–24.

Hall, D.T., and Associates. (1986). *Career Development in Organizations.* San Francisco, CA: Jossey-Bass.

Hambrick, D.C., ed. (1988). "The Executive Effect: Concepts and Methods for Studying Top Managers." In H. Thomas and D.E. Schendel, *Strategic Management Policy and Planning: A Multi-Volume Treatise, 2.* Greenwich, CT: JAI Press.

Hammer, T.H., and J.M. Turk. (1987). "Organizational Determinants of Leader Behavior and Authority." *Journal of Applied Psychology, 72*(4), 674–682.

Handy, C. (1987). *The Making of Managers: A Report on Management Education, Training and Development in the USA, West Germany, France, Japan and the UK.* London: Prepared for publication by the National Economic Development Office on behalf of the National Economic Development Council, the Manpower Services Commission and the British Institute of Management.

Hannaway, J. (1989). *Managers Managing: The Workings of an Administrative System.* New York: Oxford University Press.

Hayes, R.D. (1985, January–February). "The Myth and Reality of Supervisory Development." *Business Horizons,* 75–79.

Hill, L.A., ed. (1985). "Essentials of Executive Development." *Harvard Business Review,* Special Collection.

Hill, L.A., and J. Elias. (1991). "Retraining Midcareer Managers: Career History and Self-Efficacy Beliefs." *Human Resource Management Journal, 29*(2), 197–217.

Hill, L.A., and N.A. Kamprath. (1991). "Beyond the Myth of the Perfect Mentor: Building a Network of Developmental Relationships" (Case No. 9-491-096). Boston: Harvard Business School.

Hill, R.E., and M.T. Tinkham. (1984). "The Occupational Interests of R&D Managers." *The Career Center Bulletin, 4,* 15–16. New York: Columbia University—The Center for Career Research and Human Resource Management.

Hirschhorn, L. (1988). *The Workplace Within: Psychodynamics of Organizational Life.* Cambridge, MA: MIT Press.

Hodgison, R.C., D.J. Levinson, and A. Zaleznik. (1965). *The Executive Role Constellation.* Cambridge, MA: Harvard University Press.

Houston, P. (1990, September). "48 Hours: Case Study, A CEO's Calendar." *Business Month,* 42–49.

Howard, A., and D.W. Bray. (1988). *Managerial Lives in Transition: Advancing Age and Changing Times.* New York: Guildford Press.

Hunt, J.G., et al. (1984). *Leaders and Managers: International Perspectives on Managerial Behavior and Leadership.* New York: Pergamon Press.

Ipsen, E. (1984, November). "A Day in the Life of a Superbroker." *Institutional Investor,* 135–138.

Ives, B., and M.H. Olson. (1981). "Manager or Technician? The Nature of the Information Systems Manager's Job." *MIS Quarterly,* 49–63.

Jenks, S. (1984, August). "Solving the Executive Development Dilemma: The Case of High-Tech Entrepreneurs." In R. Kaplan, chair, *What's Different About Developing Executives (Once They've Already Become Executives)?* Symposium conducted at the 1984 Annual National Meeting, Academy of Management, Boston, MA.

Jereski, L. (1988, February). "I'm a Bad Manager." *Forbes,* 134–135.

Jick, T.D. (1979, December). "Mixing Qualitative and Quantitative Methods: Triangulation in Action." *Administrative Science Quarterly, 24,* 602–611.

Johnson, R.A., J.P. Neelankavil, and A. Jadhav. (1986, November–December). "Developing the Executive Resource." *Business Horizons,* 29–33.

Johnston, J., Jr., et al. (1986). *Educating Managers: Executive Effectiveness through Liberal Learning.* San Francisco, CA: Jossey-Bass.

Jones, G.R. (1983). "Psychological Orientation and the Process of Organizational Socialization: An Interactionist Perspective." *Academy of Management Review, 8*(3), 464–474.

———. (1986). "Socialization Tactics, Self-Efficacy, and Newcomers' Adjustments to Organizations." *Academy of Management Journal, 29,* 262–279.

Joseph, H., R. Aldag, and J. Keenan. (1987). "Identity as a Manager: Measurement, Determinants, and Career Consequences." *Academy of Management,* 66.

Kahn, R.L., et al. (1984). *Organizational Stress: Studies in Role Conflict Ambiguity.* New York: John Wiley.

Kanter, R.M. (1989, November–December). "The New Managerial Work." *Harvard Business Review,* 85–92.

Kaplan, R.E. (1989, April). *The Expansive Executive* (Report No. 135). Greensboro, NC: Center for Creative Leadership.

———. (1990, August). *Character Shifts: The Challenge of Improving Executive Performance through Personal Growth* (Report No. 143). Greensboro, NC: Center for Creative Leadership.

Kaplan, R.E., M.M. Lombardo, and M.S. Mazique. (1983, January). *A Mirror for Managers: Using Simulation to Develop Management Teams* (Technical Report No. 21). Greensboro, NC: Center for Creative Leadership.

Katz, D., and R.L. Kahn. (1978). *The Social Psychology of Organizations,* 2d ed. New York: John Wiley.

Katz, R.L. (1974, September–October). "Skills of an Effective Administrator." *Harvard Business Review,* 90–103.

Katz, R., and M.L. Tushman. (1981). "An Investigation into the Managerial Roles and Career Paths of Gatekeepers and Project Supervisors in a Major R&D Facility." *R&D Management, 11*, 103–110.

————. (1983). "A Longitudinal Study of the Effects of Boundary Spanning Supervision on Turnover and Promotion in Research and Development." *Academy of Management Journal, 26*(3), 437–456.

Kaye, B.L., and C. Farren. (1982, November–December). "Management Readiness: A Program and Its Players." *Personnel Magazine*, 65–72.

Kelley, B. (1989, September). "Who Says You Can't Go Home Again?" *Sales and Marketing Management*, 38–44.

Kerr, S., K. Hill, and L. Broedling. (1986). "The First-Line Supervisor: Phasing Out or Here to Stay?" *Academy of Management Review, 11*(1), 103–117.

Kiechell, W., III. (1983, March). "Just Promoted." *Fortune*, 143–144.

Klerman, G.L., and D.J. Levinson. (1969). "Becoming the Director: Promotion as a Phase in Person-Professional Development. *Psychiatry, 32*, 411–426.

Kobasa, S.C. (1979). "Stressful Life Events, Personality, and Health: An Inquiry into Hardiness." *Journal of Personality and Social Psychology, 37*, 1–11.

Kofodimos, J.R. (1990, Summer); "Why Executives Lose Their Balance." *Organizational Dynamics*, 59–73.

Kohn, M.L., and C. Schooler. (1982, May). "Job Conditions and Personality: A Longitudinal Assessment of Their Reciprocal Effects." *American Journal of Sociology, 87*(6), 1257–1286.

Kolb, D.A., and D.M. Wolfe. (1984). "Career Development, Personal Growth, and Experiential Learning." In D.A. Kolb et al., eds., *Organizational Psychology: Readings on Human Behavior in Organizations*, 4th ed. (124–152). Englewood Cliffs, NJ: Prentice-Hall.

Kotter, J.P. (1982). *The General Managers.* New York: Free Press.

————. (1988). *The Leadership Factor.* New York: Free Press.

Kouzes, J., and B. Posnor. (1987). *The Leadership Challenge: How to Get Extraordinary Things Done in Organizations.* San Francisco, CA: Jossey-Bass.

Kovach, B.E. (1986, Autumn). "The Derailment of Fast-Track Managers." *Organizational Dynamics*, 41–48.

Kram, K.E. (1988). *Mentoring at Work: Developmental Relationships in Organizational Life.* Lanham, MD: University Press of America.

Kram, K.E., and L.A. Isabella. (1985). "Mentoring Alternatives: The Role of Peer Relationships in Career Development." *Academy of Management Journal, 28*(1), 110–132.

Kraut, A., et al. (1989, November). "The Role of the Manager: What's Really Important in Different Management Jobs." *The Academy of Management Executive, III*(4), 286–293.

LaBelle, C., et al. (1983). *Finding, Selecting, Developing and Retaining Data Processing Professionals Through Effective Human Resources Management*. New York: Van Nostrand Reinhold.

Langer, E. (1989). "Minding Matters: The Consequences of Mindlessness-Mindfulness." *Advances in Experimental Social Psychology, 22,* 137–173.

Latack, J.C. (1984). "Career Transitions Within Organizations: An Exploratory Study of Work, Nonwork, and Coping Strategies." *Organizational Behavior and Human Performance, 34,* 296–322.

Latham, G.P., and L.M. Sari. (1979). "Application of Social Learning Theory to Training Supervisors Through Behavior Modeling." *Journal of Applied Psychology, 64,* 239–246.

Lazarus, R.S., and S. Folkman. (1984). *Stress, Appraisal, and Coping*. New York: Springer.

Leana, C.R. (1986). "Predictors and Consequences of Delegation." *Academy of Management Journal, 29*(4), 754–774.

Learned, E.P. (1966, July–August). "Problems of a New Executive." *Harvard Business Review,* 20–176.

Leonard-Barton, D. (1990). "A Dual Methodology for Case Studies: Synergistic Use of a Longitudinal Single Site with Replicated Multiple Sites." *Organizational Science,* 248–266.

Levinson, D.J., et al. (1978). *The Seasons of a Man's Life*. New York: Alfred A. Knopf.

Levinson, D., Jr., and G.L. Klerman. (1967). "The Clinician-Executive—Some Problematic Issues for the Psychiatrist in Mental Health Organizations." *Psychiatry, 30,* 3–15.

Levinson, H. (1965, November–December). "Who Is to Blame for Maladaptive Managers?" *Harvard Business Review,* 143.

———. (1968). *The Exceptional Executive: A Psychological Conception*. New York: Mentor Books.

———. (1980, July–August). "Criteria for Choosing Chief Executives." *Harvard Business Review,* 113–120.

———, ed. (1989). *Designing and Managing Your Career*. Boston: Harvard Business School Press.

Levinson, H., and S. Rosenthal. (1984). *CEO Corporate Leadership in Action*. New York: Basic Books.

Lewin, K. (1935). *A Dynamic Theory of Personality*. New York: McGraw-Hill.

Lewis, M. (1989). *Liar's Poker: Rising Through the Wreckage on Wall Street*. New York: W.W. Norton.

Lieberman, S.G. (1956). "The Effects of Changes in Roles on the Attitudes of Role Occupants." *Human Relations, 9*, 467–486.

Livingston, J.S. (1969, July–August). "Pygmalion in Management." *Harvard Business Review, 81*.

———. (1971). "Myth of the Well-Educated Manager, with Letters of Comment from HBR Readers." *Harvard Business Review*, Reprint No. 71108.

Loen, R.O. (1964, May–June). "Sales Managers Must Manage." *Harvard Business Review, 107–114*.

London, M. (1985). *Developing Managers: A Guide to Motivating and Preparing People for Successful Managerial Careers*. San Francisco, CA: Jossey-Bass.

Longenecker, C.O., and D.A. Giola. (1988, Winter). "Neglected at the Top—Executives Talk About Executive Appraisal." *Sloan Management Review, 41–47*.

Lorsch, J.W., ed. (1987). *Handbook of Organizational Behavior*. Englewood Cliffs, NJ: Prentice-Hall.

Lorsch, J.W., and P.F. Mathias. (1987, July–August). "When Professionals Have to Manage." *Harvard Business Review, 78–83*.

Louis, M.R. (1980a, June). "Surprise and Sense Making: What Newcomers Experience in Entering Unfamiliar Organizational Settings." *Administrative Science Quarterly, 25*, 226–250.

———. (1980b). "Career Transitions: Varieties and Commonalities." *Academy of Management Review, 5*(3), 329–340.

———. (1982, Spring). "Managing Career Transitions: A Missing Link in Career Development." *Organizational Dynamics, 68–77*.

———. (1990). "Acculturation in the Workplace: Newcomers as Lay Ethnographers." In Benjamin Schneider, ed. *Organizational Climate and Culture* (85–129). San Francisco, CA: Jossey-Bass.

Louis, M.R., B.Z. Posner, and G.N. Powell. (1983). "The Availability and Helpfulness of Socialization Practices." *Personnel Psychology, Inc., 36,* 857–866.

Luthans, F., R.M. Hodgetts, and S.A. Rosenkrantz. (1988). *Real Managers.* Cambridge, MA: Ballinger.

Lynton, E.A. (1984). *The Missing Connection between Business and the Universities.* New York: Macmillan.

McCall, G.J., and J.L. Simmons. (1978). *Identities and Interactions: An Examination of Human Association in Everyday Life.* New York: Free Press.

McCall, M., M. Lombardo, and A. Morrison. (1988). *The Lessons of Experience.* Lexington, MA: Lexington Books.

McCall, M.W., Jr.. Morrison, A.M., and Hannan, R.L. (1978). *Studies of Managerial Work: Results and Methods* (Technical Report No. 9). Greensboro, NC: Center for Creative Leadership.

McCall, M.W., and C.A. Segrist. (1980). *In Pursuit of the Manager's Job: Building on Mintzberg* (Technical Report No. 14). Greensboro, NC: Center for Creative Leadership.

McClelland, D.C., and Burnham, D.H. (1976, March–April). "Power Is the Great Motivator." *Harvard Business Review,* 100–110.

McClintock, C.C., D. Brannon, and S. Maynard-Moody. (1979, December). "Applying the Logic of Sample Surveys to Qualitative Case Studies: The Case Cluster Method." *Administrative Science Quarterly, 24,* 612–613.

McGrath, J.E. (1983). "Stress and Behavior in Organizations." In Martin D. Dunnette, ed., *Handbook of Industrial and Organizational Psychology* (1351–1395). New York: John Wiley.

McLean, J.W. (1990). *So You Want to Be the Boss: A CEO's Lessons in Leadership.* Englewood, NJ: Prentice-Hall.

Manz, C., and H.P. Sims, Jr. (1981). "Vicarious Learning: The Influences of Modeling on Organizational Behavior." *Academy of Management Review, 6,* 105–118.

Marshall, J., and C.L. Cooper. (1981). "The Causes of Managerial Job Stress, Research Note on Methods and Initial Findings." In E.N. Corlett and J. Richardson, eds., *Stress, Work Design, and Productivity* (115–128). New York: John Wiley.

Medcof, J.W. (1985, January–February). "Training Technologists to Become Managers." *Research Management, 28,* 18–21.

Mezirow, J., and Associates. (1990). *Fostering Critical Reflection in Adulthood.* San Francisco, CA: Jossey-Bass.

Miles, M.B., and A.M. Huberman. (1984). *Qualitative Data Analysis: A Sourcebook of New Methods.* Beverly Hills, CA: Sage Publications.

Miller, D.B. (1986). *Managing Professionals in Research and Development.* San Francisco, CA: Jossey-Bass.

Mintzberg, H. (1973). *The Nature of Managerial Work.* New York: Harper & Row.

———. (1975, July–August). "The Manager's Job: Folklore and Fact." *Harvard Business Review,* 49–61.

Moore, W.E. (1969). "Occupational Socialization." In D.A. Goslin, ed., *Handbook of Socialization Theory and Research* (861–885). Chicago: Rand McNally.

Morrison, R.F. (1977). "Career Adaptivity: The Effective Adaptation of Managers to Changing Role Demands." *Journal of Applied Psychology, 62*(5), 549–558.

Mortimer, J.T., and J. Lorence. (1979). "Work Experience and Occupational Value Socialization: A Longitudinal Study." *American Journal of Sociology, 84,* 1361–1385.

Mortimer, J.T., and R.G. Simmons. (1978). "Adult Socialization." *Annual Review of Sociology, 4,* 421–454.

Mumford, A. (1980). *Making Experience Pay: Management Success Through Effective Learning.* London: McGraw-Hill.

———. (1987). "Helping Managers Learn to Learn." *Journal of Management Development, 6*(5), 49–60.

Myerhoff, B.G. (1982). "Rites of Passage: Process and Paradox." In V. Turner, ed., *Celebration* (109–135). Washington, DC: Smithsonian Institution.

Narisetti, R. (1991, August 21). "Business Schools Revamp to Win Students." *The Wall Street Journal,* B-1.

Nelson, D.L. (1987). "Organizational Socialization: A Stress Perspective." *Journal of Occupational Behavior, 8,* 311–324.

Nicholson, N. (1984). "A Theory of Work Role Transitions." *Administrative Science Quarterly, 29,* 172–191.

Nicholson, N., and M.A. West. (1988). *Managerial Job Change: Men and Women in Transition.* Cambridge, England: Cambridge University Press.

Nord, W., ed. (1990, October). Special book-review section [Roundtable on Porter and McKibbin's *Management Education and Development*]. *Academy of Management Review, 15,* 694–705.

297

O'Connor, D.J., and D.M. Wolfe. (1987). "On Managing Midlife Transitions in Career and Family." *Human Relations, 40*(12), 799–816.

Pearlin, L.I., et al. (1981, December). "The Stress Process." *Journal of Health and Social Behavior, 22,* 337–356.

Pedler, M., J. Burgoyne, and J. Boydell. (1978). *A Manager's Guide to Self-Development.* New York: McGraw-Hill.

Peter, Dr. L.J. (1985). *Why Things Go Wrong.* New York: William Morrow.

Phillips, J.J. (1985). *Improving Supervisors' Effectiveness.* San Francisco, CA: Jossey-Bass.

———. (1986, January). "Training: Corporate Boot Camp for Newly Appointed Supervisors." *Personnel Journal,* 70–74.

Phillips, J.J., and S.L. Oswald. (1987). *Recruiting, Training, and Retraining New Employees: Managing the Transition from College to Work.* San Francisco, CA: Jossey-Bass.

Plato. (1956) *The Meno.* (W.K.C. Guthrie, translator). London: Penguin Books.

Porter, L.W., and L.E. McKibbin. (1988). *Management Education and Development: Drift or Thrust into the 21st Century?* New York: McGraw-Hill.

Raelin, J.A. (1980). *Building a Career: The Effect of Initial Job Experiences and Related Work Attitudes on Later Employment.* Kalamazoo, MI: W.E. Upjohn.

———. (1985). *The Clash of Cultures.* Boston: Harvard Business School Press.

———. (1987, January). "The Dual Ladder Is a Flexible Concept." *Personnel Journal,* 96–101.

———. (1989). "An Anatomy of Autonomy: Managing Professionals." *The Academy of Management Executive, 3*(3), 216–228.

Rappaport, S.P., ed. (1988). *Management on Wall Street: Making Securities Firms Work.* Homewood, IL: Dow Jones-Irwin.

Revans, R.W. (1979). "The Nature of Action Learning." *Management Education and Development, 10*(1), 3–23.

Robertson, I.T., and P.A. Iles. (1988). "Approaches to Managerial Selection." In C.L. Cooper and I. Robertson, eds., *International Review of Industrial and Organizational Psychology* (159–211). New York: John Wiley.

Roethlisberger, F.J. (1945, Spring). "The Foreman: Master and Victim of Doubletalk." *Harvard Business Review,* 283–298.

Rosenbaum, J.E. (1984). *Career Mobility in a Corporate Hierarchy.* Orlando, FL: Harcourt Brace Jovanovich.

Roth, L.M. (1982). *A Critical Examination of the Dual Ladder Approach to Career Advancement* (monograph). New York: Management Institute, Columbia Business School.

Ruekert, R.W., and O.C. Walker. (1987, January). "Marketing's Interaction with Other Functional Units: A Conceptual Framework and Empirical Evidence." *Journal of Marketing, 51,* 1–19.

Russell, C.J. (1987). "Person Characteristics Versus Role Congruency Explanation for Assessment Center Ratings." *Academy of Management Journal, 30*(4), 817–826.

Ryans, A.B., and C.B. Weinberg. (1981, Fall). "Sales Force Management: Integrating Research Advances." *California Management Review, 15,* 82–104.

Rychlak, J.F. (1983). *Personality and Life-Style of Young Male Managers: A Logical Learning Theory Analysis.* Orlando, FL: Academic Press.

Rynes, S.L. (1987). "Career Transitions from Engineering to Management: Are They Predictable Among Students?" *Journal of Vocational Behavior, 30,* 138–154.

Sayles, L.R. (1989). *Leadership-Managing in Real Organizations,* 2d ed. New York: McGraw-Hill.

Schaie, K.W. (1983). *Longitudinal Studies of Adult Psychological Development.* New York: Guilford Press.

Schein, E.H. (1961, May). "Management Development as a Process of Influence." *Industrial Management Review, 2,* 59–77.

———. (1964, November–December). "How to Break in the College Graduate." *Harvard Business Review,* 68–76.

———. (1967). "Attitude Change During Management Education." *Administrative Science Quarterly, 11,* 601–628.

———. (1968). "Organizational Socialization and the Profession of Management." *Industrial Management Review, 9,* 1–16.

———. (1975, May–June). "How 'Career Anchors' Hold Executives to Their Career Paths." *Personnel,* 11–24.

———. (1977). "Career Anchors and Career Paths: A Panel Study of Management School Graduates. In J. Van Mannen, ed., *Organizational Careers: Some New Perspectives* (49–64). New York: John Wiley.

———. (1978). *Career Dynamics: Matching Individual and Organizational Needs.* Reading, MA: Addison-Wesley.

———. (1984). "Culture as an Environmental Context for Careers." *Journal of Occupational Behavior, 5*(1), 71–81.

———. (1987). "Individuals and Careers." In J. Lorsch, ed., *Handbook of Organizational Behavior* (155–171). Englewood Cliffs, NJ: Prentice-Hall.

Schlesinger, L., and J. Klein. (1987). "The First-Line Supervisor: Past, Present and Future." In J. Lorsch, ed., *Handbook of Organizational Behavior* (370–384). Englewood Cliffs, NJ: Prentice-Hall.

Schön, D.A. (1983). *The Reflective Practitioner: How Professionals Think in Action.* New York: Basic Books.

———. (1990). *Educating the Reflective Practitioner.* San Francisco, CA: Jossey-Bass.

Shuchman, M. (1991, May 9). "When a Young Doctor Errs, Open Discussion Is Advised." *New York Times,* B-16.

Siegel, S. (1982, February). "What Makes a Good Branch Manager." *Institutional Investor,* 135–141.

Sims, R.R. (1983). "Kolb's Experimental Learning Theory: A Framework for Assessing Person–Job Interaction." *Academy of Management Review,* 8(3), 501–508.

Skinner, W., and W.E. Sasser. (1977, November–December). "Managers with Impact: Versatile and Inconsistent." *Harvard Business Review,* 140–158.

Snell, R.S. (1988a). "The Phenomenological Study of Managerial Learning in Day to Day Work." *Current Research in Business Studies, 1*(1), 31–57.

———. (1988b). "The Emotional Cost of Managerial Learning at Work." *Management Education and Development, 19*(4), 322–340.

———. (1988c). *Learning at Work: Creating the Opportunities.* Luton, England: Local Government Training Board.

Sofer, C. (1970). *Men in Mid-Career: A Study of British Managers and Technical Specialists.* Cambridge, England: Cambridge University Press.

Sonnenfeld, J. (1985). "Demystifying the Magic of Training." In R. Walton and P. Lawrence, eds., *HRM Trends and Challenges for the 1980s* (285–318). Boston: Harvard Business School Press.

Sonnenfeld, J., and J.P. Kotter. (1982). "The Maturation of Career Theory." *Human Relations, 35*(1), 19–46.

[Staff]. (1987, September 29). "Rookie Managers as Boss." *Boston Globe*, 34.

[Staff]. (1988, April). "Study Finds Companies Give 'A Lot of Lip Service' to Developing Managers but Little More." *The Wall Street Journal*, 27.

[Staff]. (1989, May 10). "Computer Wizards Make Unlikely Bosses." *The Wall Street Journal*, 1.

Steinmetz, L.L., and H.R. Todd, Jr. (1986). "First-Line Management: Approaching Supervision Effectively." *Business Publications, XV* (429).

Stewart, R. (1976). *Contrasts in Management: A Study of Different Types of Managers' Jobs—Their Demands and Choices.* London, England: McGraw-Hill.

———. (1982). *Choices for the Manager.* Englewood Cliffs, NJ: Prentice-Hall.

———. (1984). "Maximizing Managers' Day to Day Learning." In C. Cox and J. Beck, eds., *Management Development: Advances in Theory and Practice* (187–207). Chichester, England: John Wiley.

———. (1987). "Middle Managers: Their Jobs and Behavior." In J.W. Lorsch, ed., *Handbook of Organizational Behavior* (385–403). Englewood Cliffs, NJ: Prentice-Hall.

———. (1989). "Studies of Managerial Jobs and Behavior: The Ways Forward." *Journal of Management Studies, 26,* 1–10.

Stumm, D.A. (1985). *The New Sales Manager's Survival Guide.* New York: Amacom.

Super, D.E. (1957). *The Psychology of Careers.* New York: Harper and Row.

Sweeney, P. (1987, February). "A Day in the Life (Retail Brokers)." *Institutional Investor,* 149–153.

Thomas, E.J. (1968). "Role Theory, Personality, and the Individual." In E.F. Borgatta and W.W. Lambert, eds. *Handbook of Personality Theory and Research* (691–727). Chicago: Rand McNally.

Thomason, G.F. (1966). "Managerial Work Roles and Relationships," Part I. *Journal of Management Studies, 3,* 270–284.

———. (1967). "Managerial Work Roles and Relationships." Part II. *Journal of Management Studies, 4,* 17–30.

Thornton, G.C., and W.C. Byham. (1982). *Assessment Centers and Managerial Performance.* Orlando, FL: Academic Press.

Thornton, G.C., and J.N. Cleveland. (1990, February). "Developing Managerial Talent Through Simulation." *American Psychologist, 45,* 190–199.

Trice, H., and D. Morand. (1989). "Rites of Passage in Work Careers." In M. Arthur, D. Hall, and B. Lawrence, eds., *Handbook of Career Theory* (397–416). Cambridge, England: Cambridge University Press.

Tyagi, P.K. (1985, Summer). "Relative Importance of Key Job Dimensions and Leadership Behaviors in Motivating Salesperson Work Performance." *Journal of Marketing, 49,* 76–86.

Vaillant, G.E. (1977). *Adaptation to Life.* Boston: Little, Brown.

Van Maanen, J. (1977). "Experiencing Organizations: Notes on the Meaning of Careers and Socialization." In J. Van Mannen, ed., *Organizational Careers: Some New Perspectives* (15–45). New York: John Wiley.

———. (1978, Summer). "People Processing: Strategies of Organizational Socialization." *Organizational Dynamics, 7,* 19–36.

———, ed. (1979, December). "Reclaiming Qualitative Methods for Organizational Research: A Preface." *Administrative Science Quarterly, 24,* 520–527.

Van Mannen, J., and E.H. Schein. (1979). "Toward a Theory of Organizational Socialization." In B.M. Straw, ed., *Research in Organizational Behavior* (209–264). Greenwich, CT: JAI Press.

Van Mannen, J., E.H. Schein, and F.I. Steele, eds. (1979). *Essays in Interpersonal Dynamics.* Homewood, IL: Dorsey Press.

Vargish, T. (1991, Spring). "The Value of Humanities in Executive Development." *Sloan Management Review,* 83–91.

Waldholz, M. (1991, April 2). "Bristol Myers's Research Chief Will Leave Job." *The Wall Street Journal,* 10.

Wall, J. (1986). *Bosses.* Lexington, MA: Lexington Books.

Wallace, P.A. (1989). *MBA's on the Fast Track: The Career Mobility of Young Managers.* Cambridge, MA: Ballinger.

Webber, R.A. (1991). *Becoming a Courageous Manager: Overcoming Career Problems of New Managers.* Englewood Cliffs, NJ: Prentice-Hall.

Webster, F.E. (1983). *Field Sales Management.* New York: John Wiley.

Weick, K. (1974). [Review of H. Mintzberg's *The Nature of Managerial Work*]. *Administrative Science Quarterly, 19*, 111–118.

———. (1979). "Cognitive Processes in Organizations." In L.L. Cummings and B.M. Straw, eds., *Research in Organizational Behavior*, vol. I (41–74). Greenwich, CT.: JAI Press.

———. (1989, October). "Theory Construction as Disciplined Imagination." *Academy of Management Review, 14*, 516–531.

Weiss, R.S. (1990). *Staying the Course: The Emotional and Social Lives of Men Who Do Well at Work*. New York: Free Press.

Wells, D.L., and P.M. Muchinsky. (1985). "Performance Antecedents of Voluntary and Involuntary Managerial Turnover." *Journal of Applied Psychology, 70*(2), 329–336.

West, M.A., N. Nicholson, and A. Rees. (1987). "Transitions into Newly Created Jobs." *Journal of Occupational Psychology, 60*, 97–113.

Whetten, D.A., and K.S. Cameron. (1984). *Developing Management Skills*. Glenview, IL: Scott, Foresman.

White, R.W. (1987). *Lives in Progress*. New York: Holt, Rinehart and Winston.

Willits, R. (1984). "Suddenly a Branch Manager." In A. Cohen et al., eds., *Effective Behavior in Organizations* (736–743). Homewood, IL: Richard D. Irwin.

Wlodkowski, R.J. (1985). *Enhancing Adult Motivation to Learn*. San Francisco, CA: Jossey-Bass.

Wood, R., and A. Bandura. (1989). "Social Cognitive Theory of Organizational Management." *Academy of Management Review, 14*(3), 361–384.

Wood, R., A. Bandura, and T. Bailey. (1990). "Mechanisms Governing Organizational Performance in Complex Decision-Making Environments." *Organizational Behavior and Human Decision Processes, 46*, 181–201.

Yin, R. (1984). *Case Study Research: Design and Methods*. Beverly Hills, CA: Sage Publications.

Zaleznik, A. (1977, May–June). "Managers and Leaders: Are They Different?" *Harvard Business Review*, 67–78.

———. (1990). *Motivating People*. Chicago: Bonus Books.

Zaleznik, A., G.W. Dalton, and L.B. Barnes. (1970). *Orientation and*

Conflict in Career. Boston: Harvard University Graduate School of Business Administration, Division of Research.

Zaleznik, A., and M.F.R. Kets de Vries. (1975). *Power and the Corporate Mind*. Boston: Houghton Mifflin.

Zemke, R. (1985, August). "The Honeywell Studies: How Managers Learn to Manage." *Training*, 46–51.

APPENDIX

Research Design
and Methods

This study is an extension of research that I conducted earlier on retraining middle managers in financial services firms. For that project I interviewed more than 100 midcareer managers about their careers and organizations. During these interviews I was struck by the disproportionate attention these managers devoted to and the vehemence with which they described their earliest experiences as manager. One manager in his early fifties commented that it was as if it (his first year as a manager) had happened only yesterday.

I became intrigued by the apparent potency of managers' first experiences on the job and began to explore the literature. The managerial press had countless reports of new manager incompetence, attrition, and burnout. I soon learned, however, that few systematic or rigorous studies had been done on the transition to management and that we knew surprisingly little about how managers learned to do their jobs. Moreover, much of that limited research on career transitions treated the transition as an event rather than a process and usually ignored the more person-centered aspects of the transition—that is, the subjective experience and its social psychological consequences.[1] Weick and others have commented that much is to be gained from knowing how individuals think about and make sense of their organizational and career experiences.[2] A virtual canon in education is to "always start where the student is." If management development initiatives are to truly address the needs of new managers, they must be based on an understanding of how new managers think and feel about the experience of becoming a manager.

To begin to fill this void, I decided to conduct an exploratory field-based study of the transition from individual contributor to manager. From a theoretical viewpoint becoming a manager begins when a person is promoted from individual contributor to manager and ends when the individual understands and masters the managerial role as successfully as he or she can given his or her ability and organizational resources and constraints.[3] My objective was to describe the experience of becoming a manager from the new manager's point of view: What do new managers find most challenging? How do they learn to be managers? On what resources, individual and organizational, do they rely?

Although my interest was primarily driven by a practical agenda, the theoretical implications of such a project—for careers, managerial behavior, managerial learning, role theory, and socialization—seemed self-evident. I was neither testing theory nor seeking to develop a theory, however. I hoped to provide a conceptual framework for making sense of the transition to management and to generate fruitful hypotheses for further investigation.

EVOLUTION OF THE RESEARCH PROJECT

The phenomenon of interest nearly always dictates the methodology for studying it. Because this research was focused on "how" and "why" questions about contemporary events, it seemed that a qualitative field study was the logical approach.[4] With research on this topic so sparse, it seemed premature to adopt a priori a conceptual scheme to guide my efforts. Although some systematic research methods were used, I deliberately decided to be opportunistic in collecting data and to remain open to unfolding events.

I collected any data, qualitative and quantitative, which came my way. I relied on observation, formal interviews and informal conversations (in the hallways, at meals, during breaks in formal meetings), well- and ill-informed informants, and archival and published materials. The primary sources of data were semistructured interviews and unstructured observations. As the research progressed and patterns seemed to form, I probed more deeply the issues that appeared to dominate and to question more precisely and make more focused observations. As I established credibility and rapport with the participants in the study, I raised increasingly more sensitive issues.

Admittedly, hazards lie in depending on self-report as a primary source of evidence, especially about personal change.[5] But it is difficult to imagine how else to explore the new manager's internal frame of reference about the transition experience. I was impressed by the candor and helpfulness shown by almost everyone I spoke with and how quickly people became accustomed to my presence.

In short, during their first year on the job, I periodically visited, observed, and interviewed by telephone each of nineteen new managers. For each manager, I invested, on average, twelve days. This total includes time spent with them individually and also with their senior management, human resource managers, experienced peer managers, and representatives of their immediate superiors, subordinates, and peers in other functional areas. It also includes time spent in selected orientation and training sessions held for the managers. Clearly, the work of becoming a manager was not completed by the end of the first year: none of them felt they had mastered the job by their first anniversary.[6] But due to practical considerations, I considered only the new managers' first-year experiences.

The research strategy can thus be described as evolutionary, qualitative, descriptive, and inductive. The merits of such an approach to research have been widely debated.[7] The more in-depth and real-time a longitudinal field study can be, the more elaborate and contextual will be the data collected. Paradoxically, though, one must be all the more cautious about their generalizability, reliability, and validity. Among other complications, one must consider the researcher's influence on the phenomenon being studied. It appeared that my presence did indeed influence the new managers' experiences. As described earlier, they were relieved to have someone to whom they could confide their anxieties and questions. For many, I served as a sounding board. On rare occasions (because the manager specifically requested assistance with a problem), I played adviser. It was clear to the managers that participating in the study forced them to reflect on their experiences and that this reflection made it easier for them to make sense of and consolidate the lessons gathered from their experiences.

The Participants

Because the primary objective in this research was to study in depth the subjective experience of becoming a manager, the sample was kept small and manageable. I sought two research sites in which I could study from ten to twenty managers within one functional area. I used three criteria to assess potential sites: (1) Was it large enough to have a sizable cohort of new managers for the time period the investigation would last? (2) Were they leaders in their industry? and (3) Did they have a reputation for providing significant opportunities for management training and development and upward mobility? To set some benchmarks in selecting and developing managers, I chose to study the transition to management under the best of circumstances. I focused on sales and marketing because I was familiar with these functions, and also because very little research had been done on the transition to sales management, although much anecdotal evidence showed that many new sales managers failed to make the transition successfully. Prior research focused principally on three populations—foremen, technical managers, and professionals.

As stated, the participants were new first-line sales managers in a securities firm and a computer company. That the findings are generalizable can be proven only when supplemented with research on more managers in various functions and settings. The evidence strongly suggests that managerial jobs are remarkably similar in their basic responsibilities. Evidence shows too, however, that function does influence the significance of specific tasks and activities across positions.[8] In fact, I have interviewed and observed (though less systematically and comprehensively) new managers in other areas (including research and development, consulting, accounting, law, and museum management) with consistent results.

More importantly, this study was designed to look at the question in two rather different contexts. Because my contract with companies and individuals specifies confidentiality, I cannot provide detailed profiles of the managers and their jobs. I am sorry to deprive the reader of fuller appreciation for the individuals and their circumstances. The confidentiality agreement turned out to be more restrictive than anticipated, because the two companies had relatively few new managers at the time of the study. But I do summarize some of the differences between the securities firm managers (SFMs) and the computer company managers (CCMs), and their positions in Exhibit A-1.

I identified four companies with which I wanted to work on this research—three in the financial services industry and two in the computer industry. I chose these industries, again, partly because they were familiar to me and also because they were undergoing significant change. (Organizational change was another area that interested me, as in the earlier study on retraining.) Through my colleagues at Harvard, I was able to arrange meetings with senior executives in these firms and discuss my intentions with them (see Exhibit A-2 for form letter).

Exhibit A-1

New Manager Profile

	10 SFMs	*9 CCMs*
Job title	Branch manager	Sales manager
Job title of immediate superior	Regional director	Branch manager
Job title of salesperson position	Account executive	Sales representative
Job title of key subordinates	Account executive, Operations manager, Administrative manager	Sales representative
Number of subordinates	20–80	5–15
Sales task	Retail sale of financial products to individual and small business investors	Institutional sale of large computer systems
Average age	36	30

Exhibit A-2

Letter to Obtain Research Sites

Dear [   ]:

I am currently embarking on a major research project on the transition from salesperson to field sales manager in a variety of industries. This study is the first in a series of in-depth investigations on the transformation of an individual contributor/producer into a manager. The following questions are guiding this endeavor: (1) What are the key demands and challenges of the transition? (2) What resources do individuals most often rely upon to manage the key demands and challenges of the transition? and (3) What factors (individual, job, and organizational) are associated with successful transitions? What factors are associated with unsuccessful transitions? With this information, I hope to delineate career planning and development and job design guidelines for making this transition a smooth and successful one.

I am now identifying research sites for this investigation. Because of your position as a leading firm in the [relevant industry], I would like to work with you on this effort. Needless to say, the specifics in methodological design of the study are negotiable. I hope to conduct the study in phases. In the first phase, I would like to do one or two case studies on new managers. In the second phase, I would like to do a longitudinal study on five or more new managers. I will interview the new managers, their immediate superiors, and samples of their subordinates three times at four-month intervals. A preliminary list of the issues to be covered in the interviews is provided in the Attachment (see enclosed).

Before beginning the case studies, however, I need background or contextual information about field sales management:

Career Development System and Formal Job Design
(1) Recruitment and selection
(2) Training and development
(3) Typical career path
(4) Turnover and burnout rates
(5) Formal job description
(6) Performance evaluation and compensation plans

Perceptions of the Field Sales Management Job
(1) Critical differences between high performers and average or below-average performers
(2) Key stresses and challenges associated with the job
(3) Key rewards associated with the job

Perceptions of the Transition from Salesperson to Field Sales Manager
(1) Key stresses and challenges of the transition
(2) Resources available to manage these stresses and challenges
(3) Critical differences between those who successfully manage the transition and those who do not

To collect this information, I suspect I will have to meet with at least three groups: human resource personnel, senior sales line managers, and current field-sales managers who have been in their position for at least five years. Of course, all information will be held in strictest confidence.

I look forward to meeting you to discuss my ideas further. I will call your office next week to see when such a meeting would be convenient. Thank you for your consideration and support.

Sincerely,

Linda A. Hill

Attachment: Interview Agendas

The New Managers

The Sales Manager Job
1. Job responsibilities and authority.
2. Critical working relationships.
3. Key success factors for the job.
4. Key stresses and challenges in the job.
5. What they like about the job.
6. What they dislike about the job.

The Individual
7. Work values.
8. Motivation for pursuing a management career.
9. Assessment of knowledge, skills, and attitudes relative to the requirements and key success factors in the job.

The Change Process

10. Demands and challenges in making the transition.
11. Coping strategies used to manage the transition.
12. Role models, coaches, and/or mentors.
13. What the organization has done and can do to make the transition smooth and successful.

The Outcomes

14. Evaluation of job performance and productivity.
15. Job satisfaction.
16. Psychological well-being: self-esteem and physical and psychological symptoms of stress.

The Superiors and Subordinates

The Sales Manager Job

1. Job responsibilities and authority.
2. Critical working relationships.
3. Key success factors for the job. Differences between high performers and average performers.
4. Key stresses and challenges in the job.
5. Key rewards in the job.

The Individual

6. Assessment of the new manager's knowledge, skills, and attitudes relative to the requirements and key success factors in the job.

The Change Process

7. Perception of the demands and challenges in making the transition.
8. Key success factors for smooth and successful management of transition.
9. Organizational resources available to manage the transition.

The Outcomes

10. Evaluation of the new manager's job performance.

After the round of getting-acquainted sessions, I concluded that I would especially like to work with two of the companies, primarily for logistical reasons. I met with those executives again and formally asked them to participate in the study. Fortunately, both companies agreed to do so as long as I guaranteed them strict confidentiality. Both had difficulty with turnover and incompetence in their first-line management ranks and were eager to learn anything they could about how to improve selection and development of new managers. During these meetings we outlined the contract within which I would work and designated a company contact in the human resource function who would help coordinate the study.

Preliminary Data Collection

I began by collecting background information to ensure that I understood the context within which the new managers would be working. I interviewed senior executives in the sales and marketing functions (five in the securities firm and two in the computer company) and human resource staff responsible for new manager development (four in the securities firm and six in the computer company). I also interviewed a few relatively new managers (four in the securities company and five in the computer company who had been on the job for two years or less) and their immediate superiors. For each of these people I inquired in open-ended interviews about the issues listed in Exhibit A-3.

Then, to better understand the new managers' jobs, I asked to interview and observe the "company legends"—experienced managers whom senior management felt were the very best in their ranks. I spent a day with four such individuals in the securities firm and six in the computer company. Finally, I attended orientation and training sessions designed for new managers (two at each firm).

Having collected all this information, I was now prepared to select the participants for the study. Both companies kept rosters of those who were slated to become managers when

314

Exhibit A-3

Background Information Collected

- Career history
- Company history
- Current strategy and key success factors
- Current challenges
- Organizational structure
- Audit of managerial talent
- Recruitment and selection of managers
- Typical managerial career paths
- Training and development available to salespeople and managers
- Turnover and burnout rates
- Performance evaluation and compensation policies and procedures
- Job descriptions for the salesperson and first-line sales-manager positions
- Key success factors for these positions
- Challenges of the transition to management
- Individual and organizational differences related to the success of the transition

a position opened. I asked my company contacts to arrange interviews for me with as many of these candidates as possible. Of the first eleven I contacted in the securities firm, ten agreed to participate. The eleventh individual and I came to the mutual conclusion that he should not do so. He was quite skeptical about the benefits of such research to him personally and frankly did not believe that the company would not ask me to provide my assessment of his performance. Soon it was evident that my work was cut out for me. Because I was studying field sales managers, I would be traveling all across the country; consequently, in the computer company, I restricted the sample to prospective managers in the New England and mid-Atlantic states. The first nine individuals contacted agreed to join the project.

At the initial meetings I interviewed the managers seeking to understand their career histories, motivations for pursuing a managerial career, and expectations about managerial work.

Field Methods

I held a series of time-staggered interviews with the new managers, their immediate superiors, and representatives of their subordinates and peers. In each instance, I interviewed at least half of their subordinates. Which subordinates I interviewed was determined in a rather opportunistic fashion, although an effort always was made to interview both the least-experienced and most-experienced subordinates a new manager had. And in the securities firm, I made sure to interview not only the salespeople, but also the administrative and operations personnel. I also met with or interviewed by telephone some of the new managers' peers (thirteen in the securities company and sixteen in the computer company). Some of the peers were in staff positions in the corporate or regional headquarters, and others were in line functions, administration, operations, and technical sales support. I also had the good fortune to talk with a few of the new managers' customers. I spoke with seven customers in the securities firm and three in the computer company who just happened to be around when I was visiting.

Within the new managers' first month to six weeks on the job I made a three- to four-day visit to their offices. Before the visit, I sent the managers an interview agenda (see Exhibit A-4).

Exhibit A-4

Interview Agenda for the New Managers

Introduction

I am doing a study of the transition from being a salesperson to a sales manager. The aim of this study is to collect managers' views on this topic in order to improve the experience of those going through this transition.

Answers to all questions are voluntary and they will be kept completely confidential. Information that might identify you will be seen only by me.

I would like to get your perceptions of (1) the sales manager job and (2) the transition into sales management. I ask you to please be as specific as possible in our discussion. I want to make sure I really understand your comments and observations.

Thank you for your assistance.

The Sales Manager Position

1. Briefly describe your current position and responsibilities.
2. What does your immediate superior expect from you on the job?
3. How is your performance on the job measured or evaluated?
4. What do your salespeople expect from you on the job? How about your other subordinates?
5. To get your job done, I assume you have to interact with a variety of people. What working relationships would you describe as the critical ones—within your area? Outside your area?
6. What are the major stresses and challenges you face on the job? What is the hardest part of your job?
7. What, if anything, do you dislike about your job?
8. What rewards are associated with your job?
9. What do you like best about your job?
10. What do you think it takes to be effective or successful at your job?
11. What do you think are the critical differences between the top-performing sales managers and the average or below-average sales managers? What they do on the job and their skills, knowledge, attitudes, and job experience?
12. Think about the skills and knowledge you need to be effective on the job. How did you acquire them?
13. What do you think about your company's process for selecting new sales managers? What are its strengths? In what ways would you like to change it if you could?

The Transition

1. Why did you choose to become a sales manager?
2. Why do you think most sales managers in the Company choose to go into management?
3. What are the major stresses and challenges associated with the transition?
4. What do you find most demanding about making the transition? What is hardest for you to deal with in making the transition?
5. How are you coping with or managing these stresses, challenges, and demands?
6. What personal resources are you relying on?
7. What organizational resources are you relying on? What support are you getting from people at work?
8. What if anything, do you wish you had done differently?
9. What have been your biggest mistakes thus far?
10. Could you have avoided those mistakes? If so, how?
11. What advice would you give a new sales manager?
12. What resources do you wish had been available to you for making the transition?
13. What can the Company do to make this transition relatively smooth?
14. When do you think you will stop feeling like you are a "new manager"? How long will the transition last?

Background Information

1. How many years have you been with the Company?
2. How many years have you been in your current position?
3. What other positions have you had in the Company?
4. How many people do you have working for you? What do they do for you or what are their functions?

Conclusions

1. If you were me and doing a study of the transition into sales management, what questions would you be sure to ask a new sales manager?
2. Are there any questions you would like me to try to find answers to as I do this study?

I always began the visit by interviewing the new manager. I asked about the range of issues raised in the interview agenda: their current problems; what they had learned about their job and situation since the previous interview; how their working relationships with their superiors, subordinates, and peers had developed; how they were spending their time and with whom; any personnel or organizational changes they were contemplating; and on whom and what they relied to help them learn about and do their jobs. These interviews usually lasted three to five hours. I also interviewed samples of their subordinates. These interviews took from one to three hours and covered various topics complementary to the new manager interviews.

During my visit I shadowed the new managers as they went through their day, making every attempt to observe them meeting with subordinates and leading group meetings. Also, shortly after the site visits, I interviewed the new managers' superiors. Again, the interviews were unstructured but were designed to collect the superiors' perspective on topics comparable to those addressed in the new manager interviews; these lasted one to two hours.

In the months after (every three to four months), I periodically visited and reinterviewed the new managers and samples of their subordinates. I made one additional site visit to see nine of the new managers (during the second half of their year) and two more to see the remaining ten. Most interviews therefore were conducted by telephone, lasting thirty minutes to two hours. The managers and their subordinates were accustomed to doing business by telephone and so seemed comfortable even when talking about difficult and sensitive issues. These interviews were meant to learn anything new since the previous interview. I generally began by asking, "What's been going on?" For the new managers, if necessary, I also prompted discussion with these questions: (1) What's your typical week been looking like? Whom have you been spending time with? (2) What have you found most challenging? (3) What have you learned? (4) What have you found most enjoyable or satisfying? and (5) Whom, if anyone, have you been turning to for assistance? Evidence shows that self-report biases are reduced when we are asked to recall and describe specific events.[9] When appropriate, therefore, I encouraged the participants to provide concrete examples of whatever they were speaking about and to share their thoughts about specific incidents.

At the end of the year I asked the managers to evaluate any formal orientation or training they had received, using the interview agenda as a guide (see Exhibit A-5).

Exhibit A-5

Interview Agenda for Evaluating Formal Training

1. What are the objectives of new manager training programs?
2. How effective was the training in helping you develop this knowledge and these skills?

   a. _____ Understanding compensation and relocation policies

   b. _____ Time management skills

   c. _____ Communication skills

   d. _____ Interpreting and preparing administrative reports

   e. _____ Managing the new subordinate (coaching, counseling, and motivating skills)

   f. _____ Conducting effective sales meetings and office work nights

   g. _____ Understanding products and services

   h. _____ Recruiting and selection skills

   i. _____ Building a team atmosphere

   j. _____ Developing the experienced subordinate

   k. _____ Managing the high-producing subordinate

   l. _____ Monitoring compliance activities and resolving compliance problems (for branch managers only)

   m. _____ Developing marketing strategies (identifying strategic sales opportunities and organizing sales campaigns)

n. _____ Delegation skills
o. _____ Developing a leadership and management style
p. _____ Understanding employee policies and services
q. _____ Managing the subordinate with performance problems
r. _____ Computer skills
s. _____ Action-planning skills
t. _____ Managing home and career conflicts
u. _____ Preparing you to run your own office
Other areas?

At the end of the year I reinterviewed each manager's immediate superiors to determine from the superiors' perspective how they had progressed. I simply asked the superiors, "From your perspective, how is [the new manager] doing?" The question leads, of course, to an imperfect and incomplete evaluation of new managers' performance.[10] Most superiors supported their conclusions, however, by sharing with me (with the promise that the information would not be published) their formal performance appraisals of the manager. As described, most of the new managers (sixteen of them) made it successfully through their first year—that is, their superiors felt they had accomplished as much as could be expected from managers with their experience.

Analyzing Data

The research for this book produced more than 2,000 pages of transcriptions (about 80 percent of the interviews were taped) and field notes. Culling the managers' stories was a stimulating but daunting task. The findings presented in this book were produced by inductive analysis—iterative content analysis and interpretation of the materials. I have relied heavily on others' research to help make sense of my data. (The notes outline the theoretical foundation upon which my argument is built.) I set out to circumscribe the subject by identifying the meaningful variables and generating hypotheses about relationships among them.

I was impressed and frankly surprised that the managers' accounts were so consistent. Issues, problems, and situations repeated themselves so regularly as to make me feel I had a reasonably complete view of the transition experience. As I worked through the data, central tendencies appeared. The majority (fifteen or more) or most (ten or more) of the managers responded or behaved consistently. The majority seemed to struggle with the same challenges—the transformational quality of the transition experience and the four transformational tasks.

Because the research design was longitudinal, one of my first endeavors was to search for periodicity in the data. Much to my chagrin, no phases or stages appeared in the new managers' experiences. One memorable evening, after a frustrating day of sifting through the data, I began to reread Schön's illuminating account of the "reflective practitioner."[11] It suddenly came to me that the new managers were learning *what* they needed to learn only *when* they needed to learn it. Time was not the organizing principle that would explain my data; problems and surprises would do so. After this insight, the analytical scheme began to fall into place.

Variations did appear in the new managers' experiences. Each manager's experience seemed to be shaped partly by personal characteristics such as experience, competence, and managerial style, as well as by situational factors such as company, office size and strategy, and profile of subordinates. Some of these differences are described in this book. With a larger sample I might have been better able to exploit these differences and propose a model for understanding how individual and organizational differences mediated the transition. Because so few of the managers in this study "failed," I could not definitely ascertain why the transition went more smoothly for some than for others.

CONCLUDING REMARKS

A first-time author knows better than the most dogged critic that his or her work is never done. Thanks to the participants in the study, I was privileged to have access to unique and very rich data, analysis of which is never complete; I suspect I will be harvesting mine for years to come. Of course, I wish I had collected additional data under more systematic and rigorous conditions, especially on individual differences in the capacity to learn from experience. I wish I could say much more about how to identify and develop this critical competence.

I eagerly await insights from those who read and *use* this book. The new managers' experiences remind me how challenging and exciting managerial work can be. They have led me to reassess my priorities as a professor of business administration—what I should study and what I should teach in the classroom. Once again, I acknowledge my gratitude to the nineteen new managers who made this work possible.

NOTES

1. In reviewing the literature on careeer transitions Latack (1984) offered this critique:

> First, career transitions as a process, rather than an event, are relatively unexplored . . . it may be premature to base model building of career transitions on preexisting theory. . . . Future studies might adopt a more exploratory, hypothesis-generating approach aimed at describing and classifying how individuals react to different types of transitions, and what individual and organizational factors contribute to and alleviate stress during transitions. . . . A second research strategy concerns time as a variable. There are shortcomings in cross-sectional data to explore the process occurring over time. . . . As people move through the transition process, stress and coping processes may emerge that are not evident when we compare people who are at different points during the transition process. . . . A third methodological issue concerns whether the appropriate level of analysis is normative or ipsative. Stress is conceptualized as a highly individualized process, involving a deviation from some "normal" level

of functioning. . . . Individuals vary widely in the level of stress they experience in a particular situation and in the coping strategies they use. Thus, when we compare data across individuals who may be a different levels of "normal" to begin with, we may mask critical processes that occur intraindividually (p. 317).

2. See Burgoyne and Hodgson (1983, 1984), Morey and Luthans (1984), and Weick (1979) for discussions of the epistemological argument for a more phenomenological approach to understanding managerial action.

3. This definition is greatly influenced by Gabarro's (1987) work on taking charge:

> By taking charge, I do not mean just orienting oneself to a new assignment. Taking charge . . . refers to the process by which a manager establishes mastery and influence in a new assignment. By mastery, I mean acquiring a grounded understanding of the organization, its tasks, people, environment, and problems. By influence, I mean having an impact on the organization, its structures, practices, and performance (p. 6).

4. See Yin (1984) for a discussion of the importance of utilizing a methodological approach consistent with the topic.

5. Burgoyne and Hodgson (1983) write:

> It is of course possible, and indeed likely, that the "validity" of data collected in this way [through self-report] is constrained by the extent to which the person concerned "censors" his thoughts before articulation, and the possibility that some of the pertinent thoughts are unconscious, semi-conscious, or in a pre- or non-verbal form (p. 391).

6. I cannot say definitively how long the transformation takes. After two to three years on the job, many of the managers in the study reported that they were beginning to feel they had taken charge of their first managerial assignments. This finding, however, is based on informal conversations with some of the managers after the formal research project was completed. It is consistent, however, with related research on mastering new job assignments. See Gabarro (1987) and Louis (1980a).

7. See Benbasat et al. (1987), Eccles (1985), Leonard-Barton (1990), Mintzberg (1973), and Van Maanen (1979).

8. See Luthans et al. (1988), Mintzberg (1973), and Stewart (1976; 1982).

9. See Burgoyne and Hodgson (1984).

10. See Gabarro (1987), Kotter (1982), and Luthans et al. (1988) for descriptions of the complexities in appraising managerial performance.

11. See, Schön (1983), especially Chapter 5.

Index

Accountability
  expectations of, 20, 39–40
  living with ultimate, 78–79
  in training of new manager, 219–220
Administrator, manager as, 24–25,
    42–43, 82–83
Adviser(s)
  current boss as, 221–225
  peers as, 226–232
  previous boss as, 218
Advocate, 36, 61
Affiliation needs, 103–104, 120n4
Age
  and developmental stage, 162, 184n5
  of new manager, 136, 154n5
Agenda setting, 6, 16
  formal training in, 267
  incorporation into identity of, 84–87
  new managers' expectations of, 21–23
  subordinates' expectations of, 30–33
  superiors' expectations of, 40–41
  understanding meaning of, 79–80
Ambiguity, 181, 191–192
Apprenticeship, 94, 270–271

Aptitudes, 174–175
Assessment centers, 258
Assets, 174–175
Atmosphere, 113–115
Attention, to more-experienced subordi-
    nates, 138–141
Attitudes, 266, 281n35
Authority
  challenges to, 103, 104–105, 106, 136
  of control vs. commitment, 105–111
  expectations of, 20, 39
  of leadership, 111–117
  as reason for becoming manager, 160
  reclaiming of, 68–70
Autocratic style, 105–106, 136, 154n6
Autonomy
  authority vs., 69
  expectations of, 20
  of more-experienced subordinates, 138,
    150
  strategic, administrative, and opera-
    tional, 152, 154n11
  supportive, 219
Availability, 100–102

325

Boss(es). *See also* Superiors
  development of, 261–263
  learning from current, 221–225
  learning from previous, 214–221
  manager as, 19–29, 39–44, 105–111
  weak, 259, 280n27,28
Boundary spanner, 37, 49n16
Buddy system, 270
Buffer, 35–36, 62
Businessperson, manager as, 40–41, 84
Business school, 243n16, 274–276

Career development, 183n1
Career history, 210–214, 256, 257–258
Career insight, 279n22
Career resilience, 279n22
Career transitions, 8n3
  and identity, 169, 170, 184n7,8
  stress of, 188–190, 204n1
Case method, 240, 269, 275
Challenges, to authority, 103, 104–105, 106, 136
Character, managerial, 177–182, 257, 280n25
Classroom training, 272, 274–276
Climate, 113–115
Coaches, senior executives as, 261–263, 271–272
Cohorts, 270
Commitment, of subordinates, 105–111
Communication skills, 107–108
Community relations, 37, 89
Competence, 99–100
Complaints, 167
Compliance, 25, 48n6
Computer company managers, 4–5
Conceptual skill, 256–257, 279n19
Conflicts
  mediation of, 68
  and self-image, 172–173
  stress of, 191–192, 193
Constraints, 69
Contacts, 36–37
Control
  delegation and, 147–152
  expectations of, 20, 38
  over more-experienced subordinates, 135
  realities of, 56–57
  transition to commitment from, 105–111
Corporate culture, 113–115, 234, 243n17
Corporate office, experience in, 212–213
Corporate strategy, 31

formal training in, 267–268, 281n38
implementation of, 79–80
Corporate training. *See* Management training program
Cost, of new manager incompetence and turnover, 8n2
Cost cutting, 79, 91n1
Counselor, manager as, 34–35, 73–74, 101
Creativity, 170
Credibility, 36–37, 49n15
  transition from authority to, 97–105, 120n2
Culture, corporate, 113–115, 234, 243n17
Customers, subordinate expectations vs., 63–67

Daily realities, of managerial work, 53–57
Decisional roles, 47n1, 91n4
Decision making
  expectations of, 20–21, 39
  input into, 107–108
  self-referent factors in, 157n3
  subordinates' need for, 61
Delegation
  to subordinates, 147–152, 154n7–10
  in training of new manager, 219
Demotion, 145
Dependence, management as, 56–57, 68, 75n4,5, 106
Development
  management, 246–248, 260–265, 277n1
  of new managers' superiors, 261–263
  of subordinates, 71–72, 140–141
Developmental relationships
  with current bosses, 221–225
  encouragement of, 263–265
  in formal training programs, 269–270, 282n45,46
  with peers, 226–232
  with previous bosses, 214–221
Developmental stages, 162, 184n5, 204n5
Diversity
  acceptance of, 124–128
  responding to, 128–141, 153n1
Doer role, 28
  with less-experienced subordinates, 134
  regression to, 90–91, 251, 266
  unlearning of, 52, 53–54
Dual-career ladders, 254, 278n15,16,18

Education, 243n16, 274–276

Effectiveness, evaluation of, 165–168, 229–230, 243n14
Effective relationships, 93, 95n1, 102
Emotion(s), management of, 190–191, 198–199, 204n6, 278n11
Emotional support, from peers, 231, 243n19
Empathy, 180–181
Employees. *See* Subordinates
Entrepreneurial role, 91n4
Environment, 113–115
Evaluation, criteria for, 165–168
Expectations, 12
  and choice of management career, 248–250, 278n5
  constellation of, 17–19, 46–47
  in effective relationships, 95n1
  of new manager, 17, 19–29
  of peers, 18, 44–45
  vs. reality, 57–58, 75n6
  reconciling subordinates', 58–74
  for subordinates, 128–129
  of subordinates, 18, 29–39, 49n12–16
  of subordinates vs. customers, 63–67
  of superiors, 18, 39–44
Experience
  career history, 210–214
  expectations based on, 28, 49n10
  pitfalls of, 251, 278n9
  reflection on, 252–253
Expert, manager as, 30, 55–56, 67–68, 75n3, 99
External relations, 35–37, 49n16

Facilitator, manager as, 29, 71, 72
Failure
  fear of, 110–111, 189
  learning from, 28–29
Fairness, 127–128
Family life, 201–202
Fast-tracking, 250, 278n7
Fear, 172
Feedback
  and evaluation of efficacy, 229–231, 243n14
  from formal training program, 235–237, 240
  openness to, 241–242
  from peers, 229–231
  to problem subordinates, 144–145
  from sales vs. management position, 163, 164
  on self-image, 171–172
  from subordinates, 72, 94
  in training of new manager, 219–220
Feelings, 101
Field training officer, 271
Firing, 145–146, 200
First impression, 97–98
First-line manager
  vs. individual contributor, 3
  role of, 49n8, 83–84
Flexibility, 128
Formal authority. *See* Authority
Formal training. *See* Management training program
Frame of reference, 18, 48n3
Freedom. *See* Autonomy
Friendship, with subordinates, 103–104
Fulfillment, 170
Functional managers, 4, 13n1

Generalists, 85
General managers, 4, 13n1
Groups, leadership of, 111–117
Group interests, individual vs., 200–201
Guidance, 34–35

Heap reversal theory, 195
Hiring decisions, 32, 71–72, 146
Human problem solving, 94–95, 95n2
Humiliation, 110–111

Identity
  career transitions and, 169, 170, 184n7,8
  forging of, 63–68
  managerial, 84–90, 156
  transformation of, 5–8, 189–190, 245, 251
Impact, personal, 165–168, 169, 229–230, 243n14
Implementation, of strategy, 79–80
Impulsiveness, 179–180
Incentive, 108–111
Incompetence
  cost of, 8n2
  vs. lack of motivation, 142–143
Independence. *See* Autonomy
Individual, vs. group interests, 200–201
Individual contributor, 9n4
  vs. first-line manager, 3
  retreat into role of, 90–91, 251, 266
  unlearning of role of, 52, 53–54
Induction, 266
Influence, 120n1,5
  lasting, 86–87

Information, 31, 49n13
Informational roles, 47n1
Insecurity, 148–149
Insight, 279n22
Integrator, manager as, 42
Interface responsibilities, 84
Internal promotion, 210
Internships, 258–259
Interpersonal competence, 93–95, 95n1, 168
Interpersonal roles, 47n1, 88
Intuition, 94
Isolation, 194–196

Job change, stress of, 188–190, 204n1
Job descriptions, 3–4, 27, 49n9
Job rotation, 280n27,28
Judgment base, 94–95, 95n2

Leadership
   burdens of, 196–201
   defined, 111–112
   of group, 111–117
   management vs., 112
   new managers' understanding of, 73–74, 81–82
   sales, 21–23, 30–32, 67–68
   subordinates' expectation of, 33–35
   superiors' expectation of, 41–42
Learning, 7, 9n6,7
   from current bosses, 221–225
   from formal training, 232–241
   of managerial skills, 242n1
   personal, 155–156, 157n1, 251, 266, 278n10, 281n35
   from previous and current peers, 226–232
   from previous bosses, 214–221
   from previous experience, 210–214
Leisure time, 201–202
Liaison, manager as, 35–37, 49n16, 61, 91n4
Listening, 108, 144, 179–180
Loneliness, 194–196
Long-term planning, 22–23, 31–32, 85

Management development, 246–248, 260–265, 277n1
Management internships, 258–259
Management training program
   content of, 265–268, 281n33,34
   goals of, 265
   pedagogy of, 268–270
   prototypical, 270–274

as resource base, 253
   timing of, 272–274
   value of, 232–241
Manager(s)
   choosing to become, 248–250
   defined, 3
   effect of research study on, 271, 282n47
   expectations of, 17, 19–29
   job description of, 3–4, 27, 49n9
   purposes of, 48n1
   reasons for becoming, 159–164, 257
   satisfactions in being, 169–171, 253–254
   selection of, 254–259
   support for, 260–265
Managerial character, 177–182, 257, 280n25
Managerial identity, adoption of, 84–90, 156
Managerial role, 15–17, 46–47, 47n1, 48n7
   reframing of, 51–53, 75n1
   regression from, 251
Managerial style, 175–177
Managerial work
   critical skills of, 279n19
   daily realities of, 53–57, 266–267
   dependence of, 56–57
   leaving, 254, 278n15,16,18
   new organizations and changes in, 262, 280n31
   pace of, 54–56
   previewing of, 258–259
   stresses of, 190–202
Master of Business Administration (MBA), 243n16, 274–276
Mediation, of conflicts, 68
Medium-term planning, 22–23
Mentors, 218–219, 220–221, 222–223, 264–265
Mistakes
   learning from, 28–29
   of new managers, 220, 223–224, 243n11
   and risk management, 197–198
   by subordinates, 102, 134, 145
Money
   as incentive, 109–110
   as reason for becoming manager, 160, 183n2
Monitor, manager as, 31, 49n13, 91n4
Morale, 167
Motivation
   vs. incompetence, 142–143

for management, 159–164, 257
of subordinates, 74, 82, 106–111, 119

Needs, of subordinates, 59–63, 73
Negativity, 192–194
Neglect, of more-experienced subordinates, 138–141
Negotiator, manager as, 44–45, 86
Network building, 6, 16–17
formal training in, 268, 282n39
incorporation into identity of, 87–90
new managers' expectations of, 23–26
subordinates' expectations of, 33–37
superiors' expectations of, 41–43
understanding meaning of, 80–84
New products, 79, 91n1
Nonverbal communication, 120n2

Opportunities, 22–23, 30
Organizational culture, 113–115, 234, 243n17
Organizational socialization, 8n3
Organizer, manager as, 32–33, 49n14
Orientation, 233–234
Overload, 191
Overmanagement
of less-experienced subordinates, 132–134
of more-experienced subordinates, 136–137

Pace, of managerial work, 54–56, 75n2
Participative style, 107–108, 136, 154n6
Patience, 179
Peer(s)
building relationships with, 26, 82–83, 89
defined, 12
emotional support from, 231
expectations of, 18, 44–45
in formal training programs, 237–238, 270, 282n46
as resources, 226–232, 243n19
Peer management, 227, 230
People manager
judgment base for, 94–95, 95n2
manager as, 29–39, 71–74, 80–84, 87–88
Performance anxiety, 189
Performance evaluation, 70
Personal case law, 94, 95n2
Personal impact, 165–168, 169, 229–230, 243n14
Personality, 168, 177, 184n7

Personal learning, 155–156, 157n1, 251, 266, 278n10, 281n35
Personal lives, 201–202
Persuasion, 106–107
Pitfalls, anticipating common, 251–253
Policies, 234, 239, 267
Politician, manager as, 25–26, 83, 88–90
Positive reinforcement, 108–111
Power
vs. affiliation needs, 104, 120n4
expectations of, 20
of formal authority, 69–70
and influence, 120n5
as reason for becoming manager, 161
sharing of, 118–119
stress of, 200–201
Power bases, diversification of, 118, 121n10
Previewing, of managerial work, 258–259
Priority setting, 56, 61, 267
Problem solving
human, 94–95, 95n2
with less-experienced subordinates, 132–135
stress of, 192–194
subordinates' expectations of, 60–63
Problem subordinate, 141–146, 193–194
Professionalism, 37
Project coordinator, 211–212
Punishment, 110–111, 121n6, 145
Purposes, of manager, 48n1

Quotas, 89

Realities, of managerial work, 53–57
Recognition, 109, 163–164
Reference, frame of, 18, 48n3
Reflection, 252–253
Regional office, experience in, 212–213
Regression, to doer role, 90–91, 251, 266
Reinforcement, 108–111
Relaxation, 201–202
Resilience, 156, 279n22
Resource(s)
current boss as, 221–225
listing of, 251–252
peers as, 226–232
previous boss as, 214–221
provider of, 61
Resource base, creation of, 253, 278n13
Resource management, 88–89
Respect, 98
vs. being liked, 103–104
Responsibility, to subordinates, 178

Rewards, 108–111
  distribution of, 48n4
Risk, of dependence on subordinates,
  68–69
Risk management, 197–198, 205n10, 220
Rite of passage, training as, 238–239,
  243n18, 244n20
Role discontinuity, 189, 204n3
Role model
  manager as, 37, 41–42, 114
  for manager, 173–174
  previous boss as, 215–218
  stress of being, 198–199
  weak boss as, 259, 280n27,28
  for women managers, 243n6
Role playing, 240, 244n22, 269
Role strain, 191–192

Sales ideas, 22–23, 30–31
Sales leader, manager as, 21–23, 30–32,
  67–68
Salespeople, 124
Satisfactions, in being manager, 169–171,
  253–254
Securities firm managers, 4–5
Selection, of new managers, 254–259
Self-awareness, 249, 277n4
Self-confidence, 177–178
Self-image
  and career choices, 183n1
  discovering new aspects of, 171–174
  stress and, 172
Self-referent factors, in decision making,
  157n3
Simulations, 240, 244n22, 269
Skills, managerial, 279n19
Socialization, organizational, 8n3
Staffing, 32
Star producers, 28
Strategy, 31
  formal training in, 267–268, 281n38
  implementation of, 79–80
Strengths, managerial, 174–175
Stress
  of being role model, 198–199
  of burdens of leadership, 196–201
  of isolation, 194–196
  in managerial job, 190–202
  of managing risk, 197–198
  of negativity, 192–194
  perception of, 202–203
  on personal life, 201–202
  physical manifestations of, 187–188
  of power over people's lives, 200–201
  of role strain, 191–192

and self-image, 172, 203
of transformation, 188–190, 204n1
Style, managerial, 175–177
Subordinates
  accepting diversity of, 124–128
  assessment of, 124–125
  availability to, 100–102
  caring for, 99–101
  challenges and criticism from, 103,
    104–105, 106, 108
  commitment of, 105–111
  conflict with, 172–173
  vs. customer expectations, 63–67
  defined, 13n1
  dependence on, 56–57, 68, 75n4,5, 106
  discovering needs of, 59–63, 73
  expectations for, 128–129
  expectations of, 18, 29–39, 49n12–16
  firing of, 145–146
  friendship with, 103–104
  involvement vs. interference with,
    63–67
  less-experienced, 129–135
  mistakes of, 102, 134, 145
  more-experienced, 135–141
  motivation of, 106–111
  narrow perspective of, 70
  overmanagement of, 132–134, 136–137
  problem, 141–146, 193–194
  reconciling expectations of, 58–74
  responding to diversity of, 128–141,
    153n1
  undermanagement of, 132
Success
  definitions of, 34
  interpersonal competence and, 93,
    95n1
  learning from, 28–29
  as manager, 170–171
  as reason for becoming manager,
    160–161
  self-awareness and, 249, 277n4
  of subordinates, 71
Superiors. See also Boss(es)
  adopting point of view of, 84–90
  building relationships with, 25–26, 89
  expectations of, 18, 39–44, 79–84
  priorities of, 78–79
Supervisor, manager as, 23–24
Support
  for new manager, 260–265
  of subordinates, 71, 72, 99–100
Support group, 272

Task-force assignments, 212, 263

Task learning, vs. personal learning, 155–156, 157n1
Team building, 116–117, 121n8,9
Team leader
  manager as, 33–35, 41–42
  more-experienced subordinate as, 140
Technical expert, manager as, 30, 55–56, 67–68, 75n3, 99
Technical skill, 256, 279n19,21
Temperament, 168, 177, 184n10
Testing, by subordinates, 103, 104–105, 106, 136
Time management
  formal training in, 267
  keeping record of, 252
  realities of, 56
  stress and, 192
  and subordinates' needs, 60, 61

Trade-offs, 40–41, 86, 91n3
Training
  management. *See* Management training program
  of subordinates, 32, 71–72, 170
Transformation
  of identity, 5–8, 189–190, 245, 251
  stress of, 188–190, 204n1
Transition, work of, 104n5
Trust, 95n1, 98–105, 120n1, 149
Turnover
  cost of, 8n2
  and evaluation of impact, 167

Undermanagement, 132

Weaknesses, managerial, 168
Workload, 54–56, 75n2

FOR THE BEST IN PAPERBACKS, LOOK FOR THE

In every corner of the world, on every subject under the sun, Penguin represents quality and variety—the very best in publishing today.

For complete information about books available from Penguin—including Puffins, Penguin Classics, and Arkana—and how to order them, write to us at the appropriate address below. Please note that for copyright reasons the selection of books varies from country to country.

In the United Kingdom: Please write to *Dept. JC, Penguin Books Ltd, FREEPOST, West Drayton, Middlesex UB7 0BR.*

If you have any difficulty in obtaining a title, please send your order with the correct money, plus ten percent for postage and packaging, to *P.O. Box No. 11, West Drayton, Middlesex UB7 0BR*

In the United States: Please write to *Consumer Sales, Penguin USA, P.O. Box 999, Dept. 17109, Bergenfield, New Jersey 07621-0120.* VISA and MasterCard holders call 1-800-253-6476 to order all Penguin titles

In Canada: Please write to *Penguin Books Canada Ltd, 10 Alcorn Avenue, Suite 300, Toronto, Ontario M4V 3B2*

In Australia: Please write to *Penguin Books Australia Ltd, P.O. Box 257, Ringwood, Victoria 3134*

In New Zealand: Please write to *Penguin Books (NZ) Ltd, Private Bag 102902, North Shore Mail Centre, Auckland 10*

In India: Please write to *Penguin Books India Pvt Ltd, 706 Eros Apartments, 56 Nehru Place, New Delhi 110 019*

In the Netherlands: Please write to *Penguin Books Netherlands bv, Postbus 3507, NL-1001 AH Amsterdam*

In Germany: Please write to *Penguin Books Deutschland GmbH, Metzlerstrasse 26, 60594 Frankfurt am Main*

In Spain: Please write to *Penguin Books S. A., Bravo Murillo 19, 1° B, 28015 Madrid*

In Italy: Please write to *Penguin Italia s.r.l., Via Felice Casati 20, I-20124 Milano*

In France: Please write to *Penguin France S. A., 17 rue Lejeune, F-31000 Toulouse*

In Japan: Please write to *Penguin Books Japan, Ishikiribashi Building, 2-5-4, Suido, Bunkyo-ku, Tokyo 112*

In Greece: Please write to *Penguin Hellas Ltd, Dimocritou 3, GR-106 71 Athens*

In South Africa: Please write to *Longman Penguin Southern Africa (Pty) Ltd, Private Bag X08, Bertsham 2013*